Economics of Sericulture Farming

Economics of Sericulture Farming

Dr. Ashok Purohit
and
Prashant Kumar Sirohi

RANDOM PUBLICATIONS
NEW DELHI (INDIA)

Economics of Sericulture Farming

ISBN 978-93-5111-815-2

Published in 2016 in India by

RANDOM PUBLICATIONS

4376-A/4B, Gali Murari Lal, Ansari Road
New Delhi-110 002
Phone : +9111-43580356, 011-23289044, 011-43142548
e-mail: sales@randompublications.com,
info@randompublications.com, randomexports@gmail.com

Type Setting by : Friends Media, Delhi-110089
Printed at : Sanat Printers

Preface

Sericulture, or silk farming, is the rearing of silkworms for the production of silk. Although there are several commercial species of silkworms, Bombyx mori is the most widely used and intensively studied silkworm. Silk was first produced in China as early as the Neolithic period. Sericulture has become an important cottage industries in countries such as Brazil, China, France, India, Italy, Japan, Korea, and Russia. Today, China and India are the two main producers, with more than 60% of the world's annual production.

According to Confucian texts, the discovery of silk production dates to about 2700 BC, although archaeological records point to silk cultivation as early as the Yangshao period. By about the first half of the 1st century AD it had reached ancient Khotan, and by AD 140 the practice had been established in India. In the 6th century the Smuggling of silkworm eggs into the Byzantine Empire led to its establishment in the Mediterranean, remaining a monopoly in the Byzantine Empire for centuries. In 1147, during the Second Crusade, Roger II of Sicily attacked Corinth and Thebes, two important centres of Byzantine silk production, capturing the weavers and their equipment and establishing his own silkworks in Palermo and Calabria, eventually spreading the industry to Western Europe.

– Author

Contents

1

Economic Importance of Mulberry Sericulture Based Farming System

Agriculture in India is the single largest employer of rural labour. Agriculture remains the main source of income and livelihood for the rural population in India. With the advent of many technologies in agriculture be it by variety, soil and nutrient management, important resources management like irrigation water, labour etc., the sector is widening itself to gamut of different economic activities. For a successful farm business, it is inevitable for an appropriate decision making by the farm entrepreneur. Decision making in agriculture has been a priority issue as the farmers live in an environment under scarce resource conditions. In order to accelerate the rate of agricultural development, three major changes *viz*, institutional, technological and the infrastructural changes are essential.

While the institutional change refers to those measures which are related to agrarian relations (which make property relations favorable to the tillers of the soil) and size of the unit of cultivation which make the size of the unit of cultivation operationally viable, technological change implies a change in the method of farming and introducing yield raising technology. Stout and Rutton also defined technological change as a change in the parameters of a production function resulting directly from the use of new knowledge. Infrastructural changes include facilities like irrigation, credit, transport, marketing *etc*. In the last few decades, India has witnessed significant technological change in the agricultural sector.

Technological change ensures avenue for the use and adoption of new and improved factors, techniques, methods and know-how for more agricultural production in place of old and traditional techniques of production. Introduction of new technology in the farm or the technological change include the use of high yielding varieties of seed or plant material, chemical fertilizers, improved method of irrigation, mechanization of the farm *etc*, in place of the traditional practices. According to Pause and Singh technological change in agriculture consists of adoption of farming techniques developed through research and calculated to bring about diversification and increase of production and greater economic returns to the farmers. In view of the above, it can be said that the technological change in agriculture necessarily is a process assisting the shift in production function.

Changes pertaining to farm technology may also be distinguished with increased farm mechanization and technical knowledge, besides the adoption of improved package of practices. Of late machineries in farming have taken a lead role in reducing the cost burden in the farm. The use of new technology warrants new knowledge among the farmers. Agriculture technology dissemination is a dynamic process, wherein it can be transferred to any differentiated group in the society. New farm technology tends to decrease the unit cost of production without decreasing the output. New mechanical-biological technologies such as improved machines, seeds, fertilizers and pesticides, *etc*, have resulted in enhanced production without increasing total inputs and have helped in improving input-output relationship. By virtue of improving input – output relationships, new technology tends to reduce the cost of production and hence effects the level of agricultural prices.

Technology therefore plays a vital role in the form of increasing production as well as reducing cost and ultimately lowering the price per unit. In the recent years, farm technology has played a more significant role in enhancing the global food production and to cater to the growing food requirements, owing to demographic explosion. In the absence of rapid technological advances in agriculture, the world must have been facing gloomy prospects and even now the high rates of population growth in the less developed countries. The major changes that are noticed with the evolution and adoption of new technologies in the farm in a way has given rise to diversification in farming. Resources of production will come under extreme pressure for consumption as a result of growing demand from the farm sector.

Under the conventional farming system which mainly focuses on the growing of traditional crops for sustenance will no longer benefit the mass of rural population because of lack of market price. With the predominant small size holdings, in India, traditional agriculture has limited role to play in eradicating poverty and hunger. Possibility of increased size of holding being less, diversification in the farming sector to high value crops and enterprises may hasten farmers' income and livelihood. In this regard integrating activities which can effectively utilize the available resources at the farm level would be beneficial.

FARMING SYSTEM – DEFINITION AND CONCEPT

Farming system is an integrated set of activities that farmers perform in their farms under their resources and circumstances to maximize the productivity and net farm income on a sustainable basis. The main characteristics of the farming system specifically involve the following four basic elements:

- The farm family resources – land, labour and capital
- Household consumption needs – food, clothing, social obligations and other needs
- Farm enterprises – crops, livestock, and off-farm activities and
- The environment – physical and socio-economic

The decision making of the farmers at their farm is determined exclusively by the elements as listed above. Hence, justification to optimally utilize these elements is necessary and integrating many of the activities with in a farm arises. The integration of various activities within a farm therefore gives scope for the optimal utilization of the existing scarce resources in the farm. Integrated farming is most commonly found in many parts of Asian countries, which are having a large chunk of small farmers in the agriculture sector. The farming system takes into account the components of soil, water, crops, live stock, labour, capital, energy and other resources with the farm family at the centre, managing agricultural and other related activities in the same farm. An intensive integrated farming system addresses two issues, viz.:

- Reduction in risk with the monoculture activities and promoting enterprise diversification and value addition.
- Development of alternative income sources with efficient utilization of farm resources.

The socio economic values associated with the integrated farming system combining agricultural crops, horticultural crops, sericulture, forestry, fishery, dairy etc., can be effected through:

- Income generation – through sale proceeds of various products of the farm
- Food security - after sale proceeds are over some proportion of the food items can be put aside for home consumption
- Capital formation – savings after consumption can in turn be the net investment in production
- enhancing crop production – through the utilization of various by products from complementary enterprises
- Resource utilization – through optimal allocation of scarce resources of the farm in more effective and efficient way.
- Resource mobilization – availing credits through formal and informal sectors becomes easy.
- Social and economic status – through recognition in the society as a leader of the mass.

Various explanations and definitions were framed to define the farming system in a nutshell by many economists around the globe, some of which are as under; Wright considered farming system as bio-economic system. In this system man is attempting to control biological systems in an uncertain environment to achieve some goal which is predominantly economic in nature. Charreau opined that changes in farming system are continuously taking place because of the dynamic nature of agriculture, changes in population density, activities of man and many other reasons like changes in education, goals, income, credit institutions, availability of inputs etc.

Tejwani indicated that the farming systems research are comprehensive in nature and deals with the entire gamut of resources, inputs and management practices and operations in production of crops. Norman felt that in order to develop relevant technology, it was important to understand and analyse the existing farming systems. In his opinion, failure to recognize the interdependence between the present farming systems, the proposed improved technology and the necessary infrastructural support has often been responsible for the lack of change in indigenous farming systems. Deoghare *et al.*, defined farming systems as the entire gamut of all farm activities and related decisions with regard to development, management and allocation of all the farm resources which within the operational unit or within the combination of such units results in maximum agricultural production.

He further opined that widening of farm activities by including other enterprises such as dairying, poultry, piggery, fishery, sericulture, bee keeping and/or agro-forestry etc., with the crop husbandry is necessary because of continuously decreasing farm size in the country, particularly in case of small and marginal farmers who constitute nearly 70 per cent of the farming community. Maji described the farming as a stochastic, dynamic, biological and open system with human or social involvement.

The farming system specifically refers to a crop combination or enterprise mix. It takes into account the consumption need of the family, the economic factors, availability of farm resources, infrastructure and institutions such as irrigation, marketing facilities including storage and transportation and credit among the various technologically feasible enterprises and the preference of the individual farmers. Nagaraja *et al*, defined farming system as an integrated set of activities that farmers perform in their farms under their resources and circumstances to maximize the productivity and net farm income on a sustainable basis.

The Integrated Farming System Approach (IFSA) is an innovative and unique approach to promote integrated land use and animal management technologies as well as resource management capabilities among farmers, particularly small and marginal farmers. Integrated farming systems are probably as old as farming itself if the broadest definition of integrated farming is accepted. According to this, integration occurs when outputs (usually by-products) of one production sub-system are used as inputs by another, within the farm unit. Theoreticians used to differentiate it from mixed farming, in which production subsystems of a farm are not mutually supportive and do not depend on each other.

With an effective market access around, linking mulberry sericulture with other subsidiary enterprises has always been found to be complementary. A number of enterprises can easily be combined with mulberry sericulture for effective crop diversification. There is every scope for improving the economic efficiency of resources too. Hence various components of the farming system are clubbed together to effectively simulate the conditions of enterprise diversification.

There are quite a few diversified enterprises and crops suiting mulberry sericulture. The combination of such enterprises can be considered to be viable only if they are complementary. Dairy enterprise is one of the important activities which can suit the performance of sericulture. As it is very well known that the combination of enterprises 'silk and milk' is very popular even now in Kolar district of Karnataka. Many studies have also revealed this fact as true from the sense of effective enterprise combination. The farmers in the district are known to be highly innovative and the routine agricultural crops are combined *inter alia* with allied enterprises such as vegetables, dairy, sericulture, poultry and piggery.

One of the studies done by Komala revealed that when dairy enterprise was combined with other enterprises on scientific lines offered greater opportunities for increasing farm income and employment, particularly to the weaker sections of the rural community. Fish farming cum sericulture is commonly practiced in China.

Embankment fish culture has been practiced along with bamboo and mulberry culture in the Yangtze River delta and Pearl River delta areas of central and south China for centuries. Originally, the delta was just a waterlogged area. Farmers dug and moved soil, piling it into huge rectangular or round shapes and utilized these raised embankments for planting crops. The excavated areas became deeper, making them ideal for fish culture.

Where embankments are wide enough, mulberry, bamboo, etc., were grown. The mud is scraped from the bottom of the pond and applied as fertilizer to the embankment 2-5 times annually at a rate of 750-1 125 kg/ha/year. Different farming systems are prevailing in India primarily due to varied agricultural base, available resources, and location specific needs of humans, animals etc.

Farmers have established these farming systems through their experience to meet their food, fuel and fibre requirement in a manner that they are least dependent on the external source. However, advancement in crop production technology and need for higher food grain production compelled the nation for adoption of crop based production system.

ECONOMIC IMPORTANCE OF SERICULTURE

An attempt was made to investigate the impact of biological, chemical, mechanical technologies on income, productivity and employment in sericulture as compared to other crops. It is revealed that modern technology, which is both capitalintensive and labour-intensive, brings desirable changes in the intensity of land use, cropping and also mixture of crops, which helps in farm productivity. Use of high yielding mulberry varieties, quality compost/manure, chemical fertilizers, plant protection chemicals, disinfectants in rearing, etc, are the some important technology components, which are directly related to productivity in sericulture. Depending on the level of adoptability of these technologies, the impact on productivity, level of farm employment and income are affected. In view of the importance attached to the changes in the level of productivity, income and employment, due to the changes in the level of adoptability of technologies, a comparative analysis was done.

BRIEF REVIEWS ASSOCIATED WITH PRODUCTION IN SERICULTURE

Several studies have been conducted on the economics and employment generation pattern of mulberry sericulture and the allied crop enterprises. A review of some of the related studies was conducted in order to understand the problem in right perspective and their salient features are discussed based on the objectives of the study in this chapter.

Costs and Returns from Sericulture

Narasimhanna and Krishnaswamy outlined the possibility of obtaining 1,600 kg of bivoltine cocoons from rearing 4,000 layings and by producing 30,000 kg of leaves per hectare. The cost of leaf and cocoon production and net returns were estimated at Rs. 6,000.00 Rs.10,000.00 and Rs. 26,800.00 respectively per hectare by using improved techniques. Nataraj and Thomas conducted a study on economics of bivoltine sericulture in Karnataka and indicated that the average yield of all the bivoltine breeds for 100 Disease Free Layings (DFLs) worked out to 31 kg and the gross income aggregated to Rs. 990.00. The yield for multivoltine hybrid was estimated at 27 kg/100 dfls and the gross income at Rs. 400.00 to Rs. 500.00. It was estimated that the cost of mulberry cultivation accounted for nearly 45 per cent of the total expenditure and the balance constituted the rearing expenditure. Labour was found to account for 70 Per cent of the rearing expenditure.

The net income per acre was estimated to Rs. 6,000.00 per annum. Murthy in a study on economics of silk cocoon production in irrigated mulberry garden in Devanahalli taluk of Bangalore district observed that the average leaf per hectare was 25.38 Tonnes. Labour employed was 374.52 man days. The total cost of establishment was Rs. 1,676.55 per hectare. The net return from mulberry cultivation was Rs.7,430.61 and was maximum in the medium size group and minimum in the small size group. The yield of cocoon from a hectare of mulberry crop was 1,128.12 kg. The total cost of cocoon production was Rs.14,082.70 per hectare and operational cost accounted for 93 Per cent and the remaining was fixed cost. The net return from cocoon production was estimated to Rs. 8,202.70 per hectare and return to family labour and management amounted to Rs.10,583.85. The cost and returns from cocoon production did not show any definite trend with the size of group. The total labour force employed was 1,016 man days per hectare, of which 63.54 Per cent was family labour.

The distribution of labour was uniform through out the year. Lakshminarayan Rao estimated the establishment and cultivation costs of an hectare of mulberry leaf production to Rs.1,394.80 and Rs.7,541.50 respectively, in Anantapur district of Andhra Pradesh. The cost of production per kg of leaf was Rs. 0.27, while it was Rs.15.00 per kg of silk cocoon. Murtuza Khan studied the economics of sericulture in Anekal taluk of Bangalore Rural district and indicated that the gross return per rupee from commercial production was Rs.1.24. Marihonniah studied the income and employment generation in sericulture in Kunigal taluk of Karnataka state. The results showed that the total cost of cocoon production was Rs.13,548.95 for large, Rs.12,980.96 for marginal and Rs.12,449.62 for small farmers per hectare per year, with the over all average of Rs. 12,983.16. The average operational cost was Rs.11,711.08 per hectare per year, which accounted for 90.20 Per cent of the total cost. It was also reported that the cost of labour was 43.70 Per cent of operational cost, while the cost of mulberry leaves was 39.20 Per cent. The average gross income from cocoon production was Rs.18,906 per hectare per year and the average net income was Rs. 923.00. Sharma and Thakur in a study of economics of sericulture industry in Himachal Pradesh indicated that the total cost of rearing one ounce silk seed material was Rs. 352.00 and net returns was estimated at Rs. 596.00.

Raghavendra *et al.,* in their study of economics of bivoltine silk production estimated that the cultivation cost per acre per year for producing cross breed cocoons under irrigated conditions accounted for Rs. 4,312.05 in less than 0.50 acre, Rs. 3,037.39 in 0.50-1.00 acre and Rs. 2,514.27 in more than 1.00 acre farms. The labour cost per acre per year for these farm categories was Rs. 18,986.27, Rs.13,175.07 and Rs.11,056.45, respectively. Basavaraj in his study on income and employment generation in dry land sericulture observed that the average cost of establishing one acre of mulberry garden for large farmers was Rs.3,125.00. Lakshmanan *et al.,* studied the economic issues of production of mulberry cocoon in Tamil Nadu. It was estimated that the cost and benefit ratio for one hectare of mulberry garden was high in Dharmapuri (1: 1.41) as compared to Salem (1: 1.30). Srinivasa *et al.,* made an attempt to study the economic viability of sericulture enterprise in Kolar district of Karnataka. The results indicated that the establishment cost of mulberry gardens was Rs.6,480.00 per hectare and that of rearing assets was Rs.29,557.50. The net present value at the discount rate of 12.00 per cent was found to be Rs.70,940.08. The internal rate of return was 35.02 per cent and the benefit-cost ratio was worked out to be 2.82 at the discount rate of 12.00 per cent. Lakshmanan *et al.,* studied the economics of sericulture in four southern states namely, Karnataka, Andhra Pradesh,

Tamil Nadu and Kerala with a sample of 750 house holds during 1993-94 and 1995-96. The estimated total cost of mulberry leaf production in Karnataka indicated that farmers had incurred an average of Rs.9,580.40 and Rs.11 ,003045 during 1993-94 and '1995-96 under irrigated farms as against Rs.4,704.15and Rs.5,304.35 under rainfed farms during the above period. In Andhra Pradesh, it was worked to be Rs.9,672.00 and Rs.10,574.93 while in Tamil Nadu and Kerala, it was Rs.10,336.40 and Rs.9,854.95, Rs.9,517.55 and Rs. 6,144.20, respectively. The cost difference between years and states was due to increasing resource price and irrational use of factors of production in the farms. Lakshmanan *et al.,* compared the economic benefits in rearing of bivoltine with that of crossbreeds at farmers' level in K.R.Nagar taluk of Mysore district in Karnataka and inferred that rearing of bivoltine earned higher net return than crossbreed races owing to the prevailing suitable climate, skilled man power and technical guidance received from developmental agencies. Venkateswara Rao *et al.,* analyzed the economic viability of cocoon production in a new area (Elur, a coastal area of Andhra Pradesh) with that of traditional area (Chittoor district of Andhra Pradesh).

The cost of cocoon production was worked out to be Rs. 24,106.31 and Rs. 26,810.03 in Chittoor and Elur areas, respectively. The average yield obtained by the Chittoor farmers was higher (42.99 kg/100 dfls) than that of Elur farmers (38.50 kg/100 dfls): The Elur farmers realized the less average price for cocoon (Rs: 98.75/kg) compared to Chittoor farmers (Rs. 106.50/kg) due to non-availability of marketing facilities in that area which in turn caused deterioration of cocoon quality due to long distance transportation for marketing. The net revenue earned by Chittoor farmers was higher (Rs. 16,966.51) than that of Elur farmers (Rs. 5,863.55).

The cost benefit ratio was estimated to be Rs. 1:1.70 and 1:1.22, respectively for Chittoor and Elur areas. Srinivasa *et al.,* studied the cropping pattern and income level of both cross breed and bivoltine (CSR hybrid) silkworm rearers in Mandya district, Karnataka using linear programming technique. The model suggested 28.17 Per cent of total land holdings for mulberry for cross breed rearers. Mulberry was not suggested for rainfed area for both bivoltine and multivoltine rearers. With the suggested cropping pattern, the model offered an income of Rs.1.95 lakhs, Rs.1.53 lakhs and Rs.1. 74 lakhs, respectively for CSR hybrid, cross breed and pooled categories, which was found to be 25.90, 17.00 and 5.47 per cent higher than the existing cropping pattern. The total cost of production of cocoon was Rs. 32,786.75, Rs.37, 427.46 and Rs.34,638.31 for bivoltine (CSR hybrid) rearers, multivoltine rearers and the pooled rearers respectively. The net returns for the said categories were found to be Rs.15,756.86, Rs.20,051.16 and Rs.18,235.24, respectively. The net returns were low in the case of bivoltine rearers compared to the multivoltine rearers as the bivoltine race (CSR) was reared only from September to February, in which only three crops could be harvested as compared to 5 crops of multivoltine.

Kumaresan and Vijaya Prakash compared the economics of sericulture with that of the major crops cultivated in Gobichettipalayam taluk of Erode district in Tamil Nadu. The revenue obtained from sericulture (Rs.21, 153.51/acre/year) was comparatively higher than that of all other major crops cultivated in the area namely, paddy, sugarcane, gingelly, groundnut and sorghum except turmeric. Sabitha *et al.,* studied the comparative performance of different crops with mulberry. The study indicated that vegetable along with mulberry yielded maximum net income of Rs.2,83,500/acre/annum followed by mulberry with live stock (Rs.1,79,175 / acre / annum) and minimum net returns of Rs.56,015 / acre / annum was obtained when mulberry was grown with agro-forestry. Hiriyanna *et al.,* conducted a study to evaluate the economics of CSR hybrids *vis-à-vis* the popular multi x bi-hybrid (PM x NB D). The expenditure incurred for rearing CSR hybrids was higher than that of multi x bi-hybrid rearing due to usage of more inputs.

The cost-benefit ratio was higher with 1:1.92 for CSR hybrid compared to 1:1.35 for multi x bi-hybrid. Kumaresan *et al.,* studied the economics of bivoltine (CSR hybrid) cocoon production under PPPBST project in Karnataka. They estimated the total revenue to Rs.14,030.77 for CSR hybrid and Rs.8,016.31 for cross breed per 100 dfls.

The net revenue was estimated to Rs.3,545.66 and Rs.1,099.27 for CSR hybrids and cross breeds, respectively. The cost-benefit ratio was higher with 1:1.34 for CSR hybrids compared to 1:1.16 for cross breed. Dandin and Kumaresan estimated the cost of cocoon production as Rs. 73,516.80/acre/year and the net returns as Rs.39,883.20/acre/year. They opined from the sensitivity analysis that the silk cocoon prices significantly affected the profitability in cocoon production. In a study on the economic appraisal of silk cocoon production in the three Southern States viz., Karnataka, Andhra Pradesh and Tamil Nadu, Lakshmanan *et al.*, revealed that both the gross returns and net returns were quite high under the assured irrigated condition than the semi irrigated conditions. The profitability from sericulture was to the tune of Rs. 123059 per acre per year in case of Karnataka state, followed by Rs. 120703 per acre per year in case of Tamil Nadu and Rs. 74,607 per acre per year in case of Andhra Pradesh. The highest net return obtained in Karnataka was attributed mainly to the highest average yield of silk cocoon and price.

Employment Generation in Sericulture

Singh *et al* studied the pattern of employment of landless labourers under Integrated Rural Development Agency in Sultanpur district of Uttar Pradesh. The study revealed that the total family labour employed days were 128.75 per farm, out of which 60.94 and 67.81 days were utilized in agricultural and non-agricultural sectors, respectively on beneficiary farms. In case of non-beneficiary farms, the total family labour employed days were 133.08 per farm, out of which 82.62 and 50.46 days were utilized in both the sectors, respectively. Inder Sain and Joshi studied human labour employment in the Punjab agriculture. They estimated that family labour employed was 51 Per cent against the hired-in labour with 49 Per cent.

The study also exhibited an inverse relationship between the labour use and farm size. Ganapathi Rao *et al.,* found an inverse relationship of employment generation with the size of sericultural holdings and a direct relationship between hired labour use and size of land holdings. Tiwari and Singh in their study on employment pattern in agricultural crops and livestock, indicated that the distribution of land was quite skewed as the large farmers who comprised 14Per cent of the total households accounted for 51Per cent of the land while the marginal and small farmers who comprised 64Per cent of the households shared only 26Per cent of their land. In view of skewed distribution of land, landless, marginal and small farmers were dependent on livestock for income and employment.

On an average, the medium and large households maintained more milch animals and less work animals per household. Crop production and animal husbandry generated employment in the ratio of 2:1 on per worker basis and the ratio declined with an increase in the size while crop production generated 372 man days per household. Man days generated per livestock showed almost a negative relationship with the increase in the size of holding. Thus the results suggested that further diversification into livestock keeping would provide continuity and stability in rural employment. Pramanik *et al.,* studied the generation of agricultural employment potential in the adopted village as a result of transfer of modern high yielding technologies. As a result of the area under high yielding varieties of rice increased by 8 per cent, an additional employment was generated at the same pace through more engagement of farmers in cultivation of this crop.

It was observed that 10 per cent and 13.33 per cent of additional man days was generated in 1992 and 1993, respectively over 1991. Lakshmanan *et al.,* conducted a study on labour composition in sericulture in Salem and Dharmapuri districts of Tamil Nadu with a sample of 100 respondents. The data were post-stratified into four groups based on the operational area under mulberry. Group I having the mulberry holding of 0.01-0.50 acre utilized 73.74 man days, group II (0.51-1.00 acre) utilized 67.47 man days, group III (1.011.50 acre) utilized 64.23 man days and group IV (more than 1.51 acre) utilized 57.28 man days. In case of hired labour (male & female) engagement it was found that the hired labour use was 29 Per cent in size I and 57.75 Per cent in size IV. The family labour share showed an inverse relationship with the size of farm groups. Further, the over all farm group situations showed that the percentage of female labour participation (55.91 per cent) was more than male labour (44.09 per cent). Women contributed a higher proportion of total labour on all farm size groups. Their participation in mulberry and silkworm rearing was 58.46 per cent and 54.13 per cent, respectively.

The reason for higher female labour employment was due to the unskilled and women friendly activities in mulberry leaf production and silkworm rearing. Jayaram *et al.,* conducted a comparative study on labour employment under different mulberry farm holdings. The data were collected from 400 randomly selected farmers from Karnataka state. The estimated number of labour engaged in sericulture per acre per year under irrigated and rainfed conditions were 357 and 170 man days, respectively.

The small mulberry holdings (up to 0.50 acre) accounted for an employment of 624 and 278 man days per acre annually under irrigated and rainfed conditions, respectively. The mulberry farm of size category of 0.51 to 1.00 acre had an employment potential of 498 and 230 man days, respectively per acre annually under irrigated and rainfed conditions. The labour employed under the second category of farms (1.00 to 1.50 acre) was annually 395 and 196 man days per acre, respectively under irrigated and rainfed conditions. Similarly, the last category (above 1.50 acre) of farms generated an employment to the tune of 261 and 129 man days per acre per year, respectively under irrigated and rainfed conditions. The results revealed that the small-scale farms were good sources of income generation, as they tended to practice intensive type of cultivation.

Therefore, the average yield of cocoon under irrigated conditions was as high as 401.40 kg per acre per year under small holdings category of mulberry compared to 279.40 kg per acre per year under large mulberry holding category. The yield level per acre per year under rainfed conditions was also found to be high in the case of (171.65 kg) small holdings compared to that of large holdings (90.42 kg). Kumaresan *et al* evaluated the comparative economics and labour use pattern of shoot and shelf methods of silkworm rearing. The data were collected by using random sampling method from 30 farmers practicing shelf method of silkworm rearing in Salem taluk of Salem district and 30 farmers adopted shoot rearing method in Gobichettipalayam taluk of Erode district in Tamil Nadu.

The results indicated that 5.72 man days of male labour and 11.23 man days of female labour could be saved for rearing 100 dfls in shoot rearing over shelf rearing method. The revenue generation in cocoon production was also found to be more in shoot rearing method of silkworm rearing. Pushpa and Netaji conducted a study on income and employment pattern of farmers in various integrated fanning systems in 10 villages of Rasipuram and Namakkal taluks of Salem district.

The results indicated that the additional employment generated by poultry was 160 man days, whereas, it was 170 man days in dairy. But the maximum additional employment generated by a single enterprise was from sericulture with 515 man days. The sericulture included integrated farming systems, were able to generate high level of employment opportunities. Lakshmanan *et al.*, investigated the employment pattern and labour productivity in sericultural operations and inferred that the labour employment was more in smaller mulberry holdings, while the labour productivity was more in larger mulberry holdings.

They also found more female participation in sericulture operations when compared to male labour. Saraswathi and Sumangala studied on participation of farm women in sericulture enterprise in Dharwad district. The participation level in sericulture was categorized into high, medium and low based on mean data.

Further, to study the relationship between dependent (participation) variable with independent (income, land holdings and sericulture land holdings) variables, Karl-Pearson's product moment correlation co-efficient was worked out. The study indicated that the participation of farm women in outdoor activity (mulberry cultivation) was to the extent of 72.80 per cent while in indoor activity (silkworm rearing), it was 84.40 per cent. In harvesting and grading, inter-cultivation, pruning and management of worms during different instars, the farm women participation as a worker was also good and the observed participation was 82.89 per cent, 64.76 per cent, 46.74 per cent and 44.39 per cent, respectively.

Participation was very low in packing and marketing of cocoons, procurement of disease free layings (dfls) and incubation. Meenal and Rajan revealed the preference of sericulture enterprise in the rural Tamil Nadu for its short gestation period and low investment.

The sericulture enterprise was found to provide significant opportunity for employment in the farm. The total employment generated per acre per year among the adopters of technologies in sericulture was to the extent of 565 man days compared to 467 man days in case of non-adopters of technology. The share of family labour to the total labour employed was equivalent to 39.12 per cent and 44.95 per cent respectively, under the adopter and non-adopter categories of farmers.

MEASUREMENT OF VARIABLES USED IN THE STUDY

The respondent farmers were drawn at random form the four selected districts of Karnataka state viz., Mandya, Bangalore (Rural), Kolar and Hassan. A multistage random sampling procedure was adopted to select 240 farmers followed by an interview with a designed questionnaire (discussed in Chapter Two).

Data on important technological inputs, the impact on productivity, income and employment were elicited. For the purpose of judging the level of change in the productivity, income and employment, the data were post-classified in three different ways namely i) classification based on different categories of farmers (based on mulberry farm holding), ii) classification based on type of silkworm rearer i.e., bivoltine (CSR hybrid) silkworm rearer and cross breed silkworm rearer and iii) classification based on the sample districts i. e., Mandya, Bangalore (rural), Kolar, and Hassan. The data were subjected for evaluation based on the above classification.

The respondents in the present study were assessed in terms of variables such as age, education, size of land holding, cropping pattern, livestock possession, extension contact, mass media participation, extension participation, cosmopoliteness. The study also was further elaborated with the analysis of cost of production of mulberry sericulture as compared to other major crop enterprises specific to corresponding districts of the respondents. An attempt was also made to evaluate the level of adoption of technologies in sericulture and thereby constraints faced by the sericulturists in the adoption of technologies evolved in sericulture.

Age

Age of each of the respondents covered in the study was measured as the number of calendar years completed by the respondent at the time of the interview. A frequency table to this effect was constructed.

Education

This is operationally defined as the number of years of formal education acquired by a respondent. Education was measured by assigning the following scores;

Category	Score
Illiterate	0
Primary school	1
Middle school	2
Secondary education	3
College onwards	4

Size of Land Holding and Area under Mulberry

Data pertaining to the total acreage of the holdings in terms of dry land, wet land and garden land possessed by the respondents were recorded. Further the rearers were classified based on the mulberry land holdings under mulberry, as small, medium and large rearers by adopting the following procedure.

Type of rearer	Mulberry acreage
Small	< Mean – 1 Standard Deviation
Medium	>Mean - 1 Standard Deviation and < Mean + 1 Standard Deviation
Large	> Mean + 1 Standard Deviation

The classification was made separately for both categories *viz.*, bivoltine (CSR hybrid) silkworm rearers and cross breed silkworm rearers.

Dependents in the Family and Total Work Force in the Family

The number of dependents in the family was recorded and out of this the number of persons working on the farm as family labour was recorded and the respondents were classified accordingly.

Size of family labour	Criteria
Small	< Mean – 1 Standard Deviation
Medium	>Mean - 1 Standard Deviation and < Mean + 1 Standard Deviation
Large	> Mean + 1 Standard Deviation

Cropping Pattern

The crops grown on each of the respondent's farm was recorded and accordingly the cropping pattern of the sample respondents were worked out. The share of acreage under various crops viz., seasonal crops, annuals and perennials were recorded and is presented in acres.

Livestock Possession

The livestock possession was measured by following the scoring procedure as detailed below;

Possession of one bullock	1
Possession of one local cow or one local buffalo	1
Possession of one cross breed cow or one cross breed buffalo	2
Possession of three sheep or three goats	1
Possession of ten chickens	1

The total score obtained with respect to each of the respondent was worked out and were divided into different categories based on the mean and Standard Deviation (S.D.);

Livestock possession	Criteria
Small	< Mean – 1 Standard Deviation
Medium	>Mean - 1 Standard Deviation and < Mean + 1 Standard Deviation
Large	> Mean + 1 Standard Deviation

Extension Contact

The information from the respondents about their contact with extension worker/personnel was obtained. The frequency of meeting various extension personnel in the order of Deputy Director of Sericulture, Assistant Director of Sericulture, Sericulture Extension Officer, Sericulture Inspector, Demonstrators and so on was recorded giving appropriate score.

Extension personnel	Score
Deputy Director of Sericulture/ Assistant Director of Sericulture	3
Sericulture Extension Officer	2
Sericulture Inspector/ Demonstrators	1
None	0

The average extension contact scores of the respondents were computed and grouped into following categories;

Extension contact	Criteria
Low	< Mean – 1 Standard Deviation
Medium	>Mean - 1 Standard Deviation and < Mean + 1 Standard Deviation
High	> Mean + 1 Standard Deviation

Extension Programme Participation

A list of eight to nine extension activities viz., group discussions, field days, seminars Demonstrations, film shows, seminars, exhibitions, farm visits etc., which are normally conducted under an average village situation was prepared and the respondents were asked to indicate their participation under each of these activities. Based on the scores were obtained, the respondents were grouped into three categories using the Mean and Standard Deviation (S.D.) values.

Extension participation	Criteria
Low	< Mean – 1 Standard Deviation
Medium	>Mean - 1 Standard Deviation and < Mean + 1 Standard Deviation
High	> Mean + 1 Standard Deviation

Mass Media Participation

The mass media participation of the farmers was measured by following the scoring procedure as detailed below;

(i)	Media	Subscriber	Not a subscriber	
	Newspaper	1	0	
	Farm magazine	1	0	
(ii)	Use of the media	See/ listen	Do not see / listen	
	Rural radio programme	1	0	
	Television programmes on agriculture	1	0	
(iii)	Frequency of use	Regular/daily	Occasional	Never
	Newspaper	2	1	0
	Farm Magazine	2	1	0
	Radio	2	1	0
	Television	2	1	0

The average mass media participation scores under each category of farmers was computed and expressed in mean scores. Further the respondents were grouped into three categories of mass media participation using mean (X) and Standard Deviation (S.D.) as detailed below;

Mass media participation	Criteria
Low	< Mean – 1 Standard Deviation
Medium	>Mean - 1 Standard Deviation and < Mean + 1 Standard Deviation
High	> Mean + 1 Standard Deviation

Cosmopoliteness

The major consideration under this parameter was how the farmer was associated with the institutions catering to the needs of village community. The participation of respondents in theses institutions viz., Farmers' Service Cooperative Society, Milk Producers' Cooperative Society, Sericulture Quality Clubs, Self Help Groups, Youth Clubs etc., was scored. The average cosmopoliteness scores under each category of the farmers was computed and expressed in mean scores. The respondents were then grouped into three categories of cosmopoliteness using mean (X) and Standard Deviation (S.D.) as detailed below;

Cosmopoliteness	Criteria
Low	< Mean – 1 Standard Deviation
Medium	>Mean - 1 Standard Deviation and < Mean + 1 Standard Deviation
High	> Mean + 1 Standard Deviation

CLASSIFICATION OF RESPONDENTS

Information were collected from the sericulturists through interview method to ascertain the impact of sericultural technologies on production, employment pattern and profitability in the selected districts of Mandya,

Bangalore (rural), Kolar and Hassan districts of Karnataka. The two categories of farmers in the current study *viz*, bivoltine (CSR hybrid) silkworm rearers and cross breed silkworm rearers, were further classified based on the individual scores obtained on the adoption of different sericulture technologies. A list of 20 important sericulture related technologies which have significant impact on productivity, were prepared, and were administered while surveying. Consequent upon obtaining the individual scores, the farmers were again post-classified as 'adopters' of the sericulture technology and 'non-adopters' of the sericulture technology by deriving the adoption index for each farmer, under both the categories of respondents.

SOCIO-ECONOMIC STATUS OF SERICULTURISTS

The general characteristics of sample farmers were studied to understand the farming environment and comprehend the problem perspective. The socio-economic characteristics covered were - age of the head of the family, literacy level, family composition, farm size and land holding pattern and mulberry holding of the sample farmers.

Age of the Respondents

A large majority of the respondent farmers were found to be in the age group of 30 to 50 years. It was found that, the average age of the selected bivoltine (CSR hybrid) rearers was 38.25 years, as compared to 44. 57 years in case of cross breed silkworm rearers. While 55.73 Per cent of bivoltine (CSR hybrid) silkworm rearers were below 40 years of age, the cross breed silkworm rearers constituted up to 39.71 Per cent.

Table: Age Group Respondent Formers

Sl. No.	Age in years	Bivoltine (CSR hybrid) rearers		Crossbreed rearers	
		Number	Per cent	Number	Per cent
1	Less than 30 years	25	24.04	16	11.77
2	31 to 40 years	33	31.73	38	27.94
3	41 to 50 years	37	35.58	48	35.29
4	More than 50 years	9	8.65	34	25.00
	Total	104	100.00	136	100.00
	Average age (years)	38.25		44.57	

Educational Status of Respondents

The education status of the respondent farmers was studied and it was noted that the rate of illiteracy was up to an extent of 6.73 per cent in case of bivoltine (CSR hybrid) silkworm rearers and the same was up to 10. 30 per cent in case of cross breed silkworm rearers. It was noted that a large majority of the sample respondents had completed middle and secondary school education in both the cases.

Table: Education Status of the Respondents

Sl. No.	Particulars	Bivoltine (CSR hybrid) rearers		Crossbreed rearers	
		Number	Per cent	Number	Per cent
1	Illiterate	7	6.73	14	10.30
2	Primary school	12	11.54	15	11.03
2	Middle school	46	44.23	65	47.79
3	Secondary school	28	26.92	30	22.06
4	College education	11	10.58	12	8.82
	Total	104	-	136	-

Family Size

It was found that the average size of the family was 5.32 with respect to bivoltine (CSR hybrid) silkworm rearers and 6.85 in case of cross breed silkworm rearers. Out of the total size of the family, number of male (adult) was the highest in case of bivoltine (CSR hybrid) silkworm rearers at 2.18 number per family followed by 2.15 number in case of cross breed silkworm rearers. The children constituted 30.02 per cent and 31.09 per cent in the family of bivoltine (CSR hybrid) silkworm rearers and cross breed silkworm rearers respectively, while the female (adult) constituted 28.30 per cent and 37.52 per cent in the family of bivoltine (CSR hybrid) silkworm rearers and cross breed silkworm rearers respectively, indicating a reasonable dependency level in the families.

Table: Family Composition of the Respondents

Sl. No.	Particulars	Bivoltine (CSR hybrid) rearers		Cross breed rearers	
		Number	Per cent	Number	Per cent
1	Male (adult)	2.18	41.68	2.15	31.39
2	Female (adult)	1.48	28.30	2.57	37.52
3	Children	1.57	30.02	2.13	31.09
	Total	5.23	100	6.85	100

Land Holding Pattern

Land holding status is one of the measures of indicating the economic status of the farmers. The farmers' land holdings in terms of wet land, garden land dry and dry land were pooled and the status of holding size was determined. It was found that the average land holdings of cross breed silkworm rearers was higher (4.06 acres) than that of bivoltine (CSR hybrid) silkworm rearers (3.23

acres). A large majority of the respondent farmers had the holding size equal to less than one acre (36.54 per cent in case of bivoltine (CSR hybrid) silkworm rearers and 52.21 per cent of the cross breed silkworm rearers).

Table: Land Holiding Pattern of the Respondents

Sl. No.	Particulars	Bivoltine (CSR hybrid) rearers		Cross breed rearers	
		Number	Per cent	Number	Per cent
1	Less than one acre	38	36.54	71	52.21
2	1.00 - 3.00 acres	36	34.62	27	19.85
3	3.01 – 5.00 acres	22	21.15	18	13.24
4	More than 5.00 acres	8	7.69	20	14.71
	Total	104	100.00	136	100.00
	Average holding (acres)	3.23	-	4.06	-

Area Covered under Mulberry

The area covered under mulberry was ascertained. It was noted that a large majority of the sample respondents had mulberry acreage equal to less than one acre (44.23 per cent) in case of bivoltine (CSR hybrid) silkworm rearers and 63.97 per cent in case of cross breed silkworm rearers, indicating that the economic units of mulberry gardens were usually small. Out of total 104 bivoltine (CSR hybrid) silkworm rearers, nearly 15 (14.42 per cent) farmers owned more than two acres of mulberry garden, while 28 cross breed silkworm rearers (20.59 per cent) had the same acreage under mulberry. The average mulberry holding size of CSR hybrid rearers was up to 1.08 acres when compared to 1.25 acres of mulberry garden under cross breed silkworm rearers.

Table: Mulberry Holiding Size of the Respondents

Sl. No.	Particulars	Bivoltine (CSR hybrid) rearers		Cross breed rearers	
		Number	Per cent	Number	Per cent
1	Less than one acre	46	44.23	87	63.97
2	1.01 – 2.00 acres	43	41.35	21	15.44
3	More than 2.00 acres	15	14.42	28	20.59
	Total	104	100.00	136	100.00
	Average mulberry holding(acre)	1.08	-	1.25	-

Cropping Pattern of Respondent Farms

The existing cropping pattern under different crops of the sample respondents was worked out. The district wise, analysis revealed that the intensity of cropping was as high as 139.20 in case of Hassan district, followed by 137.54 in case of Mandya district, 131.65 in Kolar district and 120.63 in case of Bangalore (rural) district. The cropping intensity is given by the ratio of the total cropped area to total cultivated area, expressed in per cent. The major crops grown in all the districts were paddy and ragi, besides mulberry. However, Mandya (0.47 acre per household) had significant share of area under sugarcane, while Hassan district had a share of potato crop (0.91 acre per household). Kolar district also had a significant share of vegetable crops up to 0.45 acre per household. Among the respondents, the mulberry holding size was the highest in Kolar district (1.58 acres per household) followed by Bangalore (rural), Hassan and Mandya districts at the rate of 1.16 acres, 1.08 acres and 0.75 acre per household respectively.

Livestock Possession of Respondents

The livestock possession of the individual farmers was worked out and it was found that the average number of livestock units was as high as 7.51 in case of cross breed silkworm rearers when compared to 5.85 units in case of bivoltine (CSR hybrid) silkworm rearers. As the mulberry sericulture ensures a complementary relation with the dairy industry, the livestock possession with the farmers gains significance.

EXTENSION SYSTEM AND SUPPORT FOR TECHNOLOGY DISSEMINATION

Agriculture extension in developing countries has a significant influence on the rate of adoption of technologies. Various intermediaries associated with extension work, adhere to i) precise plan of work, ii) monitoring and evaluation and iii) corrective action. The introduction of various extension programmes in India, have envisaged the importance of managing agriculture extension system. In this respect the training and visit system in India introduced during eighties, has made a commendable strides in the dissemination of information to the field. The great advantage of this system of extension is the feedback it provides to the extension managers and subject matter specialists. In this respect every farmer will be accountable in acquiring knowledge and adopting the same through the change agents of the extension system. Hence in the present study an assessment of the impact of the extension system on the farmers was done. Hence a measure of rate of extension contact, extension programme participation, mass media participation and the extent of cosmopoliteness of the respondent farmers was determined.

Extension Contact

The level of extension contact of both the categories of respondent farmers was ascertained and found that, the level of extension contact was comparatively low among the non adopters (36.90 per cent) of the technology, than adopters

(25.00 per cent). However the extension contact was also low among the cross breed silkworm rearers when compared to bivoltine (CSR hybrid) silkworm rearers. The level of extension contact was highest among 28.10 per cent of non-adopters and 28.69 Per cent of adopters of technologies.

Extension Programme Participation

The extension programme participation by the respondent farmers also was studied and it was found that, the rate of extension programme participation was highest among the bivoltine (CSR hybrid) silkworm rearing farmers, than the cross breed. The adopter category farmers rearing bivoltine (CSR hybrid) silkworm (29.26 per cent) were found to have participated in more number of extension programmes than the other categories of farmers. Majority of both the adopter (49.44 per cent) and non-adopter (50.49 per cent) categories of crossbreed silkworm rearing farmers attended minimum number of extension programmes than bivoltine (CSR hybrid) silkworm rearers.

Mass Media Participation

The mass media participation of the respondent farmers were recorded and analysed. It was found that among the bivoltine (CSR hybrid) silkworm rearers, the adopter category of the farmers had more exposure to mass media (39.15 per cent) than the non-adopter category (28.85 per cent). Similarly the adopter category of cross breed silkworm rearers (33.13 per cent) had more exposure to mass media than the non-adopters (27.51 per cent). Overall it was found that the adopter category farmers had more exposure to mass media (36.14 per cent) than the non-adopters of technologies. From the above analysis it can be noted that, mass media contact in a way has a bearing on acquisition of essential knowledge and skills required in production. This is because majority of the farmers under adopter category have a high rate of mass media participation. Hence the success of the farmers was essentially brought out by the continuous exposure to mass media in the study area.

Cosmopoliteness

Similar to the other extension variables considered, the cosmopoliteness of the farmers was assessed for elucidating the entrepreneurial ability of a successful farmer in the study area. It was found that the cosmopoliteness of the bivoltine (CSR hybrid) silkworm rearers was highest when compared to that of the cross breed silkworm rearers. The cross breed silkworm reaers were found to be very poor in social activities. This was clear from the fact that nearly 84.97 Per cent of non-adopters and 88.56 Per cent adopters of cross breed silkworm rearers had a low per centage level of cosmopoliteness. Hence it can be inferred that, the bivoltine (CSR hybrid) silkworm rearers were comparatively better than the cross breed silkworm rearers in participating in various social organizations. From the above analysis it can be inferred that, the extent of adoption of technologies in sericulture were guided by the extension variables considered under the study. Efforts to strengthen the extension system at the farmers' level should be done on priority. Extension experts need to address the real basic problems of technology transfer and motivate the farmers in adopting the technologies.

IMPACT OF TECHNOLOGIES ON PRODUCTIVITY, INCOME AND EMPLOYMENT IN SERICULTURE AND ALLIED CROPS

With an objective to study the efficiency of the farm-firm and to evaluate the shares of different inputs in the production of sericulture and allied crops, an estimate of costs and returns generated in each of these selected respondents' farm were estimated. The data were later converted to a unit area of one acre and presented. A normal time period of one year was considered for assessing the efficiency of the farm. The cost concepts such as Cost A, Cost B and Cost C were worked out and presented. These distinct costs were worked out as because much of the inputs used in the respondents' farms were owned. It is mainly because the farmers try to minimize out of pocket expenses of cultivation, and that, by and large, they make maximum use of the resources they own.

VALUATION OF DIFFERENT INPUTS

A valuation of different inputs used in mulberry cultivation and silkworm rearing was attempted. Different input components were evaluated and valued keeping specific standards and these are as listed below:

1. The cost of human labour was valued at the prevailing rate paid by each farmer to male and female workers. Family labour was also imputed at the wage rate paid to the hired labour. Bullock power, both hired and owned was valued at the prevailing wage rates in the locality.
2. Farm Yard Manure (FYM) produced and purchased was valued at the local rates paid by the farmers along with other incidental charges.
3. The cost of irrigation was worked out based on the maintenance cost of pump sets, irrigation channels and open wells and the wages paid for irrigating the - garden.
4. The exact cost paid by each farmer for the Disease Free Layings (DFLs) or silkworm eggs along with other incidental charges like cost of transportation was considered as the cost of layings.
5. Mulberry leaf was valued as the actual cost of cultivation of mulberry per acre minus the cost of sold out leaves, if any plus the cost of purchased leaves, if any.
6. The cost of marketing includes the transportation cost, loading and

unloading charges besides market fee and other incidental charges actually paid by the farmers in the marketing of cocoons.

7. Land revenue was taken as the actual revenue paid by the farmers per acre per year.
8. Depreciation on equipments used in the cultivation of mulberry garden was calculated for individual farmers by straight-line method by considering the life span of the equipments.

$$\text{Annual depreciation} = \frac{\text{Purchased or construction value (Rs.)}}{\text{Useful life span of the asset (years)}}$$

The average life span of the asset as indicated by each farmer was used in compilation of the depreciation.

9. The actual cash expenditure incurred by the farmers on the wages paid for hiring human labour and bullock power, expenditure on fertilizers and FYM, irrigation charges and maintenance expenditures etc. were taken into consideration. In case of silk cocoon production, the cost of Disease Free Layings (DFLs), cost of mulberry leaf purchased, rearing house disinfection cost, transportation and marketing expenditures and miscellaneous expenses were accounted for working out interest on working capital. The interest rate on working capital was calculated at the rate of 12 per cent, which is charged by the commercial banks for crop loans.
10. Imputation of values of owned inputs like family labour, which comes from family source was accounted in computing the cost of cultivation.
11. Interest on fixed capital was calculated at the rate of 12 per cent being the opportunity cost of capital (lending rate of banks). The total interest calculated was then apportioned to mulberry crop based on the percentage of use of fixed assets for mulberry cultivation.
12. The annual apportioned establishment cost was estimated by dividing the total establishment cost by the economic life of mulberry garden (15 years). The establishment cost was estimated during the reference year by using the average physical input requirements for one acre and the corresponding average prices during the reference year. Since mulberry gardens were established during different years in the past, this procedure was adopted to bring the establishment cost of the garden to a uniform comparable basis. The establishment cost included mainly the cost of preparatory tillage, human labour, bullock power used in ploughing, cuttings or saplings, manures, fertilizers and irrigation used up to six months from the date of planting.
13. Rent on owned land was estimated on the basis of prevalent rents in the villages for identical types of land,

14. The output (cocoons) was valued as the actual price received by the farmers at the silk cocoon markets.
15. The by-products in mulberry cultivation are the residual shoot portions of mulberry plant harvested in a year. It was valued at the existing local rates. The left over leaf and litter from silkworm rearing were also valued at local rate.

ACCOUNTING COSTS AND RETURNS UNDER THE STUDY

1. The variable costs include wages for owned and hired human labour, owned and hired bullock power, cost of farmyard manures and fertilizers, interest on working capital, maintenance charges, land revenue, cost of DFLs or chawki worms, hiring charges of mountages, disinfection, marketing, maintenance and other miscellaneous expenses used in mulberry cultivation and silkworm rearing.
2. The fixed costs include apportioned costs of establishment of mulberry garden, depreciation on farm implements, equipments, rearing house and appliances and interest on fixed capital.
3. The gross income was valued at total value of cocoons sold in the market plus returns from by-products namely, the stems, left over leaves and litter, which is the rearing bed refuse.
4. Net income was arrived at by deducting the total cost of production from gross income.
5. The costs and returns were worked out for one acre and for one year. Simple tabular analysis was used to estimate the costs, returns and employment generation in mulberry cultivation and silkworm rearing.

COST CONCEPTS AND PROCEDURE FOR EVALUATION

For determining the cost structure, of the farms, a method similar to the farm management studies has been adopted. There are a few important cost concepts such as Cost A , Cost A , Cost B , Cost B , Cost C and Cost C , which have been worked out in the current study. On the basis of these concepts, total costs of inputs per acre were worked out for sericulture as well as other important crop enterprises in the selected districts. The cost computation was done for the individual groups of adopter and non adopter categories of technologies in sericulture. The estimates of gross income per acre for the sericulture and other important crops were also estimated based on the prevailing market price and presented. The estimates of gross income were also worked out for the adopter and non adopter categories of technologies of sericulture. The important measures of farm profit are net farm income, farm investment income, family labour income and farm business income. The estimates of measures of farm profit per acre from sericulture and other competing crop enterprises have been worked out and presented as follows:

- Productivity of inputs, distribution of costs and gross income earned from sericulture in selected districts of Karnataka state
- Productivity of inputs, distribution of costs and gross income earned from sericulture under different mulberry holding sizes:
  - Bivoltine (CSR hybrid) silkworm rearers;
  - Cross breed silkworm rearers
- Productivity of inputs, distribution of costs and gross income earned from sericulture among different adopter categories:
  - Bivoltine (CSR hybrid) silkworm rearers;
  - Cross breed silkworm rearers
- Productivity of inputs, distribution of costs and gross income earned from other major crops in the selected districts:
  - Mandya district;
  - Bangalore (rural) district;
  - Kolar district;
  - Hassan district

PRODUCTIVITY OF INPUTS, DISTRIBUTION OF COSTS AND GROSS INCOME EARNED FROM SERICULTURE IN SELECTED DISTRICTS OF KARNATAKA STATE

It is observed that in terms of the per cent contribution, the human labour was the single largest item of cost (for cultivation of mulberry and rearing of silkworm). The individual input costs were worked out both for the production of mulberry as well as silk cocoon. The gross income gained through the sale of silk cocoon and its by-products was worked out.

Cost of Cultivation of Mulberry

On these farms, the average cost of production of mulberry leaf is worked out to Rs. 21,467.06 per acre per year. However, the cost of production of mulberry leaf was the least in Bangalore (rural) at Rs. 17,504.60 per acre per year followed by Mandya (Rs. 19,084.43), Hassan (Rs. 23,519.20) and Kolar (Rs. 26,104.89) districts. Among the cost components, labour was the major item amounting to Rs. 5997.14 per acre per year, which accounted for nearly 28 Per cent of production cost of mulberry. The expenditure incurred on Farm Yard Manure was the next highest cost in production of mulberry. The average input cost of FYM was found to be Rs. 4992.23 per acre per year which accounted for nearly 23 per cent of total production cost of mulberry. The cost of fertilizers in mulberry leaf production (Rs. 4375.78 per acre per year) accounted for nearly 20 Per cent of the production cost of mulberry. Mulberry being a perennial crop, the costs incurred on establishment of mulberry garden was apportioned to the economic life span of mulberry garden, which was considered as 15 years, and accounted as fixed costs in working out the cost of mulberry. The fixed cost incurred was thus worked out to Rs. 738.59 per acre per year, which accounted for 3.44 Per cent of the total cost.

Cost of Silkworm Rearing

The total silkworm rearing cost was the highest in case of Kolar district (Rs. 37,002.10 per acre per year), followed by Hassan district (Rs. 33.485.00 per acre per year), Mandya district (Rs. 32,787.60 per acre per year) and Bangalore (rural) district (Rs. 29,837.90 per acre per year). The average cost of labour was found to be the most prominent and a major component in the cost of silkworm rearing too. The average cost of human labor in silkworm rearing was found to Rs. 13795.70 per acre per year, which is equivalent to 41 per cent of total silkworm rearing cost. The second highest cost contribution was from depreciation cost.

The average cost of depreciation on rearing building and equipments was found to be Rs. 7691.99 per acre per year, which accounted for nearly 23 per cent of the silkworm rearing cost. The total cost of silk cocoon production was found to be on an average Rs. 54,745.20 per acre per year. The total cost of silk cocoon production was highest in case of Kolar district (Rs. 63,107.00 per acre per year) followed by Hassan district (Rs. 57,004.20 per acre per year), Mandya district (Rs. 51,872.10 per acre per year). Finally the total income derived was found to be on an average Rs. 94,361.80 per acre per year.

The income derived from sericulture was highest in Kolar district (Rs. 112077.00 per acre per year), followed by Hassan district (Rs. 103769.00 per acre per year), Mandya district (Rs. 82,477.50 per acre per year) and Bangalore (rural) district (Rs. 79,124.00 per acre per year). The average yield of silk cocoon was found to be 62.28 kg/100 dfls. However, among the districts, the productivity of silk cocoon was highest in case of Kolar district (70.43 kg/100 dfls) followed by Hassan district (66.94 kg/100 dfls), Bangalore (rural) district (56.81 kg/100 dfls) and Mandya district (54.93 kg/100 dfls).

Cost concepts, Distribution of Costs, and Measure of Profits from Sericulture in the Selected Districts of Karnataka State

Distribution of costs on various inputs in production provides an indicator of the pattern of use of various inputs as well as their relative importance in the total cost of production. In the present study, the distribution of costs in the production of silk cocoon, into Cost A, Cost B and Cost C were worked out for the selected districts. The cost A which comprises all cash and kind expenses showed a wide variation between the districts. The cost A per cropped area was found to be Rs. 42,713.66 per acre per year. There was a clear distinction between each of the costs considered in the study. Further, a higher rate of costs per acre per year was noticed in the districts of Kolar (Cost C at Rs. 63,106.97 per acre per year) and Hassan (Cost C at Rs. 57,004.24 per acre per year) than in the districts of Mandya (Cost C at Rs. 51,872.06 per acre per year) and Bangalore (Rural) at Rs. 47,342.54 per acre per year. It is evidenced that the different costs such as Cost A , cost A , Cost B , Cost B and Cost C are normally higher in the more progressive areas than in less progressive areas. Hence the districts of Kolar and Hassan in Karnataka, can very well be adjudged as the most progressive areas for sericulture than, Mandya and Bangalore (Rural) districts, considered in the study.

It is estimated that the gross income from sericulture was Rs. 94,361.81 per acre per year. However, the estimated gross income in the selected districts were in the order of Rs.1,12,077.01 (Kolar district), Rs.1,037,68.78 (Hassan district), Rs.82,477.48 (Mandya district) and Rs.79,123.95 (Bangalore (rural) district). The net farm income was highest at Rs. 48,970 per acre per year in case of Kolar district followed by Rs. 46,764 per acre per year, Rs. 31,781 per acre per year and Rs. 30,605.42 per acre per year in case of Hassan, Bangalore (rural) and Mandya districts respectively. The family labour income which refers to the return to family labour and management, was highest in case of Kolar district (Rs. 60,055.09 per acre per year) followed by Hassan district (Rs. 53,932.69 per acre per year), Bangalore (Rural) district (Rs. 40,927.96 per acre per year) and Mandya district (Rs. 38,696.90 per acre per year).

Employment Generation in Sericulture in the Selected Districts of Karnataka

The employment potential of sericulture indicated engagement of nearly 363 mandays of labour per acre per year. It was found that the engagement of labour in mulberry cultivation was to the tune of 84 man days, while that of silkworm rearing, it was 279 man days. The major activities included in mulberry cultivation included intercultural operations, weeding, spraying chemicals etc., while the activities in silkworm rearing included mulberry leaf/ shoot harvest, feeding silkworm, disinfection of rearing house, cleaning, spraying bed disinfectants, mounting ripened larvae, harvesting silk cocoon etc. Due to the continuous changes taking place in terms of biological and mechanical innovations in sericulture, it is expected to have an impact on productivity, cropping intensity, gross income and employment.

Hence, the enterprise has a potential to absorb the labour force significantly. An attempt was made to estimate the number of hired labour employed in sericulture and it was found that nearly 55 per cent (200 mandays per acre per year) of the total labour was hired for engaging in various activities of sericulture. The district wise engagement of labour in sericulture was estimated and the number of man days engaged in sericulture was found to be the highest in case of Mandya district (416 mandays), followed by Bangalore (Rural) district (401 mandays), Hassan district (331 mandays) and Kolar district (306 mandays).

PRODUCTIVITY OF INPUTS, DISTRIBUTION OF COSTS AND GROSS INCOME EARNED FROM SERICULTURE UNDER DIFFERENT MULBERRY HOLDING SIZES

A classification of respondents (both cross breed silkworm rearers and bivoltine (CSR hybrid) silkworm rearers based on the land holding under mulberry, yielded three distinct categories, which were further sub-classified as small scale silkworm rearers also called small farmers, medium scale silkworm rearers also called medium farmers and large scale rearers also called big farmers. An attempt was made to estimate the returns, costs associated and employment generated under these categories.

Bivoltine (CSR hybrid) Silkworm Rearers

The mulberry land holding size wise classification of bivoltine (CSR hybrid) rearers, yielded three distinct categories of farmers such as small scale silkworm rearers i.e., small farmers, medium scale silkworm rearers i.e. medium farmers and large scale rearers i.e. big farmers. An analysis of costs associated in production, returns generated and employment potential of these three categories are presented as follows.

Out of the total cost of production the cost of human labour was (for cultivation of mulberry and rearing of silkworm) as high as Rs. 21,800 per acre per year (37 per cent of total cost of production) in case of small farmers, followed by Rs. 20,550 per acre per year (39 per cent of total cost of production) in case of large farmers and Rs. 18,966 per acre per year (38 per cent of total cost of production) in case of medium farmers. The total cost of production was found to be Rs. 57,847 per acre per year in case of small farmers, followed by Rs. 51,782 per acre per year in case of large farmers and Rs. 50,378 per acre per year in case of medium farmers.

Cost of Cultivation of Mulberry

On these farms, the average cost of production of mulberry leaf is worked out to Rs. 22,925 per acre per year in case of large farmers, followed by Rs. 21,219 per acre per year in case of medium farmers and Rs. 19,974 per acre per year in case of small farmers. Among the cost components, labour was the major item contributing Rs. 7,166.53 per acre per year (31 per cent) in case of large farmers, followed by Rs. 6,717.71 per acre per year (34 per cent) in case of small farmers and Rs. 6,702.38 per acre per year (31 per cent) in case of medium farmers. The expenditure incurred on Farm Yard Manure was found to be Rs. 4505.26, Rs. 4245.24 and Rs. 3559.21 per acre per year respectively under large, medium and small farmers. Similarly, the cost of fertilizers was found to be Rs. 5243.16, Rs. 4760.48 and Rs. 4718.42 per acre per year respectively under large, medium and small farmers. Further the costs incurred on establishment of mulberry garden was apportioned to the economic life span of mulberry garden and accounted as fixed costs in working out the cost of mulberry and found that the apportioned cost was Rs. 614.70, Rs. 608.25 and Rs. 568.43 per acre per year under large, medium and small farmers respectively.

Cost of Silkworm Rearing

The costs incurred on rearing silkworm and the revenue generated thereby among the different size holdings was analysed. The total silk worm rearing cost was highest in case of small farmers at Rs. 37,873 per acre per year, followed by Rs. 29,158 per acre per year in case of medium farmers and Rs. 28,257 in case of large farmers. The average cost of labour was found to be the most prominent and a major component in the cost of silkworm rearing too. The average cost of human labor in silkworm rearing was found to be Rs. 15,082.89 per acre per year (40 per cent of the cost of silkworm rearing) in case of small farmers, followed by Rs. 13,383.86 per acre per year (46 per cent of the cost of silkworm rearing) in case of large farmers and Rs. 12,264.26 per acre per year (42 per cent of the cost of silkworm rearing) in case medium farmers.

The second highest cost contribution was from depreciation cost. The average cost of depreciation on rearing building and equipments was found to be Rs. 8,020 per acre per year in case of small farmers followed by Rs. 7,480.81 per acre per year in case of medium farmers and Rs. 6,681.81 per acre per year in case of large farmers. The total cost of silk cocoon production was found to be as high as Rs. 57,847.55 per acre per year in case of small farmers followed by Rs. 51,782.54 per acre per year in case of large farmers and Rs. 50,378.05 per acre per year in case of medium farmers.

The total income derived was found to be highest in case of small farmers (Rs. 1,02,970 per acre per year) followed by large farmers (Rs. 92,696.60 per acre per year) and medium farmers (Rs. 84,238.91 per acre per year). The net income derived was found to be highest in case of small farmers (Rs. 45,122 per acre per year) followed by big farmers (Rs. 40,914 per acre per year) and medium farmers (Rs. 33,861 per acre per year). The average yield of silk cocoon was found to be highest among the medium farmers (63.04 kg/100 dfls) followed by large farmers (62.92 kg/100 dfls) and small farmers (60.74 kg/100 dfls).

Cost Concepts, Distribution of Costs, and Measure of Profits from Sericulture under Different Mulberry Holding Sizes

Distribution of costs on various inputs in production provides an indicator of the pattern of use of various inputs as well as their relative importance in the total cost of production. The details of distribution of costs under different size groups was done and presented as below. The cost A1 which comprises of all cash and kind expenses showed a wide variation between the districts. The cost A1 per cropped area was found to be Rs. 42,848 per acre per year in case of small farmers followed by Rs. 40,431 per acre per year in case of big farmers and Rs. 38,987 per acre per year in case of medium farmers. There was a clear distinction between each of the costs considered in the study. Further, a higher rate of costs per acre per year was noticed in the case of small farmers (Cost C2 at Rs. 57,848 per acre per year) followed by big farmers (Cost C2 at Rs. 51,783 per acre per year) and medium farmers (Cost C2 at Rs. 50,378 per acre per year).

The net farm income was found to be as high as Rs. 45,122 per acre per year in case of small farmers followed by big farmers (Rs. 40,914 per acre per year) and medium farmers (Rs. 33,861 per acre per year) The family labour income which refers to the return to family labour and management, was highest in case of small farmers (Rs. 57,130 per acre per year) followed by big farmers (Rs. 49,253 per acre per year) and medium farmers (Rs. 42,141 per acre per year).

Employment Generation in Sericulture Under Different Mulberry Holding Sizes

The employment potential of sericulture in different size group farms was found to be 439 man days per acre per year, 349 man days per acre per year and 328 man days per acre per year respectively under small, big and medium size group farmers taking up bivoltine sericulture. It was found that the engagement of labour in mulberry cultivation was to the tune of 94 mandays per acre, 90 mandays per acre and 89 mandays per acre respectively under big farmers, medium farmers and small farmers, while that of silkworm rearing, it was 350 man days per acre, 255 mandays per acre and 238 mandays per acre respectively under small farmers, big farmers and medium farmers respectively.

The overall man days engaged in sericulture under these categories was to the tune of 439 mandays in case of small farmers, 349 mandays in case of big farmers and 328 mandays in case of medium farmers. The number of hired labour employed in sericulture was found to be up to the tune of 212 man days per acre per year in case of big farmers followed by 202 mandays per acre per year in case of small farmers and 189 man days per acre per year in case of medium farmers.

Crossbreed Silkworm Rearers

The mulberry land holding size wise classification of cross breed silkworm rearers, also yielded three distinct categories of farmers such as small scale rearers, medium scale rearers and large scale rearers. An analysis of costs associated in production, returns generated and employment potential of these three categories are presented as follows. Out of the total cost of production the cost of human labour was (for cultivation of mulberry and rearing of silkworm) as high as Rs. 20,908 per acre per year (45 per cent of total cost of production) in case of big farmers, followed by Rs. 19,749 per acre per year (34 per cent of total cost of production) in case of small farmers and Rs. 17,699 per acre per year (26 per cent of total cost of production) in case of medium farmers. The total cost of production was found to be Rs. 67,351 per acre per year in case of medium farmers, followed by Rs. 57,339 per acre per year in case of small farmers and Rs. 46,115 per acre per year in case of big farmers.

Cost of Cultivation of Mulberry

On these farms, the average cost of production of mulberry leaf is worked out to Rs. 26,258 per acre per year in case of medium farmers, followed by Rs. 24,586 per acre per year in case of small farmers and Rs. 15,561 per acre per year in case of big farmers. Among the cost components, labour was the major item contributing Rs. 6,799 per acre per year (44 per cent) in case of large farmers, followed by Rs. 5,016 per acre per year (20 per cent) in case of small farmers and Rs. 3,974 per acre per year (15 per cent) in case of medium farmers. The expenditure incurred on Farm Yard Manure was found to be Rs. 7492, Rs. 7180 and Rs. 2358 per acre per year respectively under medium, small and big farmers. Similarly the cost of fertilizers was found to be Rs. 5171, Rs. 5060 and Rs. 2108 per acre per year respectively under medium, small and big farmers. Further the costs incurred on establishment of mulberry garden was apportioned to the economic life span of mulberry garden and accounted as fixed costs in working out the cost of mulberry and found that the apportioned cost was highest in case of medium farmers (Rs. 1691 per acre per year) followed by small farmers (Rs. 852 per acre per year) and big farmers (Rs. 561 per acre per year).

Cost of Silkworm Rearing

The costs incurred on rearing silkworm and the revenue generated thereby among the different size holdings was analysed. The total silk worm rearing cost was highest in case of medium farmers at Rs. 41,093 per acre per year, followed by Rs. 32,752 per acre per year in case of small farmers and Rs. 30,553 in case of big farmers. The average cost of labour was found to be the most prominent and a major component in the cost of silkworm rearing too. The average cost of human labour in silkworm rearing was found to be Rs. 14,733 per acre per year (45 per cent of the cost of silkworm rearing) in case of small farmers, followed by Rs. 14,108 per acre per year (46 per cent of the cost of silkworm rearing) in case of big farmers and Rs. 13,725 per acre per year (33 per cent of the cost of silkworm rearing) in case medium farmers. The second highest cost contribution was from depreciation cost. The average cost of depreciation on rearing building and equipments was found to be Rs. 10,908 per acre per year in case of medium farmers followed by Rs. 5,358 per acre per year in case of small farmers and Rs. 4,032 per acre per year in case of big farmers.

The total cost of silk cocoon production was found to be as high as Rs. 67,351 per acre per year in case of medium farmers followed by Rs. 57,339 per acre per year in case of small farmers and Rs. 46,115 per acre per year in case of big farmers. The total income derived was found to be the highest in case of small farmers (Rs. 1,09,748 per acre per year) followed by medium farmers (Rs.1,05,049 per acre per year) and big farmers (Rs. 72,585 per acre per year). The average yield of silk cocoon was found to be the highest among the small farmers (68.81 kg/100 dfls) followed by medium farmers (68.08 kg/100 dfls) and big farmers (51.34 kg/100 dfls).

Cost Concepts, Distribution of Costs, and Measure of Profits from Sericulture under Different Mulberry Holding Sizes

Distribution of costs on various inputs in production provides an indicator of the pattern of use of various inputs as well as their relative importance in the total cost of production. The details of distribution of costs under different size groups was done and presented as below. The cost A which comprises all cash and kind expenses showed a wide variation between the districts. The cost A per cropped area was found to be Rs. 53,836 per acre per year in case of medium farmers followed by Rs. 43,5111 per acre per year in case of small farmers and Rs. 33,236 per acre per year in case of big farmers.

There was a clear distinction between each of the costs considered in the study. Further, a higher rate of costs per acre per year was noticed in the case of medium farmers (Cost C at Rs. 67,351 per acre per year) followed by big farmers (Cost C at Rs. 57,339 per acre per year) and big farmers (Cost C at Rs. 46,115 per acre per year). The net farm income was found to be as high as Rs. 52,410 per acre per year in case of small farmers followed by medium farmers (Rs. 37,698 per acre per year) and big farmers (Rs. 26,470 per acre per year) The family labour income which refers to the return to family labour and management was highest in case of small farmers (Rs. 63,034 per acre per year) followed by medium farmers (Rs. 47,274 per acre per year) and big farmers (Rs. 37,363 per acre per year).

Employment Generation in Sericulture under Different Mulberry Holding Sizes

The employment potential of sericulture in different size group farms was found to be 434 mandays per acre per year, 348 man days per acre per year and 278 mandays per acre per year respectively under big, medium and small size group farmers taking up cross breed silkworm race. It was found that the engagement of labour in mulberry cultivation was to the tune of 91 mandays per acre, 82 mandays per acre and 72 mandays per acre respectively under big farmers, small farmers and medium farmers, while that of silkworm rearing, it was 343 mandays per acre, 276 mandays per acre and 197 mandays per acre under big farmers, medium farmers and small farmers respectively. The number of hired labour employed in sericulture was found to be up to the tune of 202 mandays per acre per year in case of big farmers followed by 160 mandays per acre per year in case of medium farmers and 127 mandays per acre per year in case of small farmers. per acre per year).

PRODUCTIVITY OF INPUTS, DISTRIBUTION OF COSTS AND GROSS INCOME EARNED FROM SERICULTURE AMONG DIFFERENT ADOPTER CATEGORIES

A classification of respondents (both cross breed silkworm rearers and bivoltine (CSR hybrid) silkworm rearers) based on the level of adoption of technologies of mulberry sericulture using the technology adoption index scores of each farmer was made. The farmers were then classified into adopter and nonadopter categories, based on the mean value of technology adoption index. An attempt was made to estimate the returns, costs associated and employment generated under these categories.

Bivoltine (CSR hybrid) Silkworm Rearers

The classification of bivoltine (CSR hybrid) rearers into adopter and nonadopter categories was made and an analysis of costs associated in production, returns generated and employment potential were made and presented as below. Out of the total cost of production the cost of human labour was (for cultivation of mulberry and rearing of silkworm) as high as Rs. 21,546 per acre per year (37 per cent of total cost of production) in case of adopters, followed by Rs. 19,284 per acre per year (39 per cent of total cost of production) in case of non-adopters. The total cost of production was found to be Rs. 58,658 per acre per year in case of adopters, followed by Rs. 50,031 per acre per year in case of non-adopters. The cost of production was found to be Rs. 54,096 per acre per year in case of overall bivoltine farmers.

Cost of Cultivation of Mulberry

On these farms, the average cost of production of mulberry leaf is worked out to Rs. 22,658 per acre per year in case of adopter category farmers, followed by Rs. 20,820 per acre per year in case of non-adopter category of bivoltine silkworm rearing farmers. Among the cost components, labour was the major item contributing Rs. 7,039 per acre per year (34 per cent) in case of non-adopter category of farmers, followed by Rs. 6,530 per acre per year (29 per cent) in case of adopter category of bivoltine silkworm rearing farmers. The expenditure incurred on farmyard manure was found to be Rs. 4,992 and Rs. 3163 per acre per year respectively under adopter and non-adopter categories of bivoltine silkworm rearing farmers. Similarly the cost of fertilizers was found to be Rs. 5032 and Rs. 4660 per acre per year respectively under adopter and non-adopter categories of bivoltine silkworm rearing farmers. Further the apportioned cost of mulberry garden worked out to Rs. 552 and Rs. 632 per acre per year under adopter and non-adopter categories of bivoltine silkworm rearing farmers.

Cost of Silkworm Rearing

The costs incurred on rearing silkworm and the revenue generated thereby among the different size holdings was analysed. The total silk worm rearing cost was highest in case of adopter category of bivoltine silkworm rearing farmers at Rs. 35,999 per acre per year, followed by Rs. 29,212 per acre per year in case of nonadopter category of bivoltine silkworm rearing farmers. The average cost of labour was found to be the most prominent and a major component in the cost of silkworm rearing too. The average cost of human labor in silkworm rearing was found to be Rs. 15,017 per acre per year (42 per cent of the cost of silkworm rearing) in case of adopter category of bivoltine silkworm rearing farmers, followed by Rs. 12,245 per acre per year (42 per cent of the cost of silkworm rearing) in case of non-adopter category of bivoltine silkworm rearing farmers.

The second highest cost contribution was from depreciation cost. The average cost of depreciation on rearing building and equipments was found to be Rs. 9,632 per acre per year in case of adopter category farmers followed by Rs. 5,638 per acre per year in case of non-adopter category farmers. The total cost of silk cocoon production was found to be as high as Rs. 58,658 per acre per year in case of adopter category farmers followed by Rs. 50,031 per acre per year in case of non-adopter category farmers. The total income derived was found to be the highest in case of adopter category farmers (Rs. 1,10,555 per acre per year) followed by non-adopter category farmers (Rs. 77,231 per acre per year).

The net income derived was found to be highest in case of adopter category of bivoltine silkworm rearing farmers (Rs. 51,897 per acre per year) followed by non-adopter category of bivoltine rearing farmers (Rs. 27,199 per acre per year). The average yield of silk cocoon was found to be the highest among the adopter category of bivoltine rearing farmers (63.85 kg/100 dfls) followed by nonadopter category of bivoltine rearing farmers (60.58 kg/100 dfls).

Cost Concepts, Distribution of Costs, and Measure of Profits from Sericulture under Different Mulberry Holding sizes (BV)

Distribution of costs on various inputs in production provides an indicator of the pattern of use of various inputs as well as their relative importance in the total cost of production. The details of distribution of costs under different adopter categories was assessed and presented as below. The cost A which comprises all cash and kind expenses showed a wide vide variation between the adopter and non-adopter categories. The cost A per cropped area was found to be Rs. 45,594 per acre per year in case of adopter category farmers, followed by Rs. 36,593 per acre per year in case of non-adopter category of bivoltine silkworm rearing farmers.

There was a clear distinction between each of the costs considered in the study. Further, a higher rate of costs per acre per year was noticed in the case of adopter category farmers (Cost C at Rs. 58,658 per acre per year) followed by non-adopter category of bivoltine silkworm rearing farmers (Cost C at Rs. 50,031 per acre per year). Further the estimates of gross income per acre per year from bivoltine sericulture among the adopter and non-adopter categories was done. The net farm income was found to be as high as Rs. 51,897 per acre per year in case of adopter category of farmers followed by Rs. 27,199 per acre per year in case of nonadopter category of farmers who were rearing bivoltine silkworm. The family labour income which refers to the return to family labour and management, was highest in case of adopter category farmers (Rs. 61,032 per acre per year) followed by non-adopter category farmers (Rs. 37,245 per acre per year) practicing bivoltine sericulture.

Employment Generation in Sericulture among Different Adopter Categories of Bivoltine Silkworm Rearers

The employment potential of sericulture under the different adopter categories of farmers taking up bivoltine silkworm rearing was found to be 395 man days per acre per year (adopters) and 356 man days per acre per year (non-adopters) respectively. It was found that the engagement of labour in mulberry cultivation was to the tune of 94 mandays per acre, 86 mandays per acre respectively under non-adopter and adopter categories of farmers, while that of silkworm rearing, it was 309 mandays per acre and 262 mandays per acre per year respectively under adopter and non-adopter categories of farmers respectively taking up bivoltine silkworm rearing. The number of hired labour employed in sericulture was found to be up to the tune of 225 mandays per acre per year in case of adopter category of farmers followed by 174 mandays per acre per year in case of non-adopter category of farmers practicing bivolitne sericulture.

Crossbreed Silkworm Rearers

The classification of cross breed silkworm rearers, into adopter and nonadopter categories was made and an analysis of costs associated in production, returns generated and employment potential were made and presented as below. Out of the total cost of production the cost of human labour was (for cultivation of mulberry and rearing of silkworm) as high as Rs. 20,258 per acre per year (34 per cent of total cost of production) in case of adopters, followed by Rs. 20,182 per acre per year (41 per cent of total cost of production) in case of non-adopters. The total cost of production was found to be Rs. 59,353 per acre per year in case of adopters, followed by Rs. 49,222 per acre per year in case of non-adopters. The cost of production was found to be Rs. 52,873 per acre per year in case of overall cross breed silkworm rearing farmers.

Cost of Cultivation of Mulberry

On these farms, the average cost of production of mulberry leaf is worked out to Rs. 21,892 per acre per year in case of adopter category farmers, followed by Rs. 15,372 per acre per year in case of non-adopter category of cross breed silkworm rearing farmers. Among the cost components, labour was the major item contributing Rs. 6,546 per acre per year (43 per cent) in case of non-adopter category of farmers, followed by Rs. 5,431 per acre per year (25 per cent) in case of adopter category of cross breed silkworm rearing farmers. The expenditure incurred on Farm Yard Manure was found to be Rs. 5,824 and Rs. 2372 per acre per year respectively under adopter and non-adopter categories of cross breed silkworm rearing farmers. Similarly the cost of fertilizers was found to be Rs. 4209 and Rs. 2111 per acre per year respectively under adopter and nonadopter categories of cross breed silkworm rearing farmers. Further the apportioned cost of mulberry garden worked out to Rs. 1021 and Rs. 553 per acre per year under adopter and non-adopter categories of cross breed silkworm rearing farmers.

Cost of Silkworm Rearing

The costs incurred on rearing silkworm and the revenue generated thereby among the different size holdings was analysed. The total silk worm rearing cost was highest in case of adopter category of cross breed silkworm rearing farmers at Rs. 37,462 per acre per year, followed by Rs. 33,850 per acre per year in case of nonadopter category of cross breed silkworm rearing farmers. The average cost of labour was found to be the most prominent and a major component in the cost of silkworm rearing too.

The average cost of human labor in silkworm rearing was found to be Rs. 14,827 per acre per year (40 per cent of the cost of silkworm rearing) in case of adopter category of cross breed silkworm rearing farmers, followed by Rs. 13,636 per acre per year (40 per cent of the cost of silkworm rearing) in case of non-adopter category of cross breed silkworm rearing farmers. The second highest cost contribution was from depreciation cost. The average cost of depreciation on rearing building and equipments was found to be Rs. 8,477 per acre per year in case of adopter category farmers followed by Rs. 7,718 per acre per year in case of non-adopter category farmers. The total cost of silk cocoon production was found to be as high as Rs. 59,353 per acre per year in case of adopter category farmers followed by Rs. 49,222 per acre per year in case of non-adopter category farmers. The total income derived was found to be highest in case of adopter category farmers (Rs. 92,693 per acre per year) followed by non-adopter category farmers (Rs.71,605 per acre per year). The net income derived was found to be highest in case of adopter category of cross breed silkworm rearing farmers (Rs. 33,340 per acre per year) followed by non-adopter category of cross breed silkworm rearing farmers (Rs. 22,383 per acre per year). The average yield of silk cocoon was found to be highest among the adopter category of cross breed silkworm rearing farmers (63.13 kg/100 dfls) followed by non-adopter category of cross breed silkworm rearing farmers (51.66 kg/100 dfls).

Cost Concepts, Distribution of Costs, and Measure of Profits from Sericulture among different adopter categories

Distribution of costs on various inputs in production provides an indicator of the pattern of use of various inputs as well as their relative importance in the total cost of production. The details of distribution of costs under different adopter categories was assessed and presented as below. The cost A1 which comprises all cash and kind expenses showed a wide vide variation between the adopter and non-adopter categories. The cost A per cropped area was found to be Rs. 47,557 per acre per year in case of adopter category farmers, followed by Rs. 36,798 per acre per year in case of non-adopter category of cross breed silkworm rearing farmers.

There was a clear distinction between each of the costs considered in the study. Further, a higher rate of costs per acre per year was noticed in the case of adopter category farmers (Cost C at Rs. 59,353 per acre per year) followed by non-adopter category of cross breed silkworm rearing farmers (Cost C at Rs. 49,222 per acre per year). Further the estimates of gross income per acre per year from rearing cross breed silkworm among the adopter and non-adopter categories was done. The net farm income was found to be as high as Rs. 33,340 per acre per year in case of adopter category of farmers followed by Rs. 22,383 per acre per year in case of non-adopter category of farmers rearing cross breed silkworm. The family labour income which refers to the return to family labour and management was highest in case of adopter category farmers (Rs. 41,957 per acre per year) followed by non-adopter category farmers (Rs. 31,923 per acre per year) rearing cross breed silkworm.

Employment Generation in Sericulture among Different Adopter Categories of Crossbreed Silkworm Rearers

The employment potential of sericulture under the different adopter categories of farmers rearing cross breed silkworm was found to be 432 mandays per acre per year in case of non-adopter category followed by 365 mandays per acre per year in case of adopter category of cross breed silkworm rearers. It was found that the engagement of labour in mulberry cultivation was to the tune of 87 man days per acre per year in case of non-adopter category followed by 84 man days per acre in case of adopter category of farmers, while that of silkworm rearing, it was 345 man days per acre per year and 281 man days per acre per year respectively under non-adopter and adopter categories of farmers respectively taking up cross breed silkworm rearing. The number of hired labour employed in sericulture was found to be up to the tune of 238 man days per acre per year in case of non-adopter category of farmers followed by 210 man days per acre per year in case of adopter category of farmers rearing cross breed silkworm.

Productivity of Inputs, Distribution of Costs and Gross Income Earned from Other Major Crops in the Selected Districts

A district wise analysis of input use and income earned per acre of other major crops grown in the respondent farms was analysed and presented. The crops selected for the analysis was based on the share in the total cropped area and the economic potential, under the respondent farms. The individual input costs were worked out for each of these crop enterprises and the gross income earned thereby, were worked out. For the analysis the major crops considered were paddy, ragi (irrigated), sugarcane and pulse crops in case of Mandya district, paddy, ragi (irrigated), pulse crops and coconut in case of Bangalore (Rural) district, paddy, ragi (irrigated), tomato and mango in case of Kolar district and paddy, ragi (irrigated), potato and tobacco in case of Hassan district

Productivity of Inputs, Distribution of Costs and Gross Income Earned from Other Major Crops in Mandya district

In the district of Mandya, the major share of area under different crops with the selected respondent farms (n = 60) and the respective economic benefits were worked out. It was found that the crops such as paddy, ragi, sugarcane and pulses were comparatively as potential as mulberry sericulture. Hence an analysis of the costs associated and revenue generated from these major crops was worked out.

Cost of Cultivation of Major Crops Grown in the District

The total production cost of paddy in Mandya district was found to be Rs. 21442 per acre and that of ragi (irrigated), sugarcane and pulses was found to be Rs. 13005.48, Rs. 46323.15 and Rs. 12510.48 per acre per year respectively. Of the total cost of production, the costs associated with different inputs were worked out and presented. The total income derived from these enterprises was Rs. 38040.00 per acre in case of paddy, Rs.16376.00 per acre in case of ragi (irrigated), Rs. 69400.00 per acre in case of sugarcane and Rs. 18240.00 per acre in case of pulse crops.

Distribution of Costs and Measure of Profits from Major Crops

The distribution of costs on various inputs in production of the major crops was analysed. The details of distribution of costs under different adopter categories was assessed and presented as below. The cost A which comprises all cash and kind expenses was found to be Rs. 18706.75 per acre in case of paddy, Rs. 9459.48 per acre in case of ragi (irrigated), Rs. 39704.40 per acre in case of sugarcane and Rs. 9332.98 per acre in case of pulse crops. Similarly Cost A was found to be Rs. 18706.75 per acre in case of paddy, Rs.9459.48 per acre in case of ragi (irrigated), Rs. 39704.40 per acre in case of sugarcane and Rs. 9332.98 per acre in case of pulse crops. The cost B was found to be Rs. 19906.75 per acre in case of paddy, Rs.10299.48 per acre in case of ragi (irrigated), Rs. 42054.40 per acre in case of sugarcane and Rs. 10252.98 per acre in case of pulse crops.

The cost C was found to be Rs. 21442.00 per acre in case of paddy, Rs. 13005.48 per acre in case of ragi (irrigated), Rs. 46323.15 per acre in case of sugarcane and Rs. 12510.48 per acre in case of pulse crops. The gross income from different crops was worked out to Rs. 38040.00 per acre from paddy, Rs. 16376.00 per acre from ragi (irrigated), Rs. 69400.00 per acre from sugarcane and Rs. 18240.00 from pulse crops. The net farm income was found to be Rs. 16598.00 per acre from paddy, Rs.3370.52 per acre from ragi (irrigated), Rs.23076.85 per acre from sugarcane and Rs. 5729.52 per acre from pulse crops. Similarly the family labour income was found to be Rs. 18133.25 per acre from paddy, Rs.6076.52 per acre from ragi (irrigated), Rs.27345.60 per acre from sugarcane and Rs. 7987.02 per acre from pulse crops. In the analysis it revealed that the crop sugarcane crop yielded more income than other crops.

Productivity of Inputs, Distribution of Costs and Gross Income Earned from Other Major Crops in Bangalore (rural) district

In Bangalore (rural) district the major share of area under different crops with the selected respondent farms (n = 60) and the respective economic benefits were worked out and was found that the crops such as paddy, ragi (irrigated), pulses and coconut were comparatively better performing crops. Hence, an analysis of the costs associated and revenue generated from these major crops was worked out.

Cost of Cultivation of Major Crops Grown in the District

The total production cost of paddy in Bangalore (Rural) district was found to be Rs. 21612.11 per acre and that of ragi (irrigated), pulses and coconut was found to be Rs. 12672.80, Rs. 11864.65 and Rs. 13290 per acre per year respectively. Of the total cost of production, the costs associated with different inputs were worked out and presented. The total income derived from these enterprises was Rs. 32080.00 per acre in case of paddy, Rs.15790.00 per acre in case of ragi (irrigated), Rs. 15790.00 per acre in case of pulse crops and Rs. 24660.00 per acre in case of coconut.

Distribution of Costs and Measure of Profits from Major Crops

The distribution of costs on various inputs in production of the major crops was analysed. The details of distribution of costs under different adopter categories was assessed and presented as below. The cost A which comprises all cash and kind expenses was found to be Rs. 18342.11 per acre in case of paddy, Rs. 10047.80 per acre in case of ragi (irrigated), Rs. 9047.62 per acre in case of pulse crops and Rs. 7747.62 per acre in case of coconut. The cost B was found to be Rs. 19542.11 per acre in case of paddy, Rs.10887.80 per acre in case of ragi (irrigated), Rs. 9912.40 per acre in case of pulse crops and Rs. 10140.02 per acre in case of coconut.

The cost C was found to be Rs. 21612.11 per acre in case of paddy, Rs. 12672.80 per acre in case of ragi (irrigated), Rs. 11864.65 per acre in case of pulses and Rs. 13290.02 per acre in case of coconut. The gross income from different crops worked out to Rs. 32080.00 per acre from paddy, Rs. 15790.00 per acre from ragi (irrigated), Rs. 15790.00 per acre from pulses and Rs. 24660.00 from coconut. The net farm income was found to be Rs. 10467.89 per acre from paddy, Rs.3117.20 per acre from ragi (irrigated), Rs.3925.35 per acre from pulses and Rs. 11369.98 per acre from coconut. Similarly the family labour income was found to be Rs. 12537.89 per acre from paddy, Rs.4902.20 per acre from ragi (irrigated), Rs.5877.60 per acre from pulses and Rs. 14519.98 per acre from coconut. The net income was reasonably high in case of paddy than other crops considered in the analysis.

Productivity of Inputs, Distribution of Costs and Gross Income Earned from Other Major Crops in Kolar district

The major share of area under different crops with the selected respondent farms (n = 60) in the Kolar district and the respective economic benefits were worked out. It was found that the crops such as paddy, ragi (irrigated), vegetables and mango crops were comparatively as potential as mulberry sericulture. Hence an analysis of the costs associated and revenue generated from these major crops was worked out.

Cost of Cultivation of Major Crops Grown in the District

The total production cost of paddy in Kolar district was found to be Rs. 19170.10 per acre and that of ragi (irrigated), tomato and mango was found to be Rs. 13224.80, Rs. 24610.16 and Rs. 20900.48 per acre per year respectively.

Of the total cost of production, the costs associated with different inputs were worked out and presented. The total income derived from these enterprises was Rs. 35380.00 per acre in case of paddy, Rs.18280.00 per acre in case of ragi (irrigated), Rs. 35210.00 per acre in case of tomato and Rs. 35623.00 per acre in case of mango crops.

Distribution of Costs and Measure of Profits from Major Crops

The distribution of costs on various inputs in production of the major crops was analysed. The details of distribution of costs under different adopter categories was assessed and presented as below. The cost A which comprises all cash and kind expenses was found to be Rs. 16452.10 per acre in case of paddy, Rs. 10173.80 per acre in case of ragi (irrigated), Rs. 19898.16 per acre in case of tomato and Rs. 14152.48 per acre in case of mango.

The cost B was found to be Rs. 17652.10 per acre in case of paddy, Rs.11013.80 per acre in case of ragi (irrigated), Rs. 20998.16 per acre in case of tomato and Rs. 18842.48 per acre in case of mango. The cost C was found to be Rs. 19170.10 per acre in case of paddy, Rs. 13224.80 per acre in case of ragi (irrigated), Rs. 24610.16 per acre in case of tomato and Rs. 20900.48 per acre in case of mango. The gross income of the crops was worked out to Rs. 35380.00 per acre from paddy, Rs. 18280.00 per acre from ragi (irrigated), Rs. 35210.00 per acre from tomato and Rs. 35623.00 from mango. The net farm income was found to be Rs. 16209.90 per acre from paddy, Rs.5055.20 per acre from ragi (irrigated), Rs. 10599.84 per acre from tomato and Rs. 14722.52 per acre from mango. Similarly the family labour income was found to be Rs. 17727.90 per acre from paddy, Rs.7266.20 per acre from ragi (irrigated), Rs. 14211.84 per acre from tomato and Rs. 16780.52 per acre from mango. Among the different crop enterprises, paddy crop yielded relatively more income than others.

Productivity of Inputs, Distribution of Costs and Gross Income Earned from Other Major Crops in Hassan district

The major share of area under different crops with the selected respondent farms (n = 60) and the respective economic benefits were worked out for Hassan district. It was found that the crops such as paddy, ragi, potato and tobacco were comparatively as potential as mulberry sericulture. Hence an analysis of the costs associated and revenue generated from these major crops was worked out.

Cost of Cultivation of Major Crops Grown in the District

The total production cost of paddy in Hassan district was found to be Rs. 19820.33 per acre and that of ragi (irrigated), potato and tobacco was found to be Rs. 10923.62, Rs. 23408.80 and Rs. 53119.86 per acre per year respectively. Of the total cost of production, the costs associated with different inputs were worked out and presented. The total income derived from these enterprises was Rs. 28820.00 per acre in case of paddy, Rs.13550.00 per acre in case of ragi (irrigated), Rs. 32532.80 per acre in case of potato and Rs. 76650.00 per acre in case of tobacco.

Distribution of Costs and Measure of Profits from Major Crops

The distribution of costs on various inputs in production of the major crops was analysed. The details of distribution of costs under different adopter categories was assessed and presented as below. The cost A which comprises all cash and kind expenses was found to be Rs. 16998.83 per acre in case of paddy, Rs. 8361.62 per acre in case of ragi (irrigated), Rs. 18446.30 per acre in case of potato and Rs. 44221.86 per acre in case of tobacco. The cost B was found to be Rs. 18198.83 per acre in case of paddy, Rs.9201.62 per acre in case of ragi (irrigated), Rs. 19846.30 per acre in case of tomato and Rs. 48121.86 per acre in case of tobacco.

The cost C was found to be Rs. 19820.33 per acre in case of paddy, Rs. 10923.62 per acre in case of ragi (irrigated), Rs. 23408.80 per acre in case of potato and Rs. 53119.86 per acre in case of tobacco. The gross income from different crops was worked out to Rs. 28820.00 per acre from paddy, Rs. 13550.00 per acre from ragi (irrigated), Rs. 32532.80 per acre from potato and Rs. 76650.00 from tobacco. The net farm income was found to be Rs. 8999.67 per acre from paddy, Rs.2626.38 per acre from ragi (irrigated), Rs.9124.00 per acre from potato and Rs. 23530.14 per acre from tobacco. Similarly the family labour income was found to be Rs. 10621.17 per acre from paddy, Rs. 4348.38 per acre from ragi (irrigated), Rs. 12686.50 per acre from tomato and Rs. 28528.14 per acre from tobacco. The economic return from tobacco was found to be higher than the other crops considered in the analysis.

2

Production Planning and Control in Sericulture

PLANNING : AN OVERVIEW

Planning in organizations and public policy is both the organizational process of creating and maintaining a plan; and the psychological process of thinking about the activities required to create a desired goal on some scale. As such, it is a fundamental property of intelligent behaviour.

This thought process is essential to the creation and refinement of a plan, or integration of it with other plans, that is, it combines forecasting of developments with the preparation of scenarios of how to react to them. An important, albeit often ignored aspect of planning, is the relationship it holds with forecasting. Forecasting can be described as predicting what the future will look like, whereas planning predicts what the future should look like.

The term is also used to describe the formal procedures used in such an endeavor, such as the creation of documents, diagrams, or meetings to discuss the important issues to be addressed, the objectives to be met, and the strategy to be followed. Beyond this, planning has a different meaning depending on the political or economic context in which it is used. Two attitudes to planning need to be held in tension: on the one hand we need to be prepared for what may lie ahead, which may mean contingencies and flexible processes. On the other hand, our future is shaped by consequences of our own planning and actions.

Planning is a process for accomplishing purpose. It is a blue print of business growth and a road map of development. It helps in deciding objectives both in quantitative and qualitative terms. It is setting of goals on the basis of objectives and keeping in view the resources.

What should a Plan be?

A plan should be a realistic view of the expectations. Depending upon the activities, a plan can be long range, intermediate range or short range. It is the framework within which it must operate. For management seeking external support, the plan is the most important document and key to growth. Preparation of a comprehensive plan will not guarantee success, but lack of a sound plan will almost certainly ensure failure.

Purpose of a Plan

Just as no two organizations are alike, so also their plans. It is therefore important to prepare a plan keeping in view the necessities of the enterprise. A plan is an important aspect of business.

It serves the following three critical functions:

1. Helps management to clarify, focus, and research their business's or project's development and prospects.
2. Provides a considered and logical framework within which a business can develop and pursue business strategies over the next three to five years.
3. Offers a benchmark against which actual performance can be measured and reviewed.

Importance of the Planning Process

A plan can play a vital role in helping to avoid mistakes or recognize hidden opportunities. Preparing a satisfactory plan of the organization is essential. The planning know the business and that they have thought through its development in terms of products, management, finances, and most importantly, markets and competition.

Planning helps in forecasting the future, makes the future visible to some extent. It bridges between where we are and where we want to go. Planning is looking ahead.

Types of Plans or Planning

- Architectural planning
- Business plan
- Comprehensive planning
- Enterprise Architecture Planning
- Event Planning and Production
- Family planning
- Financial planning
- Infrastructure planning
- Land use planning
- Life planning
- Marketing plan
- Network resource planning

- Strategic planning
- Urban planning
- Operational planning

Objectives and Policies

Objectives

The objectives are general parts of the planning process. They are the end-results towards which all business activities are directed. They are needed in every aspect where performance and result directly and vitally affect the survival and success of the firm. In other words, the objective of the firm justifies its existence. Robert C. Appley, "Objectives are goals; they are aims which management and administration wish the organization to achieve." In other words, goals, aims and purposes are also used to signify objectives. Newman and Summer stated, "For managerial purposes, it is useful to think of objectives as the results we want to achieve. Objective covers firm's long-range plans specific departmental goals and short-term individual assignment also."

Policies

George R. Ferry, "Policy is a verbal, written or implied overall guide setting up boundaries that supply the general units and directions in which managerial action will take place." Policies are specific guidelines and constraints for managerial thinking on decision-making and action. Policies provide the framework within which decision-makers are expected to operate while making organizational decisions. They are the basic guides to be consistent in decision-making.

Planning Basics

Essentials of Planning

Planning is not done off hand. It is prepared after careful and extensive research.

For a comprehensive business plan, management has to:

- Clearly define the target/goal in writing.
  - It should be set by a person having authority.
  - The goal should be realistic.
  - It should be specific.
  - Acceptability
  - Easily measurable
- Identify all the main issues which need to be addressed.
- Review past performance.
- Decide budgetary requirement.

- Focus on matters of strategic importance.
- What are requirements and how will they be met?
- What will be the likely length of the plan and its structure?
- Identify shortcomings in the concept and gaps.
- Strategies for implementation.
- Review periodically.

Applications

In Organizations

Planning is also a management process, concerned with defining goals for future organizational performance and deciding on the tasks and resources to be used in order to attain those goals.

To meet the goals, managers may develop plans such as a business plan or a marketing plan. Planning always has a purpose.

The purpose may be achievement of certain goals or targets. The planning helps to achieve these goals or target by using the available time and resources. To minimize the timing and resources also require proper planning. The concept of planning is to identify what the organization wants to do by using the four questions which are "where are we today in terms of our business or strategy planning? Where are we going? Where do we want to go? How are we going to get there?..."

In Public Policy

Planning refers to the practice and the profession associated with the idea of planning an idea yourself. In many countries, the operation of a town and country planning system is often referred to as "planning" and the professionals which operate the system are known as "planners".

It is a conscious as well as sub-conscious activity. It is "an anticipatory decision making process" that helps in coping with complexities. It is deciding future course of action from amongst alternatives. It is a process that involves making and evaluating each set of interrelated decisions.

It is selection of missions, objectives and "translation of knowledge into action." A planned performance brings better results compared to an unplanned one. A manager's job is planning, monitoring and controlling. Planning and goal setting are important traits of an organization. It is done at all levels of the organization.

Planning includes the plan, the thought process, action, and implementation.Planning gives more power over the future. Planning is deciding in advance what to do, how to do it, when to do it, and who should do it. It bridges the gap from where the organization is to where it wants to be. The planning function involves establishing goals and arranging them in logical order.

CONTROL

Control is one of the managerial functions like planning, organizing, staffing and directing. It is an important function because it helps to check the errors and to take the corrective action so that deviation from standards are minimized and stated goals of the organization are achieved in desired manner.

Modern concepts, control is a foreseeing action whereas earlier concept of control was used only when errors were detected. Control in management means setting standards, measuring actual performance and taking corrective action. Thus, control comprises these three main activities.

Characteristics of Control

- Control is a continuous process
- Control is a management process
- Control is embedded in each level of organizational hierarchy
- Control is forward looking
- Control is closely linked with planning
- Control is a tool for achieving organizational activities

Elements of Control

The four basic elements in a control system:

1. The characteristic or condition to be controlled,
2. The sensor,
3. The comparator, and
4. *The activator*: Occur in the same sequence and maintain a consistent relationship to each other in every system.

The first element is the characteristic or condition of the operating system which is to be measured. We select a specific characteristic because a correlation exists between it and how the system is performing. The characteristic may be the output of the system during any stage of processing or it may be a condition that has resulted from the output of the system. For example, it may be the heat energy produced by the furnace or the temperature in the room which has changed because of the heat generated by the furnace. In an elementary school system, the hours a teacher works or the gain in knowledge demonstrated by the students on a national examination are examples of characteristics that may be selected for measurement, or control. The second element of control, the sensor, is a means for measuring the characteristic or condition.

The control subsystem must be designed to include a sensory device or method of measurement. In a home heating system this device would be the thermostat, and in a quality-control system this measurement might be performed by a visual inspection of the product.

The third element of control, the comparator, determines the need for correction by comparing what is occurring with what has been planned. Some deviation from plan is usual and expected, but when variations are beyond those considered acceptable, corrective action is required. It is often possible to identify trends in performance and to take action before an unacceptable variation from the norm occurs. This sort of preventative action indicates that good control is being achieved.

The fourth element of control, the activator, is the corrective action taken to return the system to expected output. The actual person, device, or method used to direct corrective inputs into the operating system may take a variety of forms. It may be a hydraulic controller positioned by a solenoid or electric motor in response to an electronic error signal, an employee directed to rework the parts that failed to pass quality inspection, or a school principal who decides to buy additional books to provide for an increased number of students. As long as a plan is performed within allowable limits, corrective action is not necessary; this seldom occurs in practice, however. Information is the medium of control, because the flow of sensory data and later the flow of corrective information allow a characteristic or condition of the system to be controlled. To illustrate how information flow facilitates control, let us review the elements of control in the context of information.

Relationship between the Elements of Control and Information

Controlled Characteristic or. Condition The primary requirement of a control system is that it maintain the level and kind of output necessary to achieve the system's objectives. It is usually impractical to control every feature and condition associated with the system's output. Therefore, the choice of the controlled item is extremely important. There should be a direct correlation between the controlled item and the system's operation. In other words, control of the selected characteristic should have a direct relationship to the goal or objective of the system.

Sensor

After the characteristic is sensed, or measured, information pertinent to control is fed back. Exactly what information needs to be transmitted and also the language that will best facilitate the communication process and reduce the possibility of distortion in transmission must be carefully considered. Information that is to be compared with the standard, or plan, should be expressed in the same terms or language as in the original plan to facilitate decision making. Using machine methods may require extensive translation of the information.

Since optimal languages for computation and for human review are not always the same, the relative ease of translation may be a significant factor in selecting the units of measurement or the language unit in the sensing element. In many instances, the measurement may be sampled rather than providing a complete and continuous feedback of information about the operation. A sampling procedure suggests measuring some segment or portion of the operation that will represent the total.

Comparison with Standard

In a social system, the norms of acceptable behaviour become the standard against which so-called deviant behaviour may be judged. Regulations and laws provide a more formal collection of information for society. Social norms change, but very slowly. In contrast, the standards outlined by a formal law can be changed from one day to the next through revision, discontinuation, or replacement by another. Information about deviant behaviour becomes the basis for controlling social activity. Output information is compared with the standard or norm and significant deviations are noted. In an industrial example, frequency distribution may be used to show the average quality, the spread, and the comparison of output with a standard.

If there is a significant and uncorrectable difference between output and plan, the system is "out of control." This means that the objectives of the system are not feasible in relation to the capabilities of the present design. Either the objectives must be reevaluated or the system redesigned to add new capacity or capability. For example, the traffic in drugs has been increasing in some cities at an alarming rate. The citizens must decide whether to revise the police system so as to regain control, or whether to modify the law to reflect a different norm of acceptable behaviour.

Implimentor

The activator unit responds to the information received from the comparator and initiates corrective action. If the system is a machine-to-machine system, the corrective inputs are designed into the network.

When the control relates to a man-to-machine or man-to-man system, however, the individual(s) in charge must evaluate:

- The accuracy of the feedback information,
- The significance of the variation, and
- What corrective inputs will restore the system to a reasonable degree of stability. Once the decision has been made to direct new inputs into the system, the actual process may be relatively easy. A small amount of energy can change the operation of jet airplanes, automatic steel mills, and hydroelectric power plants. The pilot presses a button, and the landing gear of the airplane goes up or down; the operator of a steel mill pushes a lever, and a ribbon of white-hot steel races through the plant; a worker at a control board directs the flow of

electrical energy throughout a regional network of stations and substations. It takes but a small amount of control energy to release or stop large quantities of input.

The comparator may be located far from the operating system, although at least some of the elements must be in close proximity to operations. For example, the measurement is usually at the point of operations. The measurement information can be transmitted to a distant point for comparison with the standard and when deviations occur, the correcting input can be released from the distant point. However, the input will be located at the operating system. This ability to control from afar means that aircraft can be flown by remote control, dangerous manufacturing processes can be operated from a safe distance, and national organizations can be directed from centralized headquarters.

Process of Controlling

- Setting performance standards.
- Measurement of actual performance.
- Comparing actual performance with standards.
- Analysing deviations.
- Correcting deviations.

Kinds of Control

Control may be grouped according to three general classifications:

1. The nature of the information flow designed into the system,
2. The kind of components included in the design, and
3. The relationship of control to the decision process.

Open- and Closed-Loop Control

A street-lighting system controlled by a timing device is an example of an open-loop system. At a certain time each evening, a mechanical device closes the circuit and energy flows through the electric lines to light the lamps. Note, however, that the timing mechanism is an independent unit and is not measuring the objective function of the lighting system. If the lights should be needed on a dark, stormy day the timing device would not recognize this need and therefore would not activate energy inputs. Corrective properties may sometimes be built into the controller but this would not close the loop. In another instance, the sensing, comparison, or adjustment may be made through action taken by an individual who is not part of the system. For example, the lights may be turned on by someone who happens to pass by and recognizes the need for additional light. If control is exercised as a result of the operation rather than because of outside or predetermined arrangements, it is a closed-loop system. The home thermostat is the classic example of a control device in a closed-loop system. When the room temperature drops below the desired point, the control mechanism closes the circuit to start the furnace and the temperature rises. The furnace-activating circuit is turned off as the temperature reaches the preselected level. The significant difference between this type of system and an open-loop system is that the control device is an element of the system it serves and measures the performance of the system. In other words, all four control elements are integral to the specific system.

An essential part of a closed-loop system is feedback; that is, the output of the system is measured continually through the item controlled, and the input is modified to reduce any difference or error toward zero. Many of the patterns of information flow in organizations are found to have the nature of closed loops, which use feedback. The reason for such a condition is apparent when one recognizes that any system, if it is to achieve a predetermined goal, must have available to it at all times an indication of its degree of attainment. In general, every goal-seeking system employs feedback. ' ==

Man and Machine Control

The elements of control are easy to identify in machine systems. For example, the characteristic to be controlled might be some variable like speed or temperature, and the sensing device could be a speedometer or a thermometer. An expectation of precision exists because the characteristic is quantifiable and the standard and the normal variation to be expected can be described in exact terms. In automatic machine systems, inputs of information are used in a process of continual adjustment to achieve output specifications. When even a small variation from the standard occurs, the correction process begins. The automatic system is highly structured, designed to accept certain kinds of input and produce specific output, and programmed to regulate the transformation of inputs within a narrow range of variation.

For an illustration of mechanical control, as the load on a steam engine increases and the engine starts to slow down, the regulator reacts by opening a valve that releases additional inputs of steam energy. This new input returns the engine to the desired number of revolutions per minute. This type of mechanical control is crude in comparison to the more sophisticated electronic control systems in everyday use. Consider the complex missile-guidance systems that measure the actual course according to predetermined mathematical calculations and make almost instantaneous corrections to direct the missile to its target.

Machine systems can be complex because of the sophisticated technology, whereas control of people is complex because the elements of control are difficult to determine. In human control systems, the relationship between objectives and associated characteristics is often vague; the measurement of the characteristic may be extremely subjective; the expected standard is difficult to define; and the amount of new inputs required is impossible to quantify. To illustrate, let us refer once more to a formalized social system in which deviant behaviour is controlled through a process of observed violation of the existing law, court hearings and trials, incarceration when the accused is found guilty and release from custody after rehabilitation of the prisoner has occurred. The speed limit established for freeway driving is one standard of performance that is quantifiable, but even in this instance, the degree of permissible variation and the amount of the actual variation are often a subject of disagreement between the patrolman and the suspected violator. The complexity of our society is reflected in many of our laws and regulations, which establish the general standards for economic, political, and social operations. A citizen may not know or understand the law and consequently would not know whether or not he was guilty of a violation.

Most organized systems are some combination of man and machine; some elements of control may be performed by machine whereas others are accomplished by man. In addition, some standards may be precisely structured whereas others may be little more than general guidelines with wide variations expected in output. Man must performanceas the controller when measurement is subjective and judgment is required. Machines such as computers are incapable of making exceptions from the specified control criteria regardless of how much a particular case might warrant special consideration. A pilot acts in conjunction with computers and automatic pilots to fly large jets. In the event of unexpected weather changes, or possible collision with another plane, he must intercede and assume direct control.

Organizational and Operational Control

The concept of organizational control is implicit in the bureaucratic theory of Max Weber. Associated with this theory are such concepts as "span of control", "closeness of supervision", and "hierarchical authority". Weber's view tends to include all levels or types of organizational control as being the same. More recently, writers have tended to differentiate the control process between that which emphasizes the nature of the organizational or systems design and that which deals with daily operations.

To illustrate the difference, we "evaluate" the performance of a system to see how effective and efficient the design proved to be or to discover why it failed. In contrast, we operate and "control" the system with respect to the daily inputs of material, information, and energy. In both instances, the elements of feedback are present, but organizational control tends to review and evaluate the nature and arrangement of components in the system, whereas operational control tends to adjust the daily inputs. The direction for organizational control comes from the goals and strategic plans of the organization. General plans are translated into specific performance measures such as share of the market, earnings, return on investment, and budgets.

The process of organizational control is to review and evaluate the performance of the system against these established norms. Rewards for meeting or exceeding standards may range from special recognition to salary increases or promotions. On the other hand, a failure to meet expectations may signal the need to reorganize or redesign. In organizational control, the approach used in the programme of review and evaluation depends on the reason for the evaluation — that is, is it because the system is not effective (accomplishing its objectives)? Is the system failing to achieve an expected standard of efficiency? Is the evaluation being conducted because of a breakdown or failure in operations? Is it merely a periodic audit-and-review process?

When a system has failed or is in great difficulty, special diagnostic techniques may be required to isolate the trouble areas and to identify the causes of the difficulty. It is appropriate to investigate areas that have been troublesome before or areas where some measure of performance can be quickly identified. For example, if an organization's output backlog builds rapidly, it is logical to check first to see if the problem is due to such readily obtainable measures as increased demand or to a drop in available man hours. When a more detailed analysis is necessary, a systematic procedure should be followed.

In contrast to organizational control, operational control serves to regulate the day-to-day output relative to schedules, specifications, and costs. Is the output of product or service the proper quality and is it available as scheduled? Are inventories of raw materials, goods-in-process, and finished products being purchased and produced in the desired quantities? Are the costs associated with the transformation process in line with cost estimates? Is the information needed in the transformation process available in the right form and at the right time? Is the energy resource being utilized efficiently?

The most difficult task of management concerns monitoring the behaviour of individuals, comparing performance to some standard, and providing rewards or punishment as indicated. Sometimes this control over people relates entirely to their output. For example, a manager might not be concerned with the behaviour of a salesman as long as sales were as high as expected. In other instances, close supervision of the salesman might be appropriate if achieving customer satisfaction were one of the sales organization's main objectives.

The larger the unit, the more likely that the control characteristic will be related to some output goal. It also follows that if it is difficult or impossible to identify the actual output of individuals, it is better to measure the performance of the entire group. This means that individuals' levels of motivation and the measurement of their performance become subjective judgments made by the supervisor. Controlling output also suggests the difficulty of controlling individuals' performance and relating this to the total system's objectives.

Problems of Control

The perfect plan could be outlined if every possible variation of input could be anticipated and if the system would operate as predicted. This kind of planning is neither realistic, economical, nor feasible for most business systems. If it were feasible, planning requirements would be so complex that the system would be out of date before it could be operated. Therefore, we design control into systems.

This requires more thought in the systems design but allows more flexibility of operations and makes it possible to operate a system using unpredictable components and undetermined input. Still, the design and effective operation of control are not without problems. The objective of the system is to perform some specified function. The purpose of organizational control is to see that the specified function is achieved; the objective of operational control is to ensure that variations in daily output are maintained within prescribed limits. It is one thing to design a system that contains all of the elements of control, and quite another to make it operate true to the best objectives of design.

Operating "in control" or "with plan" does not guarantee optimum performance. For example, the plan may not make the best use of the inputs of materials, energy, or information — in other words, the system may not be designed to operate efficiently. Some of the more typical problems relating to control include the difficulty of measurement, the problem of timing information flow, and the setting of proper standards.

Measurement of Output

When objectives are not limited to quantitative output, the measurement of system effectiveness is difficult to make and subsequently perplexing to evaluate. Many of the characteristics pertaining to output do not lend themselves to quantitative measurement. This is true particularly when inputs of human energy cannot be related directly to output. The same situation applies to machines and other equipment associated with human involvement, when output is not in specific units.

In evaluating man-machine or human-oriented systems, psychological and sociological factors obviously do not easily translate into quantifiable terms. For example, how does mental fatigue affect the quality or quantity of output? And, if it does, is mental fatigue a function of the lack of a challenging assignment or the fear of a potential injury? Subjective inputs may be transferred into numerical data, but there is always the danger of an incorrect appraisal and transfer, and the danger that the analyst may assume undue confidence in such data after they have been quantified. Let us suppose, for example, that the decisions made by an executive are rated from 1 to 10, 10 being the perfect decision. After determining the ranking for each decision, adding these, and dividing by the total number of decisions made, the average ranking would indicate a particular executive's score in his decision-making role. On the basis of this score, judgments — which could be quite erroneous — might be made about his decision-making effectiveness. One executive with a ranking of 6.75 might be considered more effective than another who had a ranking of 6.25, and yet the two managers may have made decisions under different circumstances and conditions. External factors over which neither executive had any control may have influenced the difference in "effectiveness".

Quantifying human behaviour, despite its extreme difficulty, subjectivity, and imprecision in relation to measuring physical characteristics is the most prevalent and important measurement made in large systems. The behaviour of individuals ultimately dictates the success or failure of every man-made system.

Information Flow

Another problem of control relates to the improper timing of information introduced into the feedback channel. Improper timing can occur in both computerized and human control systems, either by mistakes in measurement or in judgment. The more rapid the system's response to an error signal, the more likely it is that the system could overadjust; yet the need for prompt action is important because any delay in providing corrective input could also be crucial. A system generating feedback inconsistent with current need will tend to fluctuate and will not adjust in the desired manner.

The most serious problem in information flow arises when the delay in feedback is exactly one-half cycle, for then the corrective action is superimposed on a variation from norm which, at that moment, is in the same direction as that of the correction. This causes the system to overcorrect, and then if the reverse adjustment is made out of cycle, to correct too much in the other direction, and so on until the system fluctuates out of control. If, at Point A, the trend below standard is recognized and new inputs are added, but not until Point B, the system will overreact and go beyond the allowable limits. Again, if this is recognized at Point C, but inputs are not withdrawn until Point D, it will cause the system to drop below the lower limit of allowable variation.

One solution to this problem rests in anticipation, which involves measuring not only the change but also the rate of change. The correction is outlined as a factor of the type and rate of the error. The difficulty also might be overcome by reducing the time lag between the measurement of the output and the adjustment to input.

If a trend can be indicated, a time lead can be introduced to compensate for the time lag, bringing about consistency between the need for correction and the type and magnitude of the indicated action. It is usually more effective for an organization to maintain continuous measurement of its performance and to make small adjustments in operations constantly. Information feedback, consequently, should be timely and correct to be effective. That is, the information should provide an accurate indication of the status of the system.

Setting Standards

Setting the proper standards or control limits is a problem in many systems. Parents are confronted with this dilemma in expressing what they expect of their children, and business managers face the same issue in establishing standards that will be acceptable to employees. Some theorists have proposed that workers be allowed to set their own standards, on the assumption that when people establish their own goals, they are more apt to accept and achieve them.

Standards should be as precise as possible and communicated to all persons concerned. Moreover, communication alone is not sufficient; understanding is necessary. In human systems, standards tend to be poorly defined and the allowable range of deviation from standard also indefinite. For example, how many hours each day should a professor be expected to be available for student consultation? Or, what kind of behaviour should be expected by students in the classroom? Discretion and personal judgment play a large part in such systems, to determine whether corrective action should be taken. Perhaps the most difficult problem in human systems is the unresponsiveness of individuals to indicated correction. This may take the form of opposition and subversion to control, or it may be related to the lack of defined responsibility or authority to take action. Leadership and positive motivation then become vital ingredients in achieving the proper response to input requirements.

Most control problems relate to design; thus the solution to these problems must start at that point. Automatic control systems, provided that human intervention is possible to handle exceptions, offer the greatest promise. There is a danger, however, that we may measure characteristics that do not represent effective performance or that improper information may be communicated.

Objectives :

- *Effectiveness*: Goods to fulfill customers' needs
- *Maximising output*: Maximum output with minimum input
- *Quality control*: Product/service quality meets planned quality specifications
- *Minimise throughput time*: Conversion of RM to FG in minimum time
- *Capacity*: full utilisation of men and machines
- Minimise cost: minimum cost of production
- *Maintaining inventory*: Optimal inventory
- *Flexibility*: Flexibility in production operations
- *Coordination*: Between men and machines
- *Capacity*: Plan for current and future needs

- *Reduce bottlenecks*: Solve production problems early
- *Maximise profit*: Minimise cost
- *Production schedules*: As per plan
- *Routes and schedules*: To optimise use of men, material and machinery
- *Maintain performance*: Maintain standards

Functions of Production Planning :

- Product selection and design
- Process selection and planning
- Facility location
- Facility layout and materials handling
- Capacity planning
- Systems and procedures
- Estimating quantity/costs of production, men
- Routing operation sequence
- Job scheduling and loading

Functions of Production Control :

- Inventory control: MRP; JIT
- Time management
- Quality control
- Maintenance and Replacement
- Cost reduction and cost control
- Dispatch
- Expediting/Follow-up/Progressing

Scope of Production Planning and Control :

- *Material*: RM, components, spares; right quantity; right time
- Methods
- Machines and equipments
- Manpower
- Routing
- Estimating
- Loading and sceduling
- Dispatching
- Expediting
- Inspection
- Evaluating
- Cost control

Phases in Production Planning and Control System :

- *Planning*:
  - Pre-planning

  - Product planning and development;
  - Demand forecasting;
  - Resource planning;
  - Facilities planning;
  - Plant location and layout
- Active planning
  - Quantity planning;
  - Product mix;
  - Routing;
  - Scheduling;
  - Material planning;
  - Process planning;
  - Capacity planning;
  - Tool planning

Benefits of Production Planning and Control :

- Higher quality
- Better resource utilization
- Reduced inventory
- Reduced manufacturing cycle time
- Faster delivery
- Better customer services
- Lower production costs
- Lower capital investment
- Higher customer service
- Improved sales turnover
- Improved market share
- Improved profitability
- Competitive advantage
- Flexibility
- Dependability
- Lower prices

Limitations of Production Planning and Control :

- Based on assumptions
- Resistance to change
- Time consuming
- Difficult due to rapid environment changes

Measuring Effectiveness of Production Planning and Control :

- Delivery
- Inventory levels
- Production/Operations Management

Requirements for Effective Production Planning and Control :

- Sound organisational structure
- Delegation of authority
- Reliable, up-to-date feedback
- Standardisation
- Trained people
- Flexibility to adapt
- Appropriate management policies
- Accurate assessment of manufacturing/procurement lead times
- Adequate plant capacity

Techniques :

- Planning and Control of Reserves;
  - Deterministic/non-deterministic systems
- Network analysis:
- PERT
  - Project Evaluation
  - Review Technique
- CPM
  - Critical Path Method
- Reliability Theory:
  - Probability
    a. Series structure
    b. Parallel structure

WORK STUDY

Work Study is the systemeatic examination of the methods of carrying out activities such as to improve the effective use of resources and to set up standards of performance for the activities carried out.

Another definition of Work Study could be: A generic term for those techniques, particularly method study and work measurement, which are used in the examination of human work in all its contexts, and which lead systematically to to the investigation of all the factors which affect the efficiency and economy of the situation being reviewed, in order to effect improvement'. This has to do with Productivity Improvement, but also improvement of Quality and Safety.

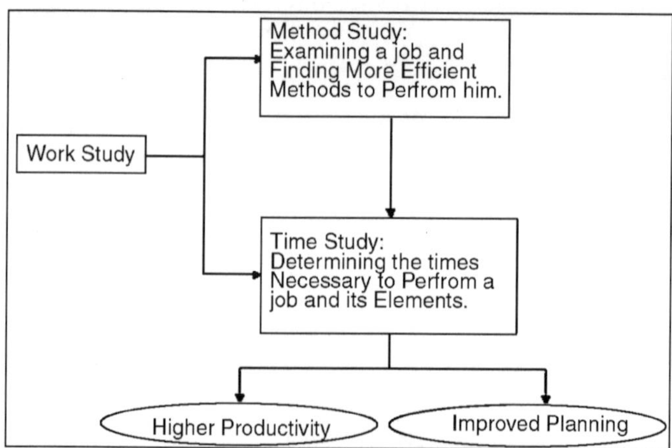

Fig. Components of Work Study

WHAT IS PRODUCTIVITY?

In this post we're going to take a deep look into the concept of productivity.

Here's our personal definition of productivity:

Productivity = Value/Time

By this definition there are two primary ways of increasing productivity:

1. Increase the value created
2. Decrease the time required to create that value

You can complicate this definition by including other factors like energy and resources, but we prefer the simplicity of time because in most cases factors like energy and resources are reducible to time anyway. Time also makes it very easy to compare different levels of productivity, such as output per hour or per day.

Apparently you can make some significant gains on the time side. There are many personal productivity optimizations which, especially if you introduce them in your youth, will produce a massive net savings of time over the course of your life. Consider your typing speed, for instance. If you invest the time to get your speed up to 90 words per minute or faster, it will be well worth the initial time investment if you happen to do a lot of typing over your lifetime, compared to allowing your speed to linger at 50 wpm or slower year after year.

The extra hours of practice will be nothing compared to the time you save typing emails, letters, or blog entries over the next few decades. Other time-based optimizations include improving your sleeping habits, minimizing commute time, or dropping time-wasting habits like smoking. The main limit of time-based optimizations is that the optimization process requires an input of time itself. It takes time to save time. So the more time you invest in optimizing time usage, the greater your initial time investment, and the greater your need for a long-term payoff to justify that investment. This limit creates an upper bound for any time-based optimizations you attempt, in accordance with the law of diminishing returns.

The more time you invest in any optimization attempt, the lower your net return, all else being equal. This law of diminishing returns points us back to the value side. While we might be stuck with diminshing returns by trying to optimize the time side alone, we may notice that working to optimize the value side is less limiting and more open-ended.

WHAT IS THE "VALUE" IN OUR PRODUCTIVITY EQUATION?

Value is a quality you must define for yourself. Hence, any definition of productity is relative to the definition of value. In circles where people can agree on a common definition of value, they can also agree on a common definition of productivity. However, in terms of your own personal productivity, you aren't obligated to define value the same way anyone else would. You are free to adopt your own definition, such that your pursuit of greater productivity becomes a personal quest that produces the value that matters most to you.

Too often we adopt a socially conditioned definition of value, which tends to be very limiting. Perhaps we define value in terms of work output within our career, number of tasks completed, number and quality of important projects finished, etc.

You may not be able to verbalize it clearly, but perhaps you have a working definition of value that feels comfortable to you. You can tell when you've had a productive day and when you haven't based on how much value you created, in accordance with your own sense of what value means.

But how much conscious thought did you put into your personal definition of value? I'm going to challenge you to put a bit more thought into your definition, which will consequently redefine your sense of productivity.

IMPACT

First, according to your definition of value, to what extent is the value provided? Who receives the value? Yourself, your boss, your coworkers, your friends, your family, your company, your customers, your team, certain investors, your community, your country, the world, your family, God, all conscious beings, etc? What degree of value is ultimately received by each person or group? Are you providing value to one person, 10 people, 100 people, 1000 people, millions of people, the whole planet? How much do you feel the value you provide ripples outward beyond those you provide it to directly? How quickly do those ripples dissipate? What's your sense of the basic level of impact of your value? Is it limited or expansive? For example, if you're the CEO of a Fortune 500 corporation or the leader of a country, you'll have a far greater ability to provide value to large numbers of people vs. if you work as a janitor. The more people you can influence, the greater your potential value. Greater leverage means greater potential impact.

ENDURANCE

Secondly, how long does the value you create endure? An hour, a day, a week, a month, a year, a decade, a lifetime, 100 years, 1000 years, 10,000 years, until the end of time? To what extent does your value carry forward in time? Is it quickly consumed and forgotten? Or does it continue to regenerate itself year after year? Does your value create ripples through time?

The Mona Lisa *is still providing value hundreds of years after its creation. But other works of art do not provide any enduring value beyond the lifetime of the artist. They are quickly abandoned and eventually replaced.*

ESSENCE

Thirdly, what is the essence of the value you produce? Do you help people survive? Entertain them? Enlighten them? How much do others value what you produce? What price would they be willing to pay for it? Do they consider your value essential, optional, or undesirable? How unique is your value? Are you the only one who can provide it, or are there plenty of equivalent choices?

The essence of value provided by a janitor is low because it is easy to find people to do such work for little pay. The essence of value of a physicist is potentially enormous because a new theoretical concept could yield a more accurate understanding of the universe.

VOLUME

Lastly, what is the volume of value you create? How much of it are you putting out in a given period of time? What is the quantity in which you produce that value? For example, Picasso was a prolific artist who created hundreds of different works over his lifetime. Other artists had a far lower volume of output.

So now we have this little formula:

Value = Impact x Endurance x Essence x Volume

And therefore:

Productivity = Impact x Endurance x Essence x Volume/Time

Now what's interesting here is that most of the productivity literature I've read focuses almost exclusively on volume and time. But those are the most limiting parts of this equation.

PRODUCTIVITY CONCEPTUAL MODEL

The Productivity Conceptual Model, takes the form of a 'productivity tree'. The roots denote the inputs to the system, the trunk the conversion process and the foliage and fruits the systems outputs.

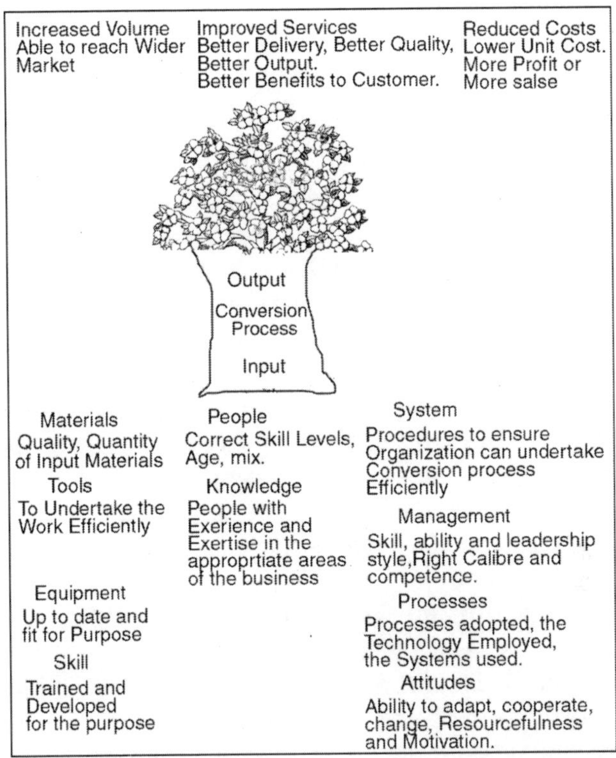

Fig. Productivity Conceptual Model

The successful management of this process, is ultimately the key to survival of any organization. It should be the concern of and a development goal for all organizational members, irrespective of their position.

METHOD STUDY

Method study is the process of subjecting work to systematic, critical scrutiny in order to make it more effective and/or more efficient.

It was originally designed for the analysis and improvement of repetitive, manual work, but it can be used for all types of activity at all levels of an organisation.

The process is often seen as a linear, described by its main steps of:

- Select;
- Record;
- Examine;
- Develop;
- Install;
- Maintain.

Although this linear representation shows the underlying simplicity of method study, in practice the process is much more one of iteration around the steps with each dominating at a different stage of the investigation. The cyclic process often starts with a quick, rough pass in which preliminary data are collected and examined, before subsequent passes provide and handle more comprehensive and more detailed data to obtain and analyse a more complete picture.

Work is selected for method study on the basis of it being an identified problem area or an identified opportunity and usually because it meets certain conditions of urgency and/or priority.Before any method study investigation is begun, it is necessary to establish clear terms of reference which define the aims, scale, scope and constraints of the investigation.

This should also include an identification of who "owns" the problem or situation and ways in which such "ownership" is shared. This may lead to a debate on the aims of the project, on reporting mechanisms and frequencies, and on the measures of success. This process is sometimes introduced as a separate and distinct phase of method study, as the "define" stage. It leads to a plan for the investigation which identifies appropriate techniques, personnel, and timescale.

The Record stage of method study is to provide sufficient data to performanceas the basis of evaluation and examination. A wide range of techniques are available for recording; the choice depends on the nature of the investigation and the work being studied, and on the level of detail required. Many of the techniques are simple charts and diagrams, but these may be supplemented by photographic and video recording, and by computer based techniques.

Especially with "hard" problems, method study often involves the construction and analysis of models, from simple charts and diagrams used to record and represent the situation to full, computerised simulations. Manipulation of and experimentation on the models leads to ideas for development.

The recorded data are subjected to examination and analysis; formalised versions of this process are critical examination and systems analysis. The aim is to identify, often through a structured, questioning process, those points of the overall system of work that require improvements or offer opportunity for beneficial change.

The Examine stage merges into the Develop stage of the investigation as more thorough analysis leads automatically to identified areas of change. The aim here is to identify possible actions for improvement and to subject these to evaluation in order to develop a preferred solution.

Sometimes it is necessary to identify short-term and long-term solutions so that improvements can be made immediately, while longer-term changes are implemented and come to fruition. The success of any method study project is realised when actual change is made 'on the ground' - change that meets the originally specified terms of reference for the project. Thus, the Install phase is very important. Making theoretical change is easy; making real change demands careful planning - and handling of the people involved in the situation under review. They may need reassuring, retraining and supporting through the acquisition of new skills. Install, in some cases,will require a parallel running of old and new systems, in others, it may need the build-up of buffer stocks, and in others..... what matters is that the introduction of new working methods is successful. There is often only one chance to make change!

Some time after the introduction of new working methods, it is necessary to check that the new method is working, that it is being adhered to, and that it has brought about the desired results. This is the Maintain phase. Method drift is common - when people start to either revert to old ways of working, or introduce new changes. Some of these may be helpful; others may be inefficient or unsafe. A methods audit can be used to formally compare practice with the defined method and identify such 'irregularities'.

WORK MEASUREMENT

Work measurement is the process of establishing the time that a given task would take when performed by a qualified worker working at a defined level of performance.

There are various ways in which work may be measured and a variety of techniques have been established.

The basic procedure, irrespective of the particular measurement technique being used, consists of three stages:

1. An analysis phase in which the job is divided into convenient, discrete components, commonly known as elements;
2. A measurement phase in which the specific measurement technique is used to establish the time required to complete each element of work;
3. A synthesis phase in which the various elemental times are added, together with appropriate allowances to construct the standard time for the complete job.

The techniques used to measure work can be classified into those that rely on direct observation of the work, and those that do not. For example, some techniques, such as predetermined motion-time systems and the use of synthetic or standard data can provide times from simulation or even visualisation of the work. However, the data on which such techniques are based were almost certainly based on earlier observation of actual work.

RATING

Direct observation techniques include a process for converting observed times to times for the "qualified worker working at a defined level of performance." The commonest of these processes is known as rating. This involves the observer making an assessment of the worker's rate of working relative to the observer's concept of the rate corresponding to standard rating. This assessment is based on the factors involved in the work - such as effort, dexterity, speed of movement, and consistency. The assessment is made on a rating scale, of which there are three or four in common usage. Thus on the 0-100 scale, the observer makes a judgement of the worker's rate of working as a percentage of the standard rate of working.

The rating is then used to convert the observed time to the basic time using the simple formula:

Basic time = observed time x observed rating/standard rating

Rating is regarded by many as a controversial area of measurement since it is a subjective assessment. Where different observers rate differently, the resulting basic times are not comparable. However, practised rating practitioners are remarkably consistent. It is important that those undertaking the rating are properly trained, and that this training is regularly updated through rating 'clinics'.

ALLOWANCES

When carrying out work over a complete shift or working day, workers obviously suffer from the fatigue imposed both by the work undertaken and the conditions under which they are working. The normal practice is to make an addition to the basic time to allow the worker to recover from this fatigue and to attend to personal needs. The amount of the allowance depends on the nature of the work and the working environment, and is often assessed using an agreed set of guidelines and scales. It is usual to allow some of the recovery period inherent in these allowances to be taken away from the workplace. Thus, work design should include the design of an effective work-rest regime. The addition of allowances should never be used to compensate for an unsafe or unhealthy working environment.

One minority school of thought suggests that relaxation allowances are unnecessary. With work which involves, say, the carrying of heavy weights, this school suggests that the observer automatically adjusts the concept of standard rating to allow for the weight. Thus, if the standard rate of performance for walking on level ground carrying no weight is equivalent to four miles per hour, then an observer rating a worker walking while carrying a weight will not expect the equivalent rate.

Thus, it is argued that the weight has been allowed for in the adjustment of standard rating and any relaxation allowance is simply a duplication of this adjustment. In many jobs there are small amounts of work that may occur irregularly and inconsistently. It is often not economic to measure such infrequent work and an additional allowance is added to cover such work and similar irregular delays. This allowance is known as a contingency allowance and is assessed either by observation, by analysis of historical records or by experience. The end result is a standard time which includes the time the work "should" take plus additional allocations in the form of allowances, where appropriate, to cover relaxation time, contingency time and, perhaps, unoccupied time which increases the overall work cycle.

CHOOSING A MEASUREMENT TECHNIQUE

The choice of a suitable measurement technique depends on a number of factors including:

- The purpose of the measurement;
- The level of detail required;
- The time available for the measurement;
- The existence of available predetermined data;
- And the cost of measurement.

To some extent there is a trade off between some of these factors. For example, techniques which derive times quickly may provide less detail and be less suitable for some purposes, such as the establishment of individual performance levels on short-cycle work.

The advantage of structured and systematic work measurement is that it gives a common currency for the evaluation and comparison of all types of work. The results obtained from work measurement are commonly used as the basis of the planning and scheduling of work, manpower planning, work balancing in team working, costing, labour performance measurement, and financial incentives. They are less commonly used as the basis of product design, methods comparison, work sequencing, and workplace design.

SERICULTURE AND SILK PRODUCTION

PROBLEM/NEED

The ancient technique of rearing silkworms for production of silk yarn (and weaving it into expensive cloth) is widely practiced today. Over Rs. 1000 crores worth of silk is produced in Indian annually by more than 27 lakh people, over half of them being women. There is a huge export market too for silk cloth and garments. However, as in so many other traditional industries, the primary producers get only a fraction of the profits which are usually cornered by middle men and trading houses. Consequently the mulberry cultivators and silk reelers, weavers, etc., continue to live in dismal conditions. They also face hardships arising from pests, non-availability or poor quality of raw materials and price manipulations. Sericulture and silk production have an enormous potential in our country provided it is made available to rural people, especially women, and its marketing is organized independently. It can serve as an excellent mode for employment generation and augmentation of income. This requires not only providing fresh technological inputs to primary producers but more importantly, evolving and establishing new systems of organizing production and marketing.

TECHNOLOGY PACKAGE

The technology of sericulture and silk production is well-known. In brief, various aspects involved in it are as follows:

- Mulberry Cultivation: Silkworms feed on mulberry leaves. Hence the rearing of silkworms involves cultivation of mulberry trees, which provide a regular supply of leaves. Worms are introduced through DFLs (Disease Free Layings, i.e. eggs) procured from a quality centre (called grainage). In India, the bulk of mulberry cultivation is done by small farmers (< 4 acres land), usually in clusters of 300-400.
- Rearing: The silkworms are actually larvae of the silkmoth. They are reared in specially made trays in rooms with controlled temperature and humidity and regularly fed mulberry leaves. At a certain stage they convert themselves into cocoons. These cocoons are made from a single filament of material secreted by the pupa and wrapped around itself for protection. These filaments upon hardening constitute silk. On an average, 1 acre of plantation would yield 240 kg of cocoons in an year, starting from 100 DFLs. Depending upon whether it is dryland or irrigated mulberry, farmers can harvest the cocoons 4 to 8 times in an year.
- Reeling: The removal of silk yarn from the cocoons is called reeling. This is done by first cooking them in water to remove the gum, which holds it together, and then unwinding the filaments (reeling). Usually 8-10 cocoons are reeled together. There are three methods for reeling: the charkha, the slightly more advanced cottage basin and the costly automatic machines.
- Twisting: Prior to weaving, the raw silk is boiled in water to remove remaining gum, dyed and bleached, and then woven into the garment – usually on handloom. In some cases the woven cloth may be dyed and bleached.
- Species of Silkworms: There are four different species of moths, cocoons of which yield differing types of silk:
  - Mulberry Silk is the most common among them contributing to nearly 95% of world's silk production. It is produced from the cocoons of the moth *Bombyx mori*. Within the species there are many varieties, mainly differentiated according to the number of generations produced annually under natural conditions. Then, hybrids of various kinds have also been developed. Multivoltine varieties (laying eggs several times a year) have been widely

propagated to push up yields, but many feel that they are more vulnerable to pests and hence risky for small farmers. The government provides DFLs of various species through its outlets.

- Eri silkworm has two varieties – a wild one and a domesticated one bred on castor leaves. The filament is neither continuous nor uniform. Hence the moths are allowed to emerge before commencing reeling. A white or bright red silk is produced.
- Tasar silkworms are wild. The Indian Tasar worm feeds on trees of Terminalia species and other minor host plants, while the Japanese and Chinese worms feed on oak and other allied species. Reeling can be done as with mulberry worms.
- Muga silkworm is found only in Assam. It feeds on two local species of shrubs – Machilus bombycina and Litsae polyantha, producing a strong, golden yellow thread.

SYSTEM DESIGN

Under the prevailing system in India, all the functions described above are usually carried out by different sets of people and there exists a well-established system of markets where the products of each stage are sold/bought. Being dominated by rich traders, it is here that most of the profits are siphoned off. Hence, in the new technology package, an alternative system is envisaged of a cooperative or collective kind where functions are decentralized yet under the larger umbrella of a people's organization. The final products are then marketed centrally. Expert inputs are made available for both technical and managerial aspects including marketing. Consequently the high prices available for silk clothes would mean higher returns to the primary producers at various stages.

PRODUCTIVITY AND PROFITABILITY IN RAINFED SERICULTURE

Sericulture plays a vital role in rural development in Karnataka, as it integrates well with the farming systems and has the potential to generate attractive income throughout the year. Karnataka produced 8196 tonnes of raw silk during 2001-02, which accounted for about 51 per cent of the country's total silk production of 15,848 tonnes. As mulberry is highly versatile in nature, it is cultivated in a variety of soil types, a wide range of agro-climatic conditions and in both rainfed and irrigated areas. Out of 1,20,119 ha of mulberry area in Karnataka, rainfed mulberry occupies 24,985 ha, accounting for 20.80 per cent of the total mulberry area. The rainfed sericulture is distinct from the irrigated sericulture. As the rainfed farming is generally characterized by uncertainty and fluctuations in rainfall and other climatic conditions, there are wide spatio-temporal variations in the productivity levels in the rainfed sericulture. Quality mulberry leaf, separate rearing house with the required rearing appliances and proper rearing management, which are essential for the production of quality cocoons are lacking with the rainfed sericulturists. In this context, the study has been taken up to analyze the resource-use pattern and profitability of dry land sericultural operations with the following specific objectives: (i) To study the resource-use efficiency and productivity in sericulture farms; (ii) To assess the profitability of sericulture operations under rainfed conditions; (iii) To analyze the extent of adoption of recommended technologies by the farmers; and (iv) To identity the problems faced by the rainfed sericulturists.

INPUTS-USE PATTERN

Optimum use of inputs is essential to obtain the potential yield of cocoons. However, as the farmers have limited resources, they make some adjustments in the allocation of their resources in order to operate the farm business at economic optimum level. The average use of farmyard manure was almost at its optimum level. Sericulture was the most feasible commercial activity in the study area. Further, mulberry is a perennial and nutrient-exhaustive crop. Hence, the farmers provided priority to the application of manures produced in their farm to mulberry fields to enrich the soil nutrients. As the family-labour availability was abundant and the scope of using the labour for other crops was limited due to seasonal nature of the agricultural crops, the availability of labour for sericultural activities was more.

Hence, the use of labour was 40.43 per cent more than the requirement for silkworm rearing and 9.67 per cent excess for mulberry cultivation. A wide gap was observed in the use of fertilizers for mulberry garden and disinfectant chemicals in silkworm rearing. As most of the respondents reared silkworms in a portion of their dwelling houses, it was difficult to use strong chemicals for disinfection of the rearing place. The farmers, therefore, tended to avoid the use of chemicals in silkworm rearing. The studies conducted by Jayram *et al.* (1996), Datta *et al.* (1999) and Geetha *et al.* (2001) also revealed that the major inputs for practising sericulture namely, silkworm seed (dfls), disinfectants, manures and fertilizers were in sub-optimal levels for mulberry cultivation and silkworm rearing by the farmers in different regions. Further, Jayram *et al.* (1996) pointed out that the major constraints in the usage of inputs in sericulture were due to lack of awareness about inputs, improper organization of channels of distribution and reluctance of farmers in accepting the improved practices generated by the research institutes.

FACTORS INFLUENCING THE COCOON PRODUCTION

A log-linear regression was fitted to study the factors influencing the cocoon production. Cocoon production was considered as a dependent variable and regressed with the factors of production such as bullock power, farm yard manure, fertilizers, human labour, quantum of leaf used for production of one kg of cocoon and cost of disinfectants. The value of coefficient of multiple determination (R2) was 0.75. The higher values of R2 testified that the selected form of the production function was the best fit. The values of the regression coefficient were less than unity for all the inputs except in the case of farmyard manure and human labour.

This shows that each of these inputs followed diminishing marginal productivity. The coefficients of bullock power, human labour, quantum of leaf used for production of one kg of cocoon, and disinfectants were positive and statistically significant.

This implied that bullock power, human labour, quantum of feeding and disinfectants were the important inputs, which significantly influenced the cocoon production. Neelakantasastry (1982), Marihonnaiah (1986), Kulkarni (1992) and Sumanta Behera (2004) identified that dfls, human labour and disinfectants had positive and significant association with cocoon production. The elasticity of production was significant but negative for farmyard manure. This could be due to improper use of poor quality organic manures for the mulberry field. The regression coefficient of fertilizers was positive but statistically not significant. But Jayaram (1991) had reported significant and positive association of farmyard manure and fertilizer with the irrigated mulberry leaf yield.

RESOURCE-USE EFFICIENCY

The marginal value of product and the cost of input were almost equal for bullock power, which implied that the bullock power was used efficiently. The ratio between marginal value of product and the acquisition cost per unit was more than unity for leaf, fertilizer and disinfectants. This indicated that leaf, fertilizer and disinfectants were used at sub-optimal levels. Hence, there is a possibility of increasing the use of these inputs to the optimum level, where the efficiency of the input-use is maximum. The allocation efficiency was higher than unity for labour, which implied that the labour was used uneconomically. As family labour was available in abundance and the scope of using it for other crops is limited in the rainfed areas, it was used excessively and inefficiently. Similar observation was made by Singh and Vasishti (1994) with respect to small farmers in the Salem district of Tamil Nadu. Farmyard manure was found to be allocated uneconomically.

ECONOMICS OF COCOON PRODUCTION

Cocoon production involves two distinct activities — production of mulberry leaf, which is a field-related activity and the rearing of silkworm that is conducted in separate rearing houses or in a portion of the dwelling houses of farmers. The leaf production cost was worked out to be Rs 4254/acre/year.

Bullock power, which is used for inter-cultivation by ploughing was the major component of the cost being Rs 1417, followed by labour (Rs 1083), farm yard manure (Rs 726) and fertilizers (Rs 383). As mulberry is a perennial crop, once it is planted, it will yield mulberry leaf from the sixth month to over fifteen years. Hence, the costs incurred during gestation period for the establishment of mulberry plantation was considered as fixed costs and apportioned for the entire life-period of the plantation by considering the economic life-period of mulberry as 15 years.

The apportioned cost of mulberry was thus worked out to be Rs 86.69. In silkworm rearing, labour cost was the major component, which worked out to be Rs 6136 (44.56 % of the total cost), followed by cost of leaf and depreciation of rearing-building and equipments, accounting for 30.90 per cent and 10.31 per cent of the total cost of production of cocoon, respectively. The cost of disinfectants was estimated at Rs 269. Most of the chemicals used for disinfection were supplied free of cost by either the State Sericulture Department or the private grainages from where the silkworm seeds were purchased.

The total cost of cocoon production was worked out as Rs 13,770. The farmers earned Rs 10534 by selling the cocoons and Rs 570 by selling the excess mulberry leaves produced in the garden to the needy farmers. The income obtained from by-products such as silkworm litter and leaf wastes, which can be used as organic manure after decomposing, worked out as Rs 462. The total revenue worked out to be Rs11,566/acre/ year, which was less than the cost incurred for cocoon production.

Hence, the net revenue was negative with (-) Rs 2204/acre/year. However, if the imputed value of family labour utilized for silkworm rearing and free disinfectants supplied by the Department of Sericulture, Government of Karnataka, for the promotion of improved technologies were excluded from the total cost, the net revenue would be positive (Rs 2704 /acre/year) and the cost-benefit ratio would become 1: 1.31.

The surplus income generated in rainfed sericulture could be just enough to meet the wages of family labour. It is evident that with the inclusion of wages for family labour in the economics, the cocoon production activity was not profitable.

The low profitability in rainfed sericulture could be attributed to less productivity and lower price fetched for the cocoons produced under the rainfed conditions. In contrast, the net returns generated in irrigated sericulture were very high, and were estimated as Rs 39,883/ acre/year by Dandin and Kumaresan (2003).

The study conducted by Kumaresan and Vijaya Prakash (2001) also indicated that irrigated sericulture was more profitable than the agricultural crops like paddy, sugarcane, gingili and groundnut.

ADOPTION LEVEL OF MULBERRY CULTIVATION AND SILKWORM REARING PRACTICES

As adoption of improved technologies is essential to realize the potential yield levels in the crop production. Improved practices such as high-yielding mulberry varieties, application of manures and chemical fertilizers, harvesting of mulberry leaf, disinfection of rearing house, maintenance of hygienic practices, maintenance of bed spacing, bed cleaning, mounting, harvesting of cocoons and control of uzifly in silkworm-rearing were practised but not as per the recommendations by majority of the sample farmers, whereas separate rearing house, rearing of crossbreed silkworm, incubation, black boxing, shoot rearing, maintenance of temperature and humidity in silkworm-rearing, dusting of vijetha (the silkworm body and bed disinfectant, which protects silkworm larvae from diseases) and control of mulberry pests and diseases were not practised by most of the surveyed farmers.

Poor economic condition did not permit the farmers to construct separate house for silkworm rearing. Lack of awareness and preference for the traditional practices were the reasons for not adopting proper incubation and black boxing techniques, which are important for uniform hatching of silkworm eggs. As most of the farmers were rearing silkworm in a portion of dwelling house itself, they were not able to disinfect the rearing space using chemicals or maintain the recommended temperature and humidity for silkworm-rearing properly.

Adoption coefficient was worked out to study the impact of socioeconomic factors on adoption of different rainfed sericultural practices. For this purpose, full adoption was scored as 2, partial adoption as 1 and non-adoption as 0 for each technology and the total score (actual score) was worked out for each farmer based on the level of adoption of the technologies or practices recommended for rainfed sericulture. Then the adoption coefficient was computed for each farmer by using the formula:

$$\text{Adoption coefficient} = \frac{\text{Actual score obtained}}{\text{Total score obtainable}} \times 100$$

The adoption coefficient was considered as dependent variable and regressed with the socio-economic factors such as age, education level, extension participation, extension contact, mass media participation and area under mulberry to evaluate the factors influencing the adoption of improved sericultural practices.

The value of coefficient of multiple determination (R^2) was 0.33, which implied that the variables included in the regression model put together explained 33 per cent of the total variations. The coefficients of extension contact and mass media participation were positive and statistically significant. Singhvi *et al.* (1994) have also found that the rate of adoption was significantly associated with sericulturist's mass media participation, extension contact and cosmopoliteness. This implied that the contact with the extension workers and mass media played an important role in educating the farmers to adopt improved technologies. The regression analysis also revealed that the size of mulberry holdings had influence on the rate of technology adoption. The other socio-economic variables, namely age and education level did not have any significant association with the technology adoption.

3

Sericulture Manufacturing by Pre-Industrial Methods

MANUFACTURING BY PRE-INDUSTRIAL METHODS

Textile manufacturing is one of the oldest human activities. The oldest known textiles date back to about 5000 B.C. In order to make textiles, the first requirement is a source of fibre from which a yarn can be made, primarily by spinning. The yarn is processed by knitting or weaving to create cloth. The machine used for weaving is the loom. Cloth is finished by what are described as wet processes to become fabric. The fabric may be dyed, printed or decorated by embroidering with coloured yarns.

The three main types of fibres are natural vegetable fibres (such as cotton, linen, jute and hemp), man-made fibres (made by industrial processes) and protein based fibres (such as wool, silk).

Almost all commercial textiles are produced by industrial methods. Textiles are still produced by pre-industrial processes in village communities in Asia, Africa and South America, as an artisan craft and a hobby in Europe and North America.

COTTON

Cotton is a soft, fluffy staple fibre that grows in a boll, or protective capsule, around the seeds of cotton plants of the genus *Gossypium*. The plant is a shrub native to tropical and subtropical regions around the world, including the Americas, Africa, India, and Pakistan. The fibre most often is spun into yarn or thread and used to make a soft, breathable textile, which is the most widely used natural-fibre cloth in clothing today. The English name derives from the Arabic *(al) qutn*, which began to be used circa 1400. The botanical purpose of cotton fibre is to aid in seed dispersal.

HISTORY

According to the Foods and Nutrition Encyclopaedia, the earliest cultivation of cotton discovered thus far in the Americas occurred in Mexico, some 8,000 years ago. The indigenous species was *Gossypium hirsutum*, which is today the most widely planted species of cotton in the world, constituting about 89.9per cent of all production worldwide. The greatest diversity of wild cotton species is found in Mexico, followed by Australia and Africa.

Cotton was first cultivated in the Old World 7,000 years ago (5th–4th millennia BC), by the inhabitants of the Indus Valley Civilization, which covered a huge swath of the northwestern part of the Indian subcontinent, comprising today parts of eastern Pakistan and northwestern India. The Indus cotton industry was well developed and some methods used in cotton spinning and fabrication continued to be used until the modern industrialization of India. Well before the Common Era, the use of cotton textiles had spread from India to the Mediterranean and beyond.

Greeks and the Arabs were apparently ignorant about cotton until the Wars of Alexander the Great, as his contemporary Megasthenes told Seleucus I Nicator of "there being trees on which wool grows" in "Indica".

According to The Columbia Encyclopaedia, Sixth Edition:

Cotton has been spun, woven, and dyed since prehistoric times. It clothed the people of ancient India, Egypt, and China. Hundreds of years before the Christian era, cotton textiles were woven in India with matchless skill, and their use spread to the Mediterranean countries. In the first century, Arab traders brought fine muslin and calico to Italy and Spain. The Moors introduced the cultivation of cotton into Spain in the 9th century. Fustians and dimities were woven there and in the 14th century in Venice and Milan, at first with a linen warp.

Little cotton cloth was imported to England before the 15th century, although small amounts were obtained chiefly for candlewicks. By the 17th century, the East India Company was bringing rare fabrics from India. Native Americans skillfully spun and wove cotton into fine garments and dyed tapestries. Cotton fabrics found in Peruvian tombs are said to belong to a pre-Inca culture.

In Iran (Persia), the history of cotton dates back to the Achaemenid era (5th century BC); however, there are few sources about the planting of cotton in pre-Islamic Iran. The planting of cotton was common in Merv, Ray and Pars of Iran. In the poems of Persian poets, especially Ferdowsi's Shahname, there are many references to cotton ("panbe" in Persian). Marco Polo (13th century) refers to the major products of Persia, including cotton. John Chardin, a famous French traveler of 17th century, who had visited the Safavid Persia, has approved the vast cotton farms of Persia.

In Peru, cultivation of the indigenous cotton species *Gossypium barbadense* was the backbone of the development of coastal cultures, such as the Norte Chico, Moche and Nazca. Cotton was grown upriver, made into nets and traded with fishing villages along the coast for large supplies of fish. The Spanish who came to Mexico and Peru in the early 16th century found the people growing cotton and wearing clothing made of it.

During the late medieval period, cotton became known as an imported fibre in northern Europe, without any knowledge of how it was derived, other than that it was a plant; noting its similarities to wool, people in the region could only imagine that cotton must be produced by plant-borne sheep. John Mandeville, writing in 1350, stated as fact the now-preposterous belief: "There grew there [India] a wonderful tree which bore tiny lambs on the endes of its branches. These branches were so pliable that they bent down to allow the lambs to feed when they are hungrie [*sic*]." (See Vegetable Lamb of Tartary.) This aspect is retained in the name for cotton in many European languages, such as German *Baumwolle*, which translates as "tree wool" (*Baum* means "tree"; *Wolle* means "wool"). By the end of the 16th century, cotton was cultivated throughout the warmer regions in Asia and the Americas.

India's cotton-processing sector gradually declined during British expansion in India and the establishment of colonial rule during the late 18th and early 19th centuries. This was largely due to aggressive colonialist mercantile policies of the British East India Company, which made cotton processing and manufacturing workshops in India uncompetitive. Indian markets were increasingly forced to supply only raw cotton and were forced, by British-imposed law, to purchase manufactured textiles from Britain.

INDUSTRIAL REVOLUTION IN BRITAIN

The advent of the Industrial Revolution in Britain provided a great boost to cotton manufacture, as textiles emerged as Britain's leading export. In 1738, Lewis Paul and John Wyatt, of Birmingham, England, patented the roller spinning machine, and the flyer-and-bobbin system for drawing cotton to a more even thickness using two sets of rollers that traveled at different speeds. Later, the invention of the spinning jenny in 1764 and Richard Arkwright's spinning frame (based on the roller spinning machine) in 1769 enabled British weavers to produce cotton yarn and cloth at much higher rates. From the late 18th century onwards, the British city of Manchester acquired the nickname *"Cottonopolis"* due to the cotton industry's omnipresence within the city, and Manchester's role as the heart of the global cotton trade. Production capacity in Britain and the United States was further improved by the invention of the cotton gin by the American Eli Whitney in 1793. Improving technology and increasing control of world markets allowed British traders to develop a commercial chain in which raw cotton fibres were (at first) purchased from colonial plantations, processed into cotton cloth in the mills of Lancashire, and then exported on British ships to captive colonial markets in West Africa, India, and China (via Shanghai and Hong Kong). By the 1840s, India was no longer capable of supplying the vast quantities of cotton fibres needed by mechanized

British factories, while shipping bulky, low-price cotton from India to Britain was time-consuming and expensive. This, coupled with the emergence of American cotton as a superior type (due to the longer, stronger fibres of the two domesticated native American species, *Gossypium hirsutum* and *Gossypium barbadense*), encouraged British traders to purchase cotton from plantations in the United States and the Caribbean. By the mid 19th century, "King Cotton" had become the backbone of the southern American economy. In the United States, cultivating and harvesting cotton became the leading occupation of slaves.

During the American Civil War, American cotton exports slumped due to a Union blockade on Southern ports, also because of a strategic decision by the Confederate government to cut exports, hoping to force Britain to recognize the Confederacy or enter the war, prompting the main purchasers of cotton, Britain and France to turn to Egyptian cotton. British and French traders invested heavily in cotton plantations and the Egyptian government of Viceroy Isma'il took out substantial loans from European bankers and stock exchanges. After the American Civil War ended in 1865, British and French traders abandoned Egyptian cotton and returned to cheap American exports, sending Egypt into a deficit spiral that led to the country declaring bankruptcy in 1876, a key factor behind Egypt's annexation by the British Empire in 1882.

During this time, cotton cultivation in the British Empire, especially India, greatly increased to replace the lost production of the American South. Through tariffs and other restrictions, the British government discouraged the production of cotton cloth in India; rather, the raw fibre was sent to England for processing. The Indian patriot Mahatma Gandhi described the process:

- English people buy Indian cotton in the field, picked by Indian labour at seven cents a day, through an optional monopoly.
- This cotton is shipped on British ships, a three-week journey across the Indian Ocean, down the Red Sea, across the Mediterranean, through Gibraltar, across the Bay of Biscay and the Atlantic Ocean to London. One hundred per cent profit on this freight is regarded as small.
- The cotton is turned into cloth in Lancashire. You pay shilling wages instead of Indian pennies to your workers. The English worker not only has the advantage of better wages, but the steel companies of England get the profit of building the factories and machines. Wages; profits; all these are spent in England.
- The finished product is sent back to India at European shipping rates, once again on British ships. The captains, officers, sailors of these ships, whose wages must be paid, are English. The only Indians who profit are a few lascars who do the dirty work on the boats for a few cents a day.

- The cloth is finally sold back to the kings and landlords of India who got the money to buy this expensive cloth out of the poor peasants of India who worked at seven cents a day. (Fisher 1932 pp 154–156)

In the United States, Southern cotton provided capital for the continuing development of the North. The cotton produced by enslaved African Americans not only helped the South, but also enriched Northern merchants. Much of the Southern cotton was transshipped through the northern ports.

Cotton remained a key crop in the Southern economy after emancipation and the end of the Civil War in 1865. Across the South, sharecropping evolved, in which free black farmers and landless white farmers worked on white-owned cotton plantations of the wealthy in return for a share of the profits. Cotton plantations required vast labour forces to hand-pick cotton, and it was not until the 1950s that reliable harvesting machinery was introduced into the South (prior to this, cotton-harvesting machinery had been too clumsy to pick cotton without shredding the fibres). During the early 20th century, employment in the cotton industry fell, as machines began to replace laborers, and the South's rural labour force dwindled during the First and Second World Wars. Today, cotton remains a major export of the southern United States, and a majority of the world's annual cotton crop is of the long-staple American variety.

TANGÜIS COTTON

In 1901, Peru's cotton industry suffered because of a fungus plague caused by a plant disease known as "cotton wilt" or, more correctly, "fusarium wilt", caused by the fungus *Fusarium vasinfectum*. The plant disease, which spread throughout Peru, entered plant's roots and worked its way up the stem until the plant was completely dried up. Fermín Tangüis, a Puerto Rican agriculturist who lived in Peru, studied some species of the plant that were affected by the disease to a lesser extent and experimented in germination with the seeds of various cotton plants. In 1911, after 10 years of experimenting and failures, Tangüis was able to develop a seed which produced a superior cotton plant resistant to the disease. The seeds produced a plant that had a 40per cent longer (between 29 mm and 33 mm) and thicker fibre that did not break easily and required little water. The Tangüis cotton, as it became known, is the variety which is preferred by the Peruvian national textile industry. It constituted 75per cent of all the Peruvian cotton production, both for domestic use and apparel exports. The Tangüis cotton crop was estimated at 225,000 bales that year.

CULTIVATION

Successful cultivation of cotton requires a long frost-free period, plenty of sunshine, and a moderate rainfall, usually from 600 to 1200 mm (24 to 48 inches). Soils usually need to be fairly heavy, although the level of nutrients does not need to be exceptional. In general, these conditions are met within the seasonally dry tropics and subtropics in the Northern and Southern hemispheres, but a large proportion of the cotton grown today is cultivated in areas with less rainfall that obtain the water from irrigation. Production of the crop for a given year usually starts soon after harvesting the preceding autumn. Planting time in spring in the Northern hemisphere varies from the beginning of February to the beginning of June.

The area of the United States known as the South Plains is the largest contiguous cotton-growing region in the world. While dryland (non-irrigated) cotton is successfully grown in this region, consistent yields are only produced with heavy reliance on irrigation water drawn from the Ogallala Aquifer. Since cotton is somewhat salt and drought tolerant, this makes it an attractive crop for arid and semiarid regions. As water resources get tighter around the world, economies that rely on it face difficulties and conflict, as well as potential environmental problems. For example, improper cropping and irrigation practices have led to desertification in areas of Uzbekistan, where cotton is a major export. In the days of the Soviet Union, the Aral Sea was tapped for agricultural irrigation, largely of cotton, and now salination is widespread.

GENETIC MODIFICATION

Genetically modified (GM) cotton was developed to reduce the heavy reliance on pesticides. The bacterium *Bacillus thuringiensis* (Bt) naturally produces a chemical harmful only to a small fraction of insects, most notably the larvae of moths and butterflies, beetles, and flies, and harmless to other forms of life. The gene coding for BT toxin has been inserted into cotton, causing cotton to produce this natural insecticide in its tissues. In many regions, the main pests in commercial cotton are lepidopteron larvae, which are killed by the BT protein in the transgenic cotton they eat. This eliminates the need to use large amounts of broad-spectrum insecticides to kill lepidopteron pests (some of which have developed pyrethroid resistance). This spares natural insect predators in the farm ecology and further contributes to no insecticide pest management.

BT cotton is ineffective against many cotton pests, however, such as plant bugs, stink bugs, and aphids; depending on circumstances it may still be desirable to use insecticides against these. A 2006 study done by Cornell researchers, the Center for Chinese Agricultural Policy and the Chinese Academy of Science on Bt cotton farming in China found that after seven years these secondary pests that were normally controlled by pesticide had increased, necessitating the use of pesticides at similar levels to non-Bt cotton and causing less profit for farmers because of the extra expense of GM seeds. However a more recent 2009 study by the Chinese Academy of Sciences, Stanford University and Rutgers University refutes this.

They concluded that the GM cotton effectively controlled bollworm. The secondary pests were mostly miridae (plant bugs) whose increase was related to local temperature and rainfall and only continued to increase in half the villages studied. Moreover, the increase in insecticide use for the control of these secondary insects was far smaller than the reduction in total insecticide use due to BT cotton adoption. The International Service for the Acquisition of Agri-biotech Applications (ISAAA) said that, worldwide, GM cotton was planted on an area of 16 million hectares in 2009.

This was 49per cent of the worldwide total area planted in cotton. The U.S. cotton crop was 93per cent GM in 2010 and the Chinese cotton crop was 68per cent GM in 2009.

The initial introduction of GM cotton proved to be a huge success in Australia - the yields were equivalent to the no transgenic varieties and the crop used much less pesticide to produce (85per cent reduction). The subsequent introduction of a second variety of GM cotton led to increases in GM cotton production until 95per cent of the Australian cotton crop was GM in 2009.

Cotton has also been genetically modified for resistance to glyphosate (marketed as Roundup in North America), an inexpensive and highly effective, but broad-spectrum herbicide.

Originally, it was only possible to achieve glyph sate resistance when the plant was young, but with the development of Roundup Ready Flex, it is possible to achieve glyphosate resistance much later in the growing season.

GM cotton acreage in India continues to grow at a rapid rate, increasing from 50,000 hectares in 2002 to 8.4 million hectares in 2009. The total cotton area in India was 9.6 million hectares (the largest in the world or, about 35per cent of world cotton area), so GM cotton was grown on 87per cent of the cotton area in 2009. This makes India the country with the largest area of GM cotton in the world, surpassing China (3.7 million hectares in 2009).

The major reasons for this increase is a combination of increased farm income ($225/ha) and a reduction in pesticide use to control the cotton bollworm.

Cotton has gossypol, a toxin that makes it inedible.

However, scientists have silenced the gene that produces the toxin, making it a potential food crop.

ORGANIC PRODUCTION

Organic cotton is generally understood as cotton, from plants not genetically modified, that is certified to be grown without the use of any synthetic agricultural chemicals, such as fertilizers or pesticides. Its production also promotes and enhances biodiversity and biological cycles.

United States cotton plantations are required to enforce the National Organic Programme (NOP). This institution determines the allowed practices for pest control, growing, fertilizing, and handling of organic crops.As of 2007, 265,517 bales of organic cotton were produced in 24 countries, and worldwide production was growing at a rate of more than 50per cent per year.

PESTS AND WEEDS

The cotton industry relies heavily on chemicals, such as fertilizers and insecticides, although a very small number of farmers are moving towards an organic model of production, and organic cotton products are now available for purchase at limited locations.

These are popular for baby clothes and diapers. Under most definitions, organic products do not use genetic engineering.

Historically, in North America, one of the most economically destructive pests in cotton production has been the boll weevil.

Due to the US Department of Agriculture's highly successful Boll Weevil Eradication Programme (BWEP), this pest has been eliminated from cotton in most of the United States. This Programme, along with the introduction of genetically engineered Bt cotton (which contains a bacterial gene that codes for a plant-produced protein that is toxic to a number of pests such as cotton bollworm and pink bollworm), has allowed a reduction in the use of synthetic insecticides. Other significant global pests of cotton include the pink bollworm, *Pectinophora gossypiella*; the chili thrips, *Scirtothrips dorsalis*; and the cotton seed bug, *Oxycarenus hyalinipennis*.

HARVESTING

Most cotton in the United States, Europe, and Australia is harvested mechanically, either by a cotton picker, a machine that removes the cotton from the boll without damaging the cotton plant, or by a cotton stripper, which strips the entire boll off the plant.

Cotton strippers are used in regions where it is too windy to grow picker varieties of cotton, and usually after application of a chemical defoliant or the natural defoliation that occurs after a freeze.

Cotton is a perennial crop in the tropics, and without defoliation or freezing, the plant will continue to grow. Cotton continues to be picked by hand in developing countries.

COMPETITION FROM SYNTHETIC FIBRES

The era of manufactured fibres began with the development of rayon in France in the 1890s. Rayon is derived from a natural cellulose and cannot be considered synthetic, but requires extensive processing in a manufacturing process, and led the less expensive replacement of more naturally derived materials. A succession of new synthetic fibres were introduced by the chemicals industry in the following decades. Acetate in fibre form was developed in 1924. Nylon, the first fibre synthesized entirely from petrochemicals, was introduced as a sewing thread by DuPont in 1936, followed by DuPont's acrylic in 1944. Some garments were created from fabrics based on these fibres, such as women's hosiery from nylon, but it was not until the introduction of polyester into the fibre marketplace in the early 1950s that the market for cotton came under threat. The rapid uptake of polyester garments in the 1960s caused economic hardship in cotton-exporting economies, especially in Central American countries, such as Nicaragua, where cotton production had boomed tenfold between 1950 and 1965 with the advent of cheap chemical pesticides. Cotton production recovered in the 1970s, but crashed to pre-1960 levels in the early 1990s.

Beginning as a self-help Programme in the mid-1960s, the Cotton Research and Promotion Programme (CRPP) was organized by U.S. cotton producers in response to cotton's steady decline in market share. At that time, producers voted to set up a per-bale assessment system to fund the Programme, with built-in safeguards to protect their investments. With the passage of the Cotton Research and Promotion Act of 1966, the Programme joined forces and began battling synthetic competitors and re-establishing markets for cotton. Today, the success of this Programme has made cotton the best-selling fibre in the U.S. and one of the best-selling fibres in the world.

Administered by the Cotton Board and conducted by Cotton Incorporated, the CRPP works to greatly increase the demand for and profitability of cotton through various research and promotion activities. It is funded by U.S. cotton producers and importers.

USES

Cotton is used to make a number of textile products. These include terrycloth for highly absorbent bath towels and robes; denim for blue jeans; chambray, popularly used in the manufacture of blue work shirts (from which we get the term "blue-collar"); and corduroy, seersucker, and cotton twill. Socks, underwear, and most T-shirts are made from cotton. Bed sheets often are made from cotton. Cotton also is used to make yarn used in crochet and knitting. Fabric also can be made from recycled or recovered cotton that otherwise would be thrown away during the spinning, weaving, or cutting process. While many fabrics are made completely of cotton, some materials blend cotton with other fibres, including rayon and synthetic fibres such as polyester. It can either be used in knitted or woven fabrics, as it can be blended with elastine to make a stretchier thread for knitted fabrics, and apparel such as stretch jeans.

In addition to the textile industry, cotton is used in fishnets, coffee filters, tents, gunpowder (see nitrocellulose), cotton paper, and in bookbinding. The first Chinese paper was made of cotton fibre. Fire hoses were once made of cotton.

The cottonseed which remains after the cotton is ginned is used to produce cottonseed oil, which, after refining, can be consumed by humans like any other vegetable oil. The cottonseed meal that is left generally is fed to ruminant livestock; the gossypol remaining in the meal is toxic to monogastric animals. Cottonseed hulls can be added to dairy cattle rations for roughage. During the American slavery period, cotton root bark was used in folk remedies as an abortifacient, that is, to induce a miscarriage.

Cotton linters are fine, silky fibres which adhere to the seeds of the cotton plant after ginning. These curly fibres typically are less than 1/8 in (3 mm) long. The term also may apply to the longer textile fibre staple lint as well as the shorter fuzzy fibres from some upland species. Linters are traditionally used in the manufacture of paper and as a raw material in the manufacture of cellulose. In the UK, linters are referred to as "cotton wool". This can also be a refined product (*absorbent cotton* in U.S. usage) which has medical, cosmetic and many other practical uses. The first medical use of cotton wool was by Dr. Joseph Sampson Gamgee at the Queen's Hospital (later the General Hospital) in Birmingham, England.

Shiny cotton is a processed version of the fibre that can be made into cloth resembling satin for shirts and suits. However, it is hydrophobic (does not absorb water easily), which makes it unfit for use in bath and dish towels (although examples of these made from shiny cotton are seen).

The term Egyptian cotton refers to the extra long staple cotton grown in Egypt and favoured for the luxury and upmarket brands worldwide. During the U.S. Civil War, with heavy European investments, Egyptian-grown cotton became a major alternate source for British textile mills. Egyptian cotton is more durable and softer than American Pima cotton, which is why it is more expensive. Pima cotton is American cotton that is grown in the southwestern states of the U.S.

INTERNATIONAL TRADE

The largest producers of cotton, currently (2009), are China and India, with annual production of about 34 million bales and 24 million bales, respectively; most of this production is consumed by their respective textile industries. The largest exporters of raw cotton are the United States, with sales of $4.9 billion, and Africa, with sales of $2.1 billion. The total international trade is estimated to be $12 billion. Africa's share of the cotton trade has doubled since 1980. Neither area has a significant domestic textile industry, textile manufacturing having moved to developing nations in Eastern and South Asia such as India and China. In Africa, cotton is grown by numerous small holders. Dunavant Enterprises, based in Memphis, Tennessee, is the leading cotton broker in Africa, with hundreds of purchasing agents. It operates cotton gins in Uganda, Mozambique, and Zambia. In Zambia, it often offers loans for seed and expenses to the 180,000 small farmers who grow cotton for it, as well as advice on farming methods. Cargill also purchases cotton in Africa for export.

The 25,000 cotton growers in the United States are heavily subsidized at the rate of $2 billion per year. The future of these subsidies is uncertain and has led to anticipatory expansion of cotton brokers' operations in Africa. Dunavant expanded in Africa by buying out local operations. This is only possible in former British colonies and Mozambique; former French colonies continue to maintain tight monopolies, inherited from their former colonialist masters, on cotton purchases at low fixed prices.

LEADING PRODUCER COUNTRIES

Table. Top Ten Cotton Producers — 2009 (480-Pound Bales).

	People's Republic of China	32.0 million bales
	India	23.5 million bales
	United States	12.4 million bales
	Pakistan	10.8 million bales
	Brazil	5.5 million bales
	Uzbekistan	4.4 million bales
	Australia	1.8 million bales
	Turkey	1.7 million bales
	Turkmenistan	1.1 million bales
	Syria	1.0 million bales

The five leading exporters of cotton in 2009 are (1) the United States, (2) India, (3) Uzbekistan, (4) Pakistan, and (5) Brazil. The largest nonproducing importers are Korea, Russia, Taiwan, Japan, and Hong Kong.

In India, the states of Maharashtra (26.63per cent), Gujarat (17.96per cent) and Andhra Pradesh (13.75per cent) and also Madhya Pradesh are the leading cotton producing states, these states have a predominantly tropical wet and dry climate.

In Pakistan, cotton is grown predominantly in the provinces of Punjab and Sindh. The leading city in cotton production is the Punjabi city of Faisalabad which is also leading in textiles within Pakistan. The Punjab has a tropical wet and dry climate throughout the year therefore enhancing the growth of cotton.

In the United States, the state of Texas led in total production as of 2004, while the state of California had the highest yield per acre.

FAIR TRADE

Cotton is an enormously important commodity throughout the world. However, many farmers in developing countries receive a low price for their produce, or find it difficult to compete with developed countries. This has led to an international dispute (see United States – Brazil cotton dispute):

On 27 September 2002, Brazil requested consultations with the US regarding prohibited and actionable subsidies provided to US producers, users and/or exporters of upland cotton, as well as legislation, regulations, statutory instruments and amendments thereto providing such subsidies (including export credits), grants, and any other assistance to the US producers, users and exporters of upland cotton.

On 8 September 2004, the Panel Report recommended that the United States "withdraw" export credit guarantees and payments to domestic users and exporters, and "take appropriate steps to remove the adverse effects or withdraw" the mandatory price-contingent subsidy measures.

In addition to concerns over subsidies, the cotton industries of some countries are criticized for employing child labour and damaging workers' health by exposure to pesticides used in production. The Environmental Justice Foundation has campaigned against the prevalent use of forced child and adult labour in cotton production in Uzbekistan, the world's third largest cotton exporter.

The international production and trade situation has led to "fair trade" cotton clothing and footwear, joining a rapidly growing market for organic clothing, fair fashion or so-called "ethical fashion". The fair trade system was initiated in 2005 with producers from Cameroon, Mali and Senegal.

TRADE

Cotton is bought and sold by investors and price speculators as a tradable commodity on 2 different stock exchanges in the United States of America.

- Cotton futures contracts are traded on the New York Mercantile Exchange (NYMEX) under the ticker symbol TT. They are delivered every year in March, May, July, October, and December.
- Cotton #2 futures contracts are traded on the New York Board of Trade (NYBOT) under the ticker symbol CT. They are delivered every year in March, May, July, October, and December.

CRITICAL TEMPERATURES

- Favourable travel temperature range: below 25°C (77°F)
- Optimum travel temperature: 21°C (70°F)
- Glow temperature: 205°C (401°F)
- Fire point: 210°C (410°F)
- Autoignition temperature: 407°C (765°F)
- Autoignition temperature (for oily cotton): 120°C (248°F)

Cotton dries out, becomes hard and brittle and loses all elasticity at temperatures above 25°C (77°F). Extended exposure to light causes similar problems. A temperature range of 25°C (77°F) to 35°C (95°F) is the optimal range for mold development.

At temperatures below 0°C (32°F), rotting of wet cotton stops. Damaged cotton is sometimes stored at these temperatures to prevent further deterioration.

BRITISH STANDARD YARN MEASURES

- 1 thread = 55 inches (about 137 cm)
- 1 skein or rap = 80 threads (120 yards or about 109 m)
- 1 hank = 7 skeins (840 yards or about 768 m)
- 1 spindle = 18 hanks (15,120 yards or about 13.826 km)

FIBRE PROPERTIES

Property	Evaluation
Shape	Fairly uniform in width, 12-20 micrometers; length varies from 1 cm to 6 cm (½ to 2½ inches); typical length is 2.2 cm to 3.3 cm (^! to 1¼ inches).
Luster	high
Tenacity (strength)	
Dry	3.0-5.0 g/d
Wet	3.3-6.0 g/d
Resiliency	low
Density	1.54-1.56 g/cm³
Moisture absorption raw:conditioned saturation mercerized:conditioned	 8.5per cent 15-25per cent 8.5-10.3per cent saturation 15-27per cent+
Dimensional stability	good
Resistance to acids alkali organic solvents sunlight microorganisms insects producing bacteria damage fibres.	damage, weaken fibres resistant; no harmful effects high resistance to most Prolonged exposure weakens fibres.Mildew and rot-Silver fish damage fibres.
Thermal reactions to heat to temperatures of 150℃ or over.	Decomposes after prolonged exposure to flame Burns readily.

The chemical composition of cotton is as follows:

- Cellulose 91.00per cent
- Water 7.85per cent
- Protoplasm, pectins 0.55per cent

- Waxes, fatty substances 0.40per cent
- Mineral salts 0.20per cent

COTTON GENOME

A public genome sequencing effort of cotton was initiated in 2007 by a consortium of public researchers. They agreed on a strategy to sequence the genome of cultivated, tetraploid cotton. "Tetraploid" means that cultivated cotton actually has two separate genomes within its nucleus, referred to as the A and D genomes. The sequencing consortium first agreed to sequence the D-genome relative of cultivated cotton (*G. raimondii*, a wild Central American cotton species) because of its small size and limited number of repetitive elements. It is nearly one-third the number of bases of tetraploid cotton (AD), and each chromosome is only present once.

The A genome of *G. arboreum* would be sequenced next. Its genome is roughly twice the size of *G. raimondii*'s. Part of the difference in size between the two genomes is the amplification of *retrotransposons* (GORGE). Once both diploid genomes are assembled, then research could begin sequencing the actual genomes of cultivated cotton varieties.

This strategy is out of necessity; if one were to sequence the tetraploid genome without model diploid genomes, the euchromatic DNA sequences of the AD genomes would co-assemble and the repetitive elements of AD genomes would assembly independently into A and D sequences respectively. Then there would be no way to untangle the mess of AD sequences without comparing them to their diploid counterparts.

The public sector effort continues with the goal to create a high-quality, draft genome sequence from reads generated by all sources. The public-sector effort has generated Sanger reads of BACs, fosmids, and plasmids as well as 454 reads. These later types of reads will be instrumental in assembling an initial draft of the D genome. They announced that they would donate their raw reads to the public. This public relations effort gave them some recognition for sequencing the cotton genome. Once the D genome is assembled from all of this raw material, it will undoubtedly assist in the assembly of the AD genomes of cultivated varieties of cotton, but a lot of hard work remains.

Yield! Maximization in the Cotton Spinning Industry (Yarn Manufacturing)

Yieldper cent shows the performance of any industry, it shows efficiency of the industry to convert the raw material into the finished goods. The industry management focuses so much on the maximization of yield so that maximum profit can be earned. Yieldper cent directly relates with profit of the industry, textile cotton spinning industry usually give the yieldper cent up to 84, this can be increased up to 1 to 2per cent, adding million in the profit of cotton spinning industry. This article presents the methodology to enhance the yield per cent of cotton spinning industry.

INTRODUCTION

Raw material consist impurities up to 4-16 per cent(according to type, region and the efficiency of the ginning), the yarn manufacturing processes (Blow-room to carding) are especially designed to remove these impurities. While removing the impurities some good fibres are also removed due to inefficient machine setting or improper machine sequence selection and there are many more causes which decrease the yield per cent. Some of the causes are discussed here which increase / decrease the yield per cent such as

- Raw material selection
- Raw martial process route selection
- Improper machine setting
- Maintenance of Machines
- Inefficient air conditioning plant
- Improper material handling

RAW MATERIAL SELECTION

Raw martial costs about 50-70per cent of the total cost of the product[1]. It is mentioned above that impurities in the cotton raw material in Pakistan ranges between 4 to 16 percent, these impurities must be removed to achieve the required quality product. If the raw material for the yarn is not properly selected than it may cause decrease in the yield per cent. Finer yarn requires more cleaning of the material than the coarser yarn because impurities present in the fine yarn create hinders in further processing and can be more visible and vice versa than coarse yarn.

Finer yarn required fine quality raw cotton which have sufficient strength and the fibre length if the cotton selected for the finer yarn is of not sufficient length and strength then the good fibres may be wasted during the processing in result of that yieldper cent is decreased.

Another main characteristic of raw material which also contribute in decrease of yield per cent is extra moisture in material because if the material has extra moister present in it then it may difficulty to separate the impurities and good fibres which required more efforts, energy, time etc such material sticks with machine parts which may go into the waste and become the cause in yieldper cent decrease.

YUCCA FIBRE

Yucca fibres were at one time widely used throughout Central America for many things. Currently they are mainly used to make twine. Yucca leaves are harvested and then cut to a standard size. The leaves are crushed in between two large rollers producing the fibres which are bundled up and dried in the sun over trellises. The dried fibres are combined into rolags. At this point it is ready to spin. The waste, a pulpy liquid that stinks, can be used as a fertilizer.

RAW MATERIAL PROCESS ROUTE SELECTION

Route selection for processing the raw material is also another important task for the management. In cotton spinning industry different lines of processing are installed in the Blow Room, routes have different beating points and according to amount of impurities present in material and quality requirement the processing route is selected.

Which reduces the wastage of good fibre, resulting increase in (production) yieldper cent. Processing route selection is based on the type of the material process *e.g.* natural and synthetic material cannot be processed on the same route even you are required to manufacturing the pc (Polyester cotton with any ration) for blend yarn you have to process both fibres separately and at any particular point blend them with required ratio.

Now a days technology facilities process and separate blending machines are available to blend the material with any ratio or you can blend the slivers of the different materials at the draw frame.

Material passage at the draw frame is also pre-decided whether material should be double (Breaker and finisher) or triple passage (breaker, intermediate and finisher).

With less passage the production increased by saving the waste per cent *i.e.* 0.5 but the quality may be effected or not if the raw material quality is enough then the intermediate process may be omitted otherwise It should be carried to improve the quality so that final product can be sold.

If after the processing product is not sold then it means whole material and efforts consumed on it are wasted and yieldper cent becomes 0. Therefore it should be kept in mind that product must be sell out.

IMPROPER MACHINE SETTING

Required quality of the product cannot be achieved without the proper setting of machine, any spinning machine setting parameters includes

- Speed
- Gauge
- Top Roller Pressure
- Air pressure

With the above mentioned setting parameters you can manufacture the required quality of yarn within the required time frame.

With the speed you can adjust the draft, production rate, beats per unit time, and many more. With the gauge and pressure (Air and top Roller) setting you can easily process the material without deteriorating its quality and properly removing the impurities to achieve the targeted product and the result of this surely contributes in the increase of yieldper cent. If any above said setting parameter is improperly set then it will deteriorate the quality and ultimately decrease the yieldper cent.

MAINTENANCE OF MACHINES:

There is old saying that machine cannot become older, if properly maintained time to time, if machine is not properly maintained then it will not deliver the required quality and may also waste good fibres and due to this yieldper cent will decrease.

E.g. if card machine is not properly overhauled and its taker-in and cylinder wires are out of order, when the material is process on such a machine then the machine is unable to remove the impurities and also unable to properly open the fibres up to individual fibre stage, then the product (sliver) delivered by the card machine is not match with requirement thus for the required quality most of good material may become useless or you have option to reprocess the material in both cases yieldper cent is ultimately decrease and any owner/ management cants bear this, therefore for improving the yieldper cent machine maintenance should be primary objective well maintained machines produces required/ targeted quality and yield.

INEFFICIENT AIR CONDITIONING PLANT

Air-conditioning plant contributes most of its share in increase / decrease of the yieldper cent, due to A.C plant the yieldper cent can be at maximum or minimum level therefore if plant is properly maintained providing proper suctions into transportation pipes, machines, atmospheric conditions with the requirement of each department then surely yieldper cent can be increase.

The main objectives of the A.C plant is to maintenance required temperature and RHper cent into every department, provide proper suction into return ducts so that the fluf and good fibres from the floor properly collected and have sufficient air filters, so that the dust, other impurities and good fibres can be separated. Each machine have also separate suction system *e.g.* at ring frame pnewmafil is collected by the internal machine suction.

Pnemafil 100per cent good fibres which and be reprocessed with minimum efforts if these are not collected then went into waste hence causing decrease in yieldper cent. Similarly A.C plant performs its job in every machine to prevent the wastage of good/processable fibre.

THE OBJECTIVES OF THE AIR-CONDITIONING PLANTS INCLUDES

- Control the RHper cent and Temperature in every department
- Collect and Control the fulf
- Properly separate the collected impurities and good fibre by the help of filters

By achieving the above mentioned objectives we can improve the efficiency of man and machine, Quality of yarn and production of plant in result of that we can achieve our target *i.e.* yield per cent maximization

IMPROPER MATERIAL HANDLING:

Improper handling of material before, during and after process decreases the yieldper cent. *E.g.* the slivers cans during transporting from the card to draw frame or from draw to comber or simplex if not properly carried and by chance material may be deteriorate by hand touching or due to other reason can fall on floor because of uneven floor or cane wheels will contribute in yieldper cent shortage.

Handling of material start when the raw material arrived and you have to plane well where to store it and in which conditions it should me stored considering that when transporting to production floor may not be effected / damage/detoriated. Material handling is also required in each department of cotton spinning staring from blow-room as the material is process through each department *e.g.* final product of blow-room is lap or final product of chute feed system is sliver of card therefore the lap/slivers are properly transported and stored so that their quality cannot be effected similarly the final product of each department is well stored, material handling also deals with the proper storage and transportation of the finished product.

PHOTOCHROMIC

Photochromism is the reversible transformation of a chemical species between two forms by the absorption of electromagnetic radiation, where the two forms have different absorption spectra.This can be described as a reversible change of colour upon exposure to light

This property is a boon for scientists doing research on intelligent textiles where they are making use of this property to store data on the surface of textile fabrics and polymer sheets. Whereas the same property of some reactive dyes is a bane for textile processors. The change in shade after dyeing creates unwanted problems in dyeing.

An optical recording medium contains, on a base, one or more dyes and a polymer which forms liquid-crystalline phases. The information is written into the uniformly oriented liquid-crystalline polymer layer, for example by means of a laser. During this procedure, the polymer heats up locally to above a phase transition temperature. By cooling, the resulting change is frozen in the glass state. The information can be erased by applying an electric field and/or heating. The recording material permits high-contrast storage and possesses high sensitivity, good resolution and excellent stability.

There are other chromatic properties called electrochromatism and thermochromatism of dyes that are affected by electric field and heat respectively.

Photochromic colours are plastisol-based inks, which are off-white when not exposed to UV radiation.

It gains colour when exposed to Sun light / UV light. The colour change is "reversible," *i.e.*, the colour will fade again and appear colour less upon removal from UV light / sun light exposure.

These inks are available in various colours. See our colour availability chart for a complete list of available colours.

The uses of Americos Photo chromic colours are:

- On garment to create novel products and promotional items like T-shirts
- On fabric/garment to print company logo / brand name to prevent duplication
- On garment which are used for party wear
- Thermometers and temperature indicators
- Security printing
- Food industry to indicate temperature of packaged food

NANO TEXTILE

WHAT IS NANOTECHNOLOGY?

Nanotechnology is the technical process of working on the nano-scale – each nano-scale molecule is one million times smaller than a grain of sand. Nanotechnology refers to not only the small size of the materials being used, but also how those materials are engineered to perform specific functions.

Traditional coatings make garments feel stiff and clog the weave of the fabric preventing breath ability.

Using nanotechnology, our treatments are small enough to attach to individual fibres, delivering superior performance characteristics without compromising the look, feel or comfort of the fabric.

COOLEST COMFORT

Night before the big job interview. Sleep elusive. Hot, then cold, then hot again. No fever, just frantic. Good thing your sheets are keeping you cool. Wake up to sunshine, fresh outlook.

Feel like a million bucks. Dress to impress. Blow them away with energy and intelligence. Career happily underway.

With Nano Textiles Coolest Comfort, you stay dry and comfortable. An advanced moisture-wicking system helps balance your body temperature to keep you feeling fresh. Keep dry, stay cool, rest easy.

- Balances body temperature

- Enhances comfort
- Retains fabric's natural softness
- Allows fabric to breathe naturally

RESISTS SPILLS

Playing hooky. Breakfast in bed. Perfect white linens. Reading the *Times*. Everything just right. Phone rings. Newspaper falls on breakfast tray. Cranberry juice flies on favourite duvet. Relaxed mood is ruined. Good thing your bed cover isn't.

Conventional methods only coat fabrics superficially. But Nano Textiles uses an innovative process to build spill resistance into the individual fibres, so fabrics hold up under the toughest spills.

You'll never sacrifice softness or durability, though - Nano Textiles technology makes your duvets, drapery, tablecloths, placemats, and even mattress pads stay looking beautiful, longer.

If it could, your bed would thank you.

- Repels liquids
- Outperforms conventional fabric treatments
- Provides long lasting protection
- Extends the life of the fabric
- Retains fabric's natural softness
- Allows fabric to breathe naturally

REPELS AND RELEASES STAINS

10th annual family reunion. More relatives than you can count. Potluck dinner. Plates piled high. Favourite tablecloth "decorated" with Grandma's special spaghetti sauce, and who knows what else. Luckily, your tablecloth is enhanced with an invisible shield.

Nano Textiles Repels and Releases Stains technology actually prevents stains from sinking into fabrics, so spills are never a problem. Easy cleaning and durable protection keeps your finery looking its finest.

- Repels spills
- Helps stains wash out easily
- Provides long lasting protection
- Extends the life of the fabric
- Retains fabric's natural softness
- Allows fabric to breathe naturally

RESISTS STATIC

Cozy evening in. An old movie in front of a roaring fire. Hot popcorn. Great date. Warm blanket- It's not the TV with the bad static, it's the blanket. Dust, lint, and dog hair getting in the way of real electricity. Fast forward. New blanket. Same great date. The right kind of attraction.

Nano Textiles provides permanent static resistance for throws and blankets. It repels hair, lint, and dust while staying soft, comfortable, and beautifully durable.

Let the sparks fly, just not between you and your blankets.

- Provides permanent static protection
- Repels lint, dust, dirt and pet hair
- Enhances appearance and comfort
- Retains fabric's natural softness
- Allows fabric to breathe naturally

ORGANIC CLOTHING: WEAR WITH AWARENESS

When picking cotton clothing, today's ecologically minded consumer has several choices. Once believed to be a pure, natural fabric, today's cotton is dosed with harmful chemicals that pollute our environment. Today, thanks to strong media awareness and a revitalization of old techniques, we have alternatives. Organically grown cotton, naturally coloured cotton and recycled cotton products give us three choices for truly natural clothing. It may cost a little more, but by supporting the natural cotton industry's growth, we're supporting ourselves and the future of our planet.

PROBLEMS WITH CONVENTIONAL COTTON

The use of cotton dates back to the Egyptians some 4,500 year ago. For thousands of years, cotton, grown using natural methods, was the primary source of textiles. Today, cotton production is far from natural. The United States alone dumps 8.5 million tons of pesticides on cotton fields annually. And that's not all. Conventionally grown cotton accounts for nearly 25 percent of the total insecticide use for crops worldwide. This chemical onslaught harms our environment by polluting ground waters and soil, resulting in the death of wildlife and natural habitats.

Most of the cotton garments sold today is made from cotton grown with chemical pesticides, bleached and then coloured with chemical dyes containing toxic heavy metals. About a third of a pound of chemicals are used to make one adult T-shirt; two-thirds of a pound of chemicals can go into a pair of jeans.

THREE ECO-FRIENDLY ALTERNATIVES

Concerned consumers are choosing clothing made from organic cotton, naturally coloured cotton, and recycled sources. Here are details on these three environmentally healthy ways of producing cotton clothing and other textiles.

ORGANICALLY GROWN COTTON

Organic cotton is grown without the use of synthetic chemical fertilizers, pesticides or defoliants. By incorporating farming practices that increase fertility and diverse eco-systems, organic farmers rely on time-honoured techniques. Crop rotation, cover crops, organic fertilizers, integrated pest management, and human labour for weed control are a few of the methods used. To be certified organic, the soil must be free of synthetic pesticides for at least three years. Farmers and processors are required to pass yearly inspections.

With the obvious environmental and health benefits of growing cotton organically, why aren't more farmers doing it? In the past, demand for organic cotton has been limited due to higher production costs. However, in recent years media attention has been strong. Some major industry players such as Levi Strauss, Nike and The Gap are blending organic cotton fibres with conventionally produced cotton. The growing public awareness of the toxicity of conventional farming methods has resulted in an increase in both the demand for organically grown cotton and the amount of acreage planted.

NATURALLY COLOURED COTTON

Until recently, chemical dyeing was counted as the only viable way to colour cotton clothing. This process requires several steps, each of which creates toxic waste. Cotton is often bleached before it is dyed and heavy metal mordants are used to adhere the dye to the fabric. Because dyes have a hard time adhering to cotton, at least half of the chemicals end up as waste water in rivers and in the soil. Even in small amounts these heavy metals are lethal.

In 1982, entomologist Sally Fox reintroduced naturally coloured cotton, eliminating the need for dyeing altogether. Cottons of different colours have always existed in nature. Like our eyes or hair, cotton is genetically encoded with colours ranging from brown to tan. Native peoples have used these wild cottons for weaving and hand spinning for centuries. Because of its short fibres and inherent weakness, however, it was unable to be processed by modern textile machinery and had limited commercial value.

With a Programme of plant breeding, Fox developed a strong, long-fibre, coloured cotton that can be used commercially. Today, coloured cotton is grown on the stem in shades of brown, reddish brown, green and yellow, totally eliminating the need for dyes. In the long run, no dyeing means a savings in our pocket.

The cost of one pound of dyed cotton including dyestuff, water, energy costs and toxic waste disposal is 20 to 40 percent higher than that of coloured cotton. And with coloured cotton there are no hidden costs to the environment. In addition coloured cotton offers:

- An eco-friendly solution. Since there is no bleaching or harmful dyestuff involved in manufacturing, no waste water is produced.

- Unlike dyed material, the colour of the fabrics made from coloured cotton actually deepens with washing.
- Coloured cotton is naturally pest and disease tolerant, making it easier to grow organically.
- Coloured cotton is suitable for chemically sensitive people.
- Coloured cotton provides new yarn and fabric design potentials.
- Without the need for abundant water or energy sources, new mill sites have many more choices for location.

In recent years, the demand for coloured cotton has increased. Large companies like Esprit and Levi have launched popular "green lines" of cotton outerwear using dye-free, unbleached, organic green cotton. The demand for these items far exceed the supply. Coloured cotton is now being grown in the United States, Europe and Australia.

RECYCLED COTTON

Another ecological choice when purchasing cotton clothing is Eco Fibre. Eco Fibre is a recycled cotton fabric made from recovered cotton that would otherwise be cast off during the spinning, weaving or cutting process. There are no harsh chemicals used in the processing of this fabric.

The next time you are shopping for cotton clothing, choose garments made from organic cotton, naturally coloured cotton or recycled cotton. By buying from these natural sources, you are supporting the demand for a new earth-friendly textile industry. Your choice makes a difference.

Hemp is naturally one of the most ecologically friendly fabrics and also the oldest. The Columbia History of the World states that the oldest relics of human industry are bits of hemp fabric discovered in tombs dating back to approximately 8,000 BC.

Hemp fibre is one of the strongest and most durable natural textile fibres. Not only is it strong, but it also holds its shape having one of the lowest percent elongation of any natural fibre. In fact, its combination of ruggedness and comfort were utilized by Levi Strauss as a lightweight duck canvas for the very first pair of jeans made in California.

Furthermore hemp has the best ratio of heat capacity of all fibres giving it superior insulation properties. As a fabric, hemp provides all the warmth and softness of other natural textiles but with a superior durability seldom found in other materials. Natural organic hemp fibre 'breathes' and is biodegradable. Hemp blended with other fibres easily incorporate the desirable qualities of both textiles. When combined with the natural strength of hemp, the soft elasticity of cotton or the smooth texture of silk create a whole new genre of fashion design.

A fibre of a hundred uses besides fabrics, hemp is also used in the production of paper. The oldest piece of paper - over 2000 years old - was discovered in China and is made from hemp. Until 1883, between 75per cent and 90per cent of all paper in the world was made with hemp fibre. The Gutenberg bible (15th century), Lewis Carroll's Alice in Wonderland (19th century) and just about everything in between was printed on hemp paper. Thomas Jefferson wrote the early drafts of the Declaration of Independence on hemp paper produced in Holland. Jefferson grew hemp on his plantation as an industrial crop, selling the dried stalk to the U.S. Navy as outfitting material. George Washington also grew hemp, harvesting the fibrous seed for a variety of commercial uses including a skin lotion.

Other uses include feed for animals and for humans in veggie burgers, salad dressings, and pastas. Hemp seed is nutritious and contains more essential fatty acids than any other source, is second only to soybeans in complete protein (but is more digestible by humans), is high in B-vitamins, and is a good source of dietary fibre. Cosmetics manufacturers include hemp oil in makeup, skin lotions, and shampoo. In Europe, hemp is used in household cleaners as a natural alternative to harsher chemicals.

Hemp is a renewable resource which grows more quickly and easily than trees making hemp more cost effective than waiting decades for trees to grow to be used in man-made fibre production such as lyocell and rayon from wood pulps. The bark of the hemp stalk contains bast fibres, which are among the Earth's longest natural soft fibres and are also rich in cellulose. The cellulose and hemi-cellulose in its inner woody core are called hurds. Hemp fibre is longer, stronger, more absorbent and more insulative than cotton fibre.

Hemp produces more pulp per acre than timber on a sustainable basis, and can be used for every quality of paper.

Hemp paper manufacturing can reduce wastewater contamination. Hemp's low lignin content reduces the need for acids used in pulping, and its creamy colour lends itself to environmentally-friendly bleaching instead of harsh chlorine compounds. Less bleaching results in less dioxin and fewer chemical by-products. Hemp fibre paper resists decomposition, and does not yellow with age when an acid-free process is used. Hemp paper more than 1,500 years old has been found. Hemp paper can also be recycled more times than wood-based paper.

According to the Department of Energy, hemp is an excellent biomass fuel producer and the hydrocarbons in hemp can be processed into a wide range of biomass energy sources, from fuel pellets to liquid fuels and gas. Development of bio-fuels could significantly reduce our consumption of fossil fuels and nuclear power.

Hemp can be grown organically easily and hemp is most often grown without herbicides, fungicides or pesticides. Hemp is also a natural weed suppressor due to the fast growth of the plant's canopy. Eco-friendly hemp can replace most toxic petrochemical products. Research is being done to use hemp in manufacturing biodegradable plastic products: plant-based cellophane, recycled plastic mixed with hemp for injection-molded products, and resins made from the oil are just a few examples.

- Properties of Hemp
- Uses for Hemp
- Hemp Fibres and Fabrics
- Manufacturing Hemp Fabric
- Dyeing and Finishing
- Ecology of Hemp
- Industrial Hemp for renewable energy
- Ramie Fibre - Another Natural fibre:

WELLNESS FINISH WITH VITAMIN E

Functional aspects for clothing textiles, which promote the wearing comfort and well-being have become a striking sales argument. The following article introduces a product idea for "Wellness Textiles". It describes a transfer system consisting of textile/cyclodextrin-vitamin E complex.

Wellness is by long more than just a buzzword for wellbeing, vitality and fitness. It has become a social phenomenon which confers the wish of 'eternal youth' to ageing persons. The term 'wellness' has become a new life philosophy and from the commercial aspect is an important pulse generator and growth motor for many trade brances.

The 'wellness' fever has also reached the field of textile finishing and blew in some 'fresh wind' to this field with innovative product ideas. The following article describes a so-called transfer system by which vitamin E is converted from the textile onto the human skin. For the first time the transfer of vitamin E from the textile material into a skin model could be proven in an experiment.

VITAMIN E (A-TOCOPHEROL)

Vitamin E belongs to the group of lipid-soluble vitamins and is found in nature in many vegetable oils. The chemical term for vitamin E is "a-Tocopherol".(alpha-Tocopherol)

In the cosmetic industry vitamin E is used as antioxidant and active substance among others because of its moisture binding capacity in aliphatic cosmetic creams, lotions, emulsions, body and face oils for dry skin care as well as for decorative cosmetics like lipsticks. Vitamin E is also successfully applied for various skin diseases.

Very much importance is attached to vitamin E in the food industry, too. Vitamin E is an important lipid-soluble antioxidant which has many positive physiological properties besides its vitamin character.

The term 'antioxidant' describes the capability of molecules neutralizing so called radicals. Thus antioxidants are often called scavengers. Radicals are atoms or molecules which have an unpaired electron in their outer shell. Free radicals also emerge by the normal cell breathing as side products and try to snatch away an electron from other structures for means of completing their outer shell.

In this way for example the cell membrane can be damaged. Antioxidants and thus also vitamin E 'deactivate' the free radicals by giving off an electron and in this way protect the cells from 'oxidative stress'.

CYCLODEXTRINS

Cyclodextrins are circular molecules produced by the enzymatic decomposition of starch and they belong to the group of oligosaccharides and consist of 6 to 8 glucose units. The interesting point about cyclodextrins is their cylindrical structure and the resulting properties and application possibilities. The polar OH groups of the individual glucose units are on the outside of the cylinder due to their steric arrangement. The outside is hydrophilic, whereas the inside of the cylinder is non polar and thus hydrophobic (resp. lipophilic).

The cavities of the cyclodextrins (host) can take in 'guest molecules' and release them again. The chemist calls this phenomenon host-guest-chemistry. Guests are all those molecules which could fit into the cavity and are non- polar enough to interact with the lipophilic cavity surface.

By this complexation the properties of the locked in molecules change. For example an increase of the water solubility of non- polar organic compounds or decrease of sightly volatile substances are obtained through complexation with cyclodextrins, but also an increase of the stability y of the locked in substances to light, oxygen and heat.

Altogether the complexation through cyclodextrins has been researched only to a small extent, although cyclodextrins have been marketed for some time now for means of odour absorption (antismell finish). Knowledge about which substances can actually be complexed, is still very fragmentary and quite some more fundamental research will be necessary in this field.

CYCLODEXTRIN-VITAMIN-E COMPLEX

Vitamin E being a lipid soluble substance is virtually predestined for complexation with cyclodextrines. Y-cyclodextrin (8 glucose units) has proven to be a particularly suitable 'active substance'. Examinations have shown that a 2:1 complex consisting of Y-cyclodextrin and vitamin E offers many more advantages in terms of stability than a 1:1 complex.

The antioxidative potential of vitamin E is based on the reactivity of the chromanoxyl radical. The main task of the cyclodextrine is to surround the ring system of the vitamin E molecule (benzopyran-6-ol) and continue to stabilize it.

In this stabilized 'packaging', vitamin E is excellently suitable for Wellness finishes of textiles worn close to the body and these products can be purchased as 'NouWell E' from CHT R Beitlich GmbH.

Fixation and proof of CD vitamin E complex on textile surfaces

As the CD vitamin E complex does not show any substantivity, only those processes are to be considered where the product application can be controlled like for example by padding, spraying, coating or printing. For permanent fixation of the complex, reactive polyurethanes have proven to be advantageous for the following reasons:

- Free from formaldehyde
- Soft handle
- Good permanence
- Applicable on all types of fibres.

Fixation of the complex is physical and particularly on CEL and WO chemical (reaction with -OH, -NH2-groups). Fixation of the charged cyclodextrins with reactant crosslinking agents is also be possible, but then only for application on CEL fibres.

The qualitative proof of vitamin E on the textile can be done through a dyeing reaction at which the reductive properties of vitamin E are taken advantage of.

- Dripping on a FeCl3-solution onto the finished textile. In the presence of vitamin E the Fe3+-Ion is reduced to Fe2+.
- Dripping on a dipyridyl solution. Dipyridyl forms with Fe2+ions a red chelate complex.

By means of this Redox reaction vitamin E can be easily and safely seen on the fabric with the restriction that this of course can only be done on white or pastel shaded fabric.

YARN FORMATION

WOOL

Wool is a protein based fibre, being the coat of a sheep. The wool is removed by shearing.

Wool is the textile fibre obtained from sheep and certain other animals, including cashmere from goats, mohair from goats, qiviut from muskoxen, vicuña, alpaca, and camel from animals in the camel family, and angora from rabbits. Wool has several qualities that distinguish it from hair or fur: it is crimped, it is elastic, and it grows in staples (clusters).

Characteristics

Wool's scaling and crimp make it easier to spin the fleece by helping the individual fibres attach to each other, so that they stay together. Because of the crimp, wool fabrics have a greater bulk than other textiles, and retain air, which causes the product to retain heat. Insulation also works both ways; Bedouins and Tuaregs use wool clothes to keep the heat out.

The amount of crimp corresponds to the fineness of the wool fibres. A fine wool like Merino may have up to 100 crimps per inch, while the coarser wools like karakul may have as few as 1 to 2. Hair, by contrast, has little if any scale and no crimp, and little ability to bind into yarn. On sheep, the hair part of the fleece is called kemp. The relative amounts of kemp to wool vary from breed to breed, and make some fleeces more desirable for spinning, felting, or carding into batts for quilts or other insulating products.

Wool fibres are hygroscopic, meaning they readily absorb moisture. Wool fibres are hollow. Wool can absorb moisture almost one-third of its own weight. Wool absorbs sound like many other fabrics. Wool is generally a creamy white colour, although some breeds of sheep produce natural colours such as black, brown, silver, and random mixes.

Wool ignites at a higher temperature than cotton and some synthetic fibres. It has lower rate of flame spread, low heat release, low heat of combustion, and does not melt or drip; it forms a char which is insulating and self-extinguishing, and contributes less to toxic gases and smoke than other flooring products, when used in carpets. Wool carpets are specified for high safety environments, such as trains and aircraft. Wool is usually specified for garments for fire-fighters, soldiers, and others in occupations where they are exposed to the likelihood of fire.

Wool is resistant to static electricity, as the moisture retained within the fabric conducts electricity. This is why wool garments are much less likely to spark or cling to the body. The use of wool car seat covers or carpets reduces the risk of a shock when a person touches a grounded object. Wool is considered by the medical profession to be hypoallergenic.

SHEEP SHEARING

Sheep shearing, shearing or clipping is the process by which the woolen fleece of a sheep is cut off. The person who removes the sheep's wool is called a *shearer*. Typically each adult sheep is shorn once each year (a sheep may be said to have been "shorn" or "sheared", depending upon dialect). The annual shearing most often occurs in a shearing shed, a facility especially designed to process often hundreds and sometimes more than 3,000 sheep per day.

History

Shearers wear moccasins to protect their feet, grip wooden floors well, and absorb sweat.

Up until the 1870s squatters washed their sheep in nearby creeks prior to shearing. Later some expensive hot water installations were constructed on some of the larger stations for the washing. Sheep washing in Australia was influenced by the Saxony sheep breeders in Germany who washed their sheep and by the Spanish practice of washing the wool after shearing. There were three main reasons for the custom in Australia:

- The English manufacturers demanded that Australian woolgrowers provide their fleeces free from vegetable matter, burrs, soil, etc.
- The dirty fleeces were hard to shear and demanded that the metal blade shears be sharpened more often.
- Wool in Australia was carted by bullock team or horse teams and charged by weight. Washed wool was lighter and did not cost as much to transport.

The practice of washing the wool rather than the sheep evolved from the fact that hotter water could be used to wash the wool, than that used to wash the sheep. When the practice of selling wool in the grease occurred in the 1890s, wool washing became obsolete.

Australia and New Zealand had to discard the old methods of wool harvesting and evolve more efficient systems to cope with the huge numbers of sheep involved. After 1888 machine shearing was introduced, reducing second cuts and shearing time. By 1915 most large sheep station sheds in Australia had installed machines, driven by steam or later by internal combustion engines.

Shearing tables were invented in the 1950s and have not proved popular, although some are still used for crutching.

MODERN SHEARING

Today, large flocks of sheep are shorn by professional shearing teams working eight hour days, most often in spring, by machine shearing. These contractor teams will consist of shearers, shed hands and a cook (in the more isolated areas). The shed staff working hours and wages are regulated by industry awards. A working day starts at 7:30 AM and the day is divided into four "runs" of two hours each. "Smoko" breaks of a half hour each are at 9:30 AM and again at 3:00 PM.

The lunch break is taken at 12:00 PM for one hour. Most shearers are paid on a piece rate, *i.e.*, per sheep. Shearers who "tally" more than 200 sheep per day are known as "gun shearers". Typical mass shearing of sheep today follows a well-defined workflow: remove the wool, throw the fleece onto the wool table, skirt, roll and class the fleece, place it in the appropriate wool bin, press and store the wool until it is transported.

In 1984 Australia became the last country in the world to permit the use of wide combs, due to previous Australian Workers Union rules. Although they were rare in sheds, women now take a large part in the shearing industry by working as pressers, wool rollers, rouse about, wool classers and also shearing, too.

REMOVING THE WOOL

A sheep is caught by the shearer from the catching pen and taken to his "stand" on the shearing board. It is then shorn using mechanical hand piece (see *Shearing devices* below). The wool is removed by following an efficient set of movements, devised by Godfrey Bowen in c. 1950, (the *Bowen Technique*) or the *Tally-Hi* method. In 1963 the Tally-hi shearing system was developed by the Australian Wool Corporation and promoted using synchronized shearing demonstrations.

Sheep struggle less using the Tally-Hi method, reducing strain on the shearer and there is a saving of about 30 seconds shearing each sheep. The shearer begins by removing the sheep's belly wool, which is separated from the main fleece by a rouseabout, while the sheep is still being shorn. A professional or "gun" shearer typically removes a fleece without badly marking or cutting the sheep in two to three minutes, depending on the size and condition of the sheep, or less than two in elite competitive shearing. The shorn sheep is moved from the board via a chute in the floor, or wall, to a counting out pen, efficiently removing it from the shed.

The CSIRO in Australia has developed a non-mechanical method of shearing sheep using an injected protein that creates a natural break in the wool fibres. After fitting a retaining net to enclose the wool, sheep are injected with the protein. When the net is removed after a week, the fleece has separated and is removed by hand. In some breeds a similar process occurs naturally (see below).

SKIRTING THE FLEECE

Once the entire fleece has been removed from the sheep, the fleece is *thrown*, clean side down, on to a wool table by a shed hand (commonly known in New Zealand and Australian sheds as a *rouseabout* or *roustie*). The wool table top consists of slats spaced approximately 12 cm apart. This enables short pieces of wool, the *locks* and other debris, to gather beneath the table separately from the fleece.

The fleece is then *skirted* by one or more wool rollers to remove the sweat fribs and other less desirable parts of the fleece. The removed pieces largely consist of shorter, seeded, burry or dusty wool etc. which is still useful in the industry. As such they are placed in separate containers and sold along with fleece wool. Other items removed from the fleece on the table, such as faeces, skin fragments or twigs and leaves, are discarded a short distance from the wool table so as not to contaminate the wool and fleece.

WOOL CLASSING

Following the skirting of the fleece, it is folded, rolled and examined for its quality in a process known as wool classing, which is performed by a registered and qualified wool classer. Based on its type, the fleece is placed into the relevant wool bin ready to be pressed (mechanically compressed) when there is sufficient wool to make a wool bale.

SHEARING DEVICES

Blade Shears

Blade shears consist of two blades arranged similarly to scissors except that the hinge is at the end farthest from the point (not in the middle). The cutting edges pass each other as the shearer squeezes them together and shear the wool close to the animal's skin. Blade shears are still used today but in a more limited way. Blade shears leave some wool on a sheep and this is more suitable for cold climates where the sheep needs some protection from the elements. For those areas where no powered-machinery is available blade shears are the only option. Blades are more commonly used to shear stud rams.

Machine Shears

Machine shears, known as hand pieces, operate in a similar manner to human hair clippers in that a power-driven toothed blade, known as a cutter, is driven back and forth over the surface of a comb and the wool is cut from the animal. The original machine shears were powered by a fixed hand-crank linked to the hand piece by a shaft with only two universal joints, which afforded a very limited range of motion. Later models have more joints to allow easier positioning of the hand piece on the animal. Electric motors on each stand have generally replaced overhead gear for driving the hand pieces. The jointed arm is replaced in many instances with a flexible shaft. Smaller motors allowed the production of shears in which the motor is in the hand piece; these are generally not used by professional shearers as the weight and heat of the motor becomes bothersome with long use.

SHEARING IN AUSTRALASIAN CULTURE

A culture has evolved out of the practice of sheep shearing, especially in post-colonial Australia and New Zealand. *Shearing the Rams*, a painting by Australian impressionist painter Tom Roberts is considered to be iconic of the livestock-growing culture or "life on the land" in Australia.

For an inversion, Michael Leunig's *Ramming the Shears* can be seen as a sign of the shifts in Australian culture, and the extent to which the dominant rural culture is being eroded by an increasingly urban population.

The expression that Australia's wealth rode on *the sheep's back* in parts of the twentieth century no longer has the currency it once had.

In 2001, Mandy Francis of Hardy's Bay, NSW constructed a black butt seat for the Street Furniture Project at Walcha, New South Wales. This seat was inspired by the combs, cutters, wool tables and grating associated with the craft and industry of shearing.

During the long weekend in June 2010, 111 machine shearers and 78 blade shearers shore 6,000 Merino ewes and 178 rams at the historic 72 stand *North Tuppal* station. Along with the shearers there were 107 wool handlers and penners-up and more than 10,000 visitors to witness this event in the restored shed. Over this weekend the scene in Tom Robert's *Shearing of the Rams* was twice re-enacted for the visitors.

Many stations across Australia no longer carry sheep due to lower wool prices, drought and other disasters, but their shearing sheds remain, in a wide variety of materials and styles, and have been the subject of books and documentation for heritage authorities. Some farmers are reluctant to remove either the equipment or the sheds, and many unused sheds remain intact.

Contests

Sheep shearing and wool handling competitions are held regularly in parts of the world, particularly Ireland, the UK, South Africa, New Zealand and Australia. As sheep shearing is an arduous task, speed shearers, for all types of equipment and sheep, are usually very fit and well trained. In Wales a sheep shearing contest is one of the events of the Royal Welsh Show, the country's premier agricultural show held near Builth Wells.

The world's largest sheep shearing and wool handling contest, the Golden Shears, is held in the Wairarapa district, New Zealand.

SCOURING

Wool straight off a sheep, known as "greasy wool" or "wool in the grease", contains a high level of valuable lanolin, as well as dirt, dead skin, sweat residue, pesticide, and vegetable matter. Before the wool can be used for commercial purposes, it must be scoured, a process of cleaning the greasy wool. Scouring may be as simple as a bath in warm water, or as complicated as an industrial process using detergent and alkali, and specialized equipment. In commercial wool, vegetable matter is often removed by chemical carbonization. In less processed wools, vegetable matter may be removed by hand, and some of the lanolin left intact through use of gentler detergents. This semi-grease wool can be worked into yarn and knitted into particularly water-resistant mittens or sweaters, such as those of the Aran Island fishermen. Lanolin removed from wool is widely used in cosmetic products such as hand creams.

QUALITY

The quality of wool is determined by the following factors, fibre diameter, crimp, yield, colour, and staple strength. Fibre diameter is the single most important wool characteristic determining quality and price.

Merino wool is typically 3-5 inches in length and is very fine (between 12-24 microns). The finest and most valuable wool comes from Merino hoggets. Wool taken from sheep produced for meat is typically more coarse, and has fibres that are 1.5 to 6 inches in length. Damage or breaks in the wool can occur if the sheep is stressed while it is growing its fleece, resulting in a thin spot where the fleece is likely to break.

Wool is also separated into grades based on the measurement of the wool's diameter in microns and also its style. These grades may vary depending on the breed or purpose of the wool. For example:

- <15.5 - Ultrafine Merino
- 15.6-18.5 - Superfine Merino
- 18.6-20 - Fine Merino
- 20.1-23 - Medium Merino
- 23< - Strong Merino
- Comeback: 21-26 microns, white, 90–180 mm long
- Fine crossbred: 27-31 microns, Corriedales etc.
- Medium crossbred: 32–35 microns
- Downs: 23-34 microns, typically lacks luster and brightness. Examples, Aussiedown, Dorset Horn, Suffolk etc.
- Coarse crossbred: 36> microns
- Carpet wools: 35-45 microns

Any wool finer than 25 microns can be used for garments, while coarser grades are used for outerwear or rugs. The finer the wool, the softer it is, while coarser grades are more durable and less prone to pilling.

The finest Australian and New Zealand Merino wools are known as 1PP which is the industry benchmark of excellence for Merino wool that is 16.9 micron and finer. This style represents the top level of fineness, character, colour, and style as determined on the basis of a series of parameters in accordance with the original dictates of British Wool as applied today by the Australian Wool Exchange (AWEX) Council. Only a few dozen of the millions of bales auctioned every year can be classified and marked 1PP.

HISTORY

As the raw material has been readily available since the widespread domestication of sheep - and of goats, another major provider of wool - the use of felted or woven wool for clothing and other fabrics characterizes some of the earliest civilizations. Prior to invention of shears - probably in the Iron Age - the wool was plucked out by hand or by bronze combs. The oldest known European wool textile, ca. 1500 BCE, was preserved in a Danish bog. Wool fibres from wild goats found in a prehistoric cave in the Republic of Georgia as far back 34,000 BCE suggest that wool fabrics were made even earlier than this. In Roman times, wool, linen, and leather clothed the European population; the cotton of India was a curiosity that only naturalists had heard of; and silk, imported along the Silk Road from China, was an extravagant luxury. Pliny the Elder records in his Natural History that the reputation for producing the finest wool was enjoyed by Tarentum, where selective breeding had produced sheep with a superior fleece, but which required special care.

In medieval times, as trade connections expanded, the Champagne fairs revolved around the production of wool cloth in small centers such as Proving; the network that the sequence of annual fairs developed meant that the woollens of Provins might find their way to Naples, Sicily, Cyprus, Majorca, Spain, and even Constantinople. The wool trade developed into serious business, the generator of capital. In the thirteenth century, the wool trade was the economic engine of the Low Countries and of Central Italy; by the end of the following century Italy predominated, though in the 16th century Italian production turned to silk. Both pre-industries were based on English raw wool exports - rivaled only by the sheepwalks of Castile, developed from the fifteenth century - which were a significant source of income to the English crown, which from 1275 imposed an export tax on wool called the "Great Custom". The importance of wool to the English economy can be shown by the fact that since the 14th Century, the presiding officer of the House of Lords has sat on the "Woolsack", a chair stuffed with wool.

Economies of scale were instituted in the Cistercian houses, which had accumulated great tracts of land during the twelfth and early thirteenth centuries, when land prices were low and labour still scarce.

Raw wool was baled and shipped from North Sea ports to the textile cities of Flanders, notably Ypres and Ghent, where it was dyed and worked up as cloth. At the time of the Black Death, English textile industries accounted for about 10per cent of English wool production; the English textile trade grew during the fifteenth century, to the point where export of wool was discouraged. Over the centuries, various British laws controlled the wool trade or required the use of wool even in burials.

The smuggling of wool out of the country, known as owling, was at one time punishable by the cutting off of a hand. After the Restoration, fine English woollens began to compete with silks in the international market, partly aided by the Navigation Acts; in 1699 English crown forbade its American colonies to trade wool with anyone but England herself.

A great deal of the value of woolen textiles was in the dyeing and finishing of the woven product.

In each of the centers of the textile trade, the manufacturing process came to be subdivided into a collection of trades, overseen by an entrepreneur in a system called by the English the "putting-out" system, or "cottage industry", and the *Verlagssystem* by the Germans.

In this system of producing wool cloth, until recently perpetuated in the production of Harris tweeds, the entrepreneur provides the raw materials and an advance, the remainder being paid upon delivery of the product. Written contracts bound the artisans to specified terms. Fernand Braudel traces the appearance of the system in the thirteenth-century economic boom, quoting a document of 1275 The system effectively by-passed the guilds' restrictions.

Before the flowering of the Renaissance, the Medici and other great banking houses of Florence had built their wealth and banking system on their textile industry based on wool, overseen by the Arte della Lana, the wool guild: wool textile interests guided Florentine policies. Francesco Datini, the "merchant of Prato", established in 1383 an *Arte della Lana* for that small Tuscan city. The sheepwalks of Castile shaped the landscape and the fortunes of the *meseta* that lies in the heart of the Iberian peninsula; in the sixteenth century, a unified Spain allowed export of Merino lambs only with royal permission. The German wool market - based on sheep of Spanish origin - did not overtake British wool until comparatively late.

Australia's colonial economy was based on sheep raising, and the Australian wool trade eventually overtook that of the Germans by 1845, furnishing wool for Bradford, which developed as the heart of industrialized woollens production. A World War I era poster sponsored by the United States Department of Agriculture encouraging children to raise sheep to provide needed war supplies.

Due to decreasing demand with increased use of synthetic fibres, wool production is much less than what it was in the past. The collapse in the price of wool began in late 1966 with a 40per cent drop; with occasional interruptions, the price has tended down. The result has been sharply reduced production and movement of resources into production of other commodities, in the case of sheep growers, to production of meat.

Superwash wool (or washable wool) technology first appeared in the early 1970s to produce wool that has been specially treated so that it is machine washable and may be tumble-dried. This wool is produced using an acid bath that removes the "scales" from the fibre, or by coating the fibre with a polymer that prevents the scales from attaching to each other and causing shrinkage. This process results in a fibre that holds longevity and durability over synthetic materials, while retaining its shape.

In December 2004, a bale of the world's finest wool, averaging 11.8 micron, sold for $3,000 per kilogram at auction in Melbourne, Victoria. This fleece wool tested with an average yield of 74.5per cent, 68 mm long, and had 40 newtons per kilotex strength. The result was $AUD279,000 for the bale. The finest bale of wool ever auctioned sold for a seasonal record of 269,000 cents per kilo during June 2008. This bale was produced by the Hillcreston Pinehill Partnership and measured 11.6 microns, 72.1per cent yield and had a 43 Newtons per kilotex strength measurement. The bale realized $247,480 and was exported to India. During 2007 a new wool suit was developed and sold in Japan that can be washed in the shower, and dries off ready to wear within hours with no ironing required. The suit was developed using Australian Merino wool and it enables woven products made from wool, such as suits, trousers and skirts, to be cleaned using a domestic shower at home.

In December 2006 the General Assembly of the United Nations proclaimed 2009 to be the International Year of Natural Fibres, so to raise the profile of wool and other natural fibres.

PRODUCTION

Global wool production is approximately 1.3 million tonnes per year, of which 60per cent goes into apparel. Australia is the leading producer of wool which is mostly from Merino sheep. New Zealand is the second-largest producer of wool, and the largest producer of crossbred wool. China is the third-largest producer of wool. Breeds such as Lincoln, Romney, Tukidale, Drysdale and Elliotdale produce coarser fibres, and wool from these sheep is usually used for making carpets.

In the United States, Texas, New Mexico and Colourado have large commercial sheep flocks and their mainstay is the Rambouillet (or French Merino). There is also a thriving home-flock contingent of small-scale farmers who raise small hobby flocks of specialty sheep for the hand spinning market. These small-scale farmers offer a wide selection of fleece.

Global woolclip (total amount of wool shorn) 2004/2005

- Australia: 25per cent of global woolclip (475 million kg greasy, 2004/2005)
- China: 18per cent
- New Zealand: 11per cent
- Argentina: 3per cent
- Turkey: 2per cent
- Iran: 2per cent
- United Kingdom: 2per cent
- India: 2per cent
- Sudan: 2per cent
- South Africa: 1per cent
- United States: 0.77per cent

Organic wool is becoming more and more popular. This wool is very limited in supply and much of it comes from New Zealand and Australia. It is becoming easier to find in clothing and other products, but these products often carry a higher price. Wool is environmentally preferable (as compared to petroleum-based Nylon or Polypropylene) as a material for carpets as well, in particular when combined with a natural binding and the use of formaldehyde-free glues.

Animal rights groups have noted issues with the production of wool, such as Mulesing.

MARKETING

About 85per cent of wool sold in Australia is sold by open cry auction. Sale by Sample is a method in which a mechanical claw takes a sample from each bale in a line or lot of wool. These grab samples are bulked, objectively measured, and a sample of not less than 4 kg is displayed in a box for the buyer to examine. The Australian Wool Exchange (AWEX) conducts sales primarily in Sydney, Melbourne, Newcastle, and Fremantle. There are about 80 brokers and agents throughout Australia.

About 7per cent of Australian wool is sold by private treaty on farms or to local wool-handling facilities. This option gives wool growers benefit from reduced transport, warehousing, and selling costs. This method is preferred for small lots or mixed butts in order to make savings on reclassing and testing.

About 5per cent of Australian wool is sold over the internet on an electronic offer board. This option gives wool growers the ability to set firm price targets, reoffer passed in wool and offer lots to the market quickly and efficiently. This method works well for tested lots as buyers use these results to make a purchase. 97per cent of wool is sold without sample inspection however as of dec 2009, 59per cent of wool listed had been passed in from auction. Growers through certain brokers can allocate their wool to a sale and what price their wool will be reserved at.

Sale by tender can achieve considerable cost savings on wool clips large enough to make it worthwhile for potential buyers to submit tenders. Some marketing firms sell wool on a consignment basis, obtaining a fixed percentage as commission.

Forward selling: Some buyers offer a secure price for forward delivery of wool based on estimated measurements or the results of previous clips. Prices are quoted at current market rates and are locked in for the season. Premiums and discounts are added to cover variations in micron, yield, tensile strength, etc., which are confirmed by actual test results when available.

Another method of selling wool includes sales direct to wool mills. The British Wool Marketing Board operates a central marketing system for UK fleece wool with the aim of achieving the best possible net returns for farmers.

Less than half of New Zealand's wool is sold at auction, while around 45per cent for farmers sell wool directly to private buyers and end-users. Some businesses in New Zealand like Blue House Yarns have turned to selling organic wool, a new trend on wool production. United States sheep producers' market wool with private or cooperative wool warehouses, but wool pools are common in many states. In some cases, wool is pooled in a local market area but sold through a wool warehouse. Wool offered with objective measurement test results is preferred. Imported apparel wool and carpet wool goes directly to central markets where it is handled by the large merchants and manufacturers.

USES

In addition to clothing, wool has been used for blankets, horse rugs, saddle cloths, carpeting, felt, wool insulation (also see links) and upholstery. Wool felt covers piano hammers, and it is used to absorb odors and noise in heavy machinery and stereo speakers. Ancient Greeks lined their helmets with felt, and Roman legionnaires used breastplates made of wool felt.

Wool has also been traditionally used to cover cloth diapers. Wool fibre exteriors are hydrophobic (repel water) and the interior of the wool fibre is hygroscopic (attracts water); this makes a wool garment able to cover a wet diaper while inhibiting wicking, so outer garments remain dry. Wool felted and treated with lanolin is water resistant, air permeable, and slightly antibacterial, so it resists the buildup of odour. Some modern cloth diapers use felted wool fabric for covers, and there are several modern commercial knitting patterns for wool diaper covers.

Initial studies of woollen underwear have found it prevented heat and sweat rashes because it more readily absorbs the moisture than other fibres.

Merino wool has been used in baby sleep products such as swaddle baby wrap blankets and infant sleeping bags.

Wool is an animal protein, and as such it can be used as a soil fertilizer, being a slow release source of nitrogen and ready made amino acids.

VIRGIN WOOL

Wool spun for the first time is called Virgin wool.

SHODDY OR RECYCLED WOOL:

It is made by cutting or tearing apart existing wool fabric and respinning the resulting fibres. As this process makes the wool fibres shorter, the remanufactured fabric is inferior to the original. The recycled wool may be mixed with raw wool, wool noil, or another fibre such as cotton to increase the average fibre length. Such yarns are typically used as weft yarns with a cotton warp. This process was invented in the Heavy Woollen District of West Yorkshire and created a micro-economy in this area for many years.

Ragg is a sturdy wool fibre made into yarn and used in many rugged applications like gloves.

Worsted is a strong, long-staple, combed wool yarn with a hard surface.

Woollen is a soft, short-staple, carded wool yarn typically used for knitting. In traditional weaving, woollen weft yarn (for softness and warmth) is frequently combined with a worsted warp yarn for strength on the loom.

EVENTS

A buyer of Merino wool, Ermenegildo Zegna, has offered awards for Australian wool producers. In 1963, the first Ermenegildo Zegna Perpetual Trophy was presented in Tasmania for growers of "Superfine skirted Merino fleece". In 1980, a national award, the Ermenegildo Zegna Trophy for Extrafine Wool Production, was launched. In 2004, this award became known as the Ermenegildo Zegna Unprotected Wool Trophy. In 1998, an Ermenegildo Zegna Protected Wool Trophy was launched for fleece from sheep coated for around nine months of the year.

In 2002, the Ermenegildo Zegna Vellus Aureum Trophy was launched for wool that is 13.9 micron and finer. Wool from Australia, New Zealand, Argentina, and South Africa may enter, and a winner is named from each country. In April 2008, New Zealand won the Ermenegildo Zegna Vellus Aureum Trophy for the first time with a fleece that measured 10.8 microns. This contest awards the winning fleece weight with the same weight in gold as a prize, hence the name.

In 2010 an ultra-fine, 10 micron fleece, from Windradeen, near Pyramul, New South Wales set a new world record in the fineness of wool fleeces when it won the Ermenegildo Zegna Vellus Aureum International Trophy.

Since 2000, Loro Piana has awarded a cup for the world's finest bale of wool that produces just enough fabric for 50 tailor-made suits. The prize is awarded to an Australian or New Zealand wool grower who produces the year's finest bale. The New England Merino Field days which display local studs, wool, and sheep are held during January, every two years (in even numbered years) around the Walcha, New South Wales district. The Annual Wool Fashion Awards, which showcase the use of Merino wool by fashion designers, are hosted by the city of Armidale, New South Wales in March each year.

This event encourages young and established fashion designers to display their talents. During each May, Armidale hosts the annual New England Wool Expo to display wool fashions, handicrafts, demonstrations, shearing competitions, yard dog trials, and more.

In July, the annual Australian Sheep and Wool Show is held in Bendigo, Victoria. This is the largest sheep and wool show in the world, with goats and alpacas as well as woolcraft competitions and displays, fleece competitions, sheepdog trials, shearing, and wool handling.

The largest competition in the world for objectively-measured fleeces is the Australian Fleece Competition, which is held annually at Bendigo. In 2008, there were 475 entries from all states of Australia with first and second prizes going to the Northern Tablelands, New South Wales fleeces.

WOOL CLASSING

Wool classing is an occupation for which people are trained to produce uniform, predictable, low risk lines of wool. This is carried out by examining the characteristics of the wool in its raw state. The characteristics which a wool classer would examine are:

Breed of the sheep: Shedding breeds will increase the risk of medulated and/or pigmented fibres. Any sheep likely to have dark fibres should be shorn last to avoid contamination.

The age of the sheep will have a bearing on the fibre diameter and value of wool, too.

Chemical usage: Ensure that all rules have been followed.

Brands, seedy jowls and *shanks*: Must be removed from fleeces and broken.

Stain: Must be removed from bellies and fleeces and identified in a separate line.

Wool crimp: The number of bends per unit length along the wool fibre approximately indicates spinning capacity of the wool. fibres with a fine crimp have many bends and usually have a small diameter. Such fibre can be spun into fine yarns, with great lengths of yarn for a given weight of wool, and greater market value. Fine fibres may be utilised in the production of fine garments such as men's suits whereas the coarser fibres may be used for the production of carpet and other sturdy products. Crimp is measured in crimps per inch or crimps per centimetre. Average diameter or mean fibre diameter is measured in micrometres (microns). For generations, English wool-handlers categorized wool along the above lines estimating spinning capacity by eye and touch. This spread worldwide as the Bradford system.

Wool Strength (also known as *tensile strength*) determines wool's ability to withstand processing. Weaker wools produce more waste in carding and spinning. Weaker wools may be used for production of felt, or combined with other fibres, etc.

Wool colour: Indicates whether wool is able to be dyed in light shades. Colour may be graded depending upon the natural colour, impurities and various stains present. Severely stained wool decreases prices dramatically. However, it is difficult to assess colour accurately without proper measurement, since some stains will wash out in the processing, whereas others are quite persistent.

The fleece is skirted to remove excess frib, seed and burr etc to leave the fleece as reasonably even as possible in good respects. The parts of wool taken from a sheep are graded separately.

The fleece forming the bulk of the yield is placed with other fleece wool as the main line, other pieces such as the neck, belly and skirtings (inferior wool from edges) are sold for such purposes where the shorter wools are required (for example: fillings, carpets, insulation).

Whilst in some places crimp may determine which grade the fleece will be placed into, this subjective assessment is not always reliable and processors prefer that wools are measured objectively by qualified laboratories. Some of the superfine wool growers do in shed wool testing, but this can only be used as a guide.

This enables wool classers to place wool into lines of a consistent quality. A shedhand, known as a wool presser, places the wool into approved wool packs in a wool press to produce a bale of wool that must meet regulations concerning its fastenings, length, weight and branding if it is to be sold at auction in Australasia. All Merino fleece wool sold at auction in Australia is objectively measured for fibre diameter, yield (including the amount of vegetable matter), staple length, staple strength and sometimes colour.

Classers are also responsible for ensuring that a pre-shearing check is made to ensure that the wool and sheep areas are free of possible contaminants. They are to supervise shed staff during shearing and train any inexperienced hands. At the end of shearing classers have to provide full documentation concerning the clip.

ROOING

In some primitive sheep (for example in many Shetlands), there is a natural break in the growth of the wool in spring. By late spring this causes the fleece to begin to peel away from the body, and it may then be plucked by hand without cutting – this is known as *rooing*. Individual sheep may reach this stage at slightly different times.

Shearing can be done with use of hand-shears or powered shears. Professional sheep shearers can shear a sheep in under a minute, without nicking the sheep.

The fleece is removed in one piece. Second cuts can be made but produce only short fibres, which are more difficult to spin. Primitive breeds, like the Scottish Soay sheep have to be plucked, not sheared, as the kemps are still longer than the soft fleece, (a process called rooing).

SKIRTING

Skirting is disposing of all wool that is unsuitable for spinning. Recovering can be attempted. It can also be done at the same time as carding.

CLEANING

The wool is cleaned. At this point the fleece is full of lanolin and often contains extraneous vegetable matter, such as sticks, twigs, burrs and straw. These may all be removed, though lanolin may be left in the wool till after the spinning, a technique known as spinning 'in the grease'. Indeed if the fabric is to be water repellent, lanolin is not removed at any stage.

Washing the wool at this stage can be a tedious process. Some people wash it a small handful at a time very carefully, and then set it out to dry on a table in the sun. Others will wash the whole fleece. Lanolin is removed by soaking the fleece in very hot water. If the fleece gets agitated, it will become felt, and then spinning is impossible. Felting, when done on purpose (with needles, chemicals, or simply rubbing the fibres against each other), can be used to create garments.

CARDING OR COMBING

It is possible to spin directly from a clean fleece, but it is much easier to spin a carded fleece. Carding by hand yields a rolag, a loose woollen roll of fibres. Using a drum carder yields a bat, which is a mat of fibres in a flat, rectangular shape. Carding mills return the fleece in a roving, which is a stretched bat; it is very long and often the thickness of a wrist.A pencil roving is a roving thinned to the width of a pencil. It can used for knitting without any spinning, or for apprentices.

One good-sized fleece may take weeks to card with a drum-carder, or an eternity by hand. If the fleece is sent to a carding mill, it must be washed before it is carded. Most mills offer washing the wool as a service, with extra fees if the wool is exceptionally dirty. Fibres can be purchased pre-carded. Combing is another method to align the fibres parallel to the yarn, and thus is good for spinning a worsted yarn, whereas the rolag from handcards produces a woolen yarn.

SPINNING

Hand spinning can be done by using a spindle or the spinning wheel. Spinning turns the carded wool fibres into yarn which can then be directly woven, knitted (flat or circular), crocheted, or by other means turned into fabric or a garment.

The spinning wheel collects the yarn on a bobbin. A woollen yarn is lightly spun so it is airey, and is a good insulator and suitable for knitting, while a worsted yarn is spun tight to exclude air, and has greater strength and is suited to weaving..

Once the bobbin is full, the spinner either puts on a new bobbin, or forms a skein, or balls the yarn. A skein is a coil of yarn twisted into a loose knot. Yarn is skeined using a niddy-noddy or other type of skein -winder. Yarn is rarely balled directly after spinning, it will be stored in skein form, and transferred to a ball only if needed. Knitting from a skein, is difficult as the yarn forms knots, in this case it is best to ball. Yarn to be plied is left on the bobbin. A skein is either formed on a niddy noddy or some other type of skein winder. Traditionally niddy-noddys looked like an uppercase "i", with the bottom half rotated 90 degrees. Now spinning wheel manufactures also make niddy-noddys that attach onto the spinning wheel for faster skein winding.

PLYING

Plying yarn is when one takes a strand of spun yarn (one strand is often called a single) and spins it together with other strands in order to make a thicker yarn. Regular plying consists of taking two or more singles and twisting them together, the against their twist. This can be done on a spinning wheel or on a spindle. If the yarn was spun clockwise (which is called a "Z" twist), to ply, the wheel must spin counter-clockwise (an "S" twist). This is the most common way. When plying from bobbins a device called a lazy kate is often used to hold them.

Most spinners (who use spinning wheels) ply from bobbins. This is easier than plying from balls because there is less chance for the yarn to become tangled and knotted if it is simply unwound from the bobbins. So that the bobbins can unwind freely, they are put in a device called a lazy kate, or sometimes simply *kate*. The simplest lazy kate consists of wooden bars with a metal rod running between them. Most hold between three and four bobbins. The bobbin sits on the metal rod. Other lazy kates are built with devices that create an adjustable amount of tension, so that if the yarn is jerked, a whole bunch of yarn is not wound off, then wound up again in the opposite direction. Some spinning wheels come with a built in lazy kate.

Navajo plying consists of making large loops, similar to crocheting.A loop about 8 inches long is made on the leader the end on the leader. (A leader is the string left on the bobbin to spin off.) The three strands together are spun in the opposite direction. When a third of the loop remains, a new loop is created and the spinning continues.

The process is repeated until the yarn is all plied. The advantage of this method is that only one single is needed and if the single is already dyed this technique allows it to be plied without ruining the colour scheme. This technique also allows the spinner to try to match up thick and thin spots in the yarn, thus making for a smoother end product.

WASHING

If the lanolin is unwanted, and has not already been washed out, this is done now. The skein is tied in six points and steeped overnight in detergent, it is rinsed and air-dried, and re-skinned.

unless the lanolin is to be left in the cloth as a water repellent. When washing a skein it works well to let the wool soak in soapy water overnight, and rinse the soap out in the morning. Dishwashing detergents are commonly used, and a special laundry detergent designed for washing wool is not required. The dishwashing detergent works and does not harm the wool. After washing, let the wool dry (air drying works best). Once it is dry, or just a bit damp, one can stretch it out a bit on a niddy-noddy. Putting the wool back on the niddy-noddy makes for a nicer looking finished skein. Before taking a skein and washing it, the skein must be tied up loosely in about six places. If the skein is not tied up, it will be very hard to unravel when done washing.

FLAX

The preparations for spinning is similar across most plant fibres, including

Flax and Hemp. Flax is the fibre used to create linen. Cotton is handled differently since it uses the fruit of the plant and not the stalk.

HARVESTING

Flax is pulled out of the ground about a month after the initial blooming when the lower part of the plant begins to turn yellow, and when the most forward of the seeds are found in a soft state. It is pulled in handfuls and several handfuls are tied together with slip knot into a 'beet'. The string is tightened as the stalks dry. The seed heads are removed and the seeds collected, by threshing and winnowing.

RETTING

Threshing and dressing flax at the Roscheider Hof Open Air Museum

Retting is the process of rotting away the inner stalk, leaving the outer fibres intact. A standing pool of warm water is needed, into which the beets are submerged. An acid is produced when retting, and it would corrode a metal container.

At 80 °F (27 °C), the retting process takes 4 or 5 days, it takes longer takes longer when colder.

When the retting is complete the bundles feel soft and slimy, The process can be overdone, and the fibres rot too.

DRESSING THE FLAX

Dressing is removing the fibres from the straw and cleaning it enough to be spun. The flax is broken, scutched and hackled in this step.

Breaking The process of breaking breaks up the straw into short segments. The beets are untied and fed between the beater of the breaking machine, the set of wooden blades that mesh together when the upper jaw is lowered. Scutching In order to remove some of the straw from the fibre a wooden scutching knife is scaped down the fibres while they hang vertically.

Heckling Fibre is pulled through various different sized heckling combs. A Heckling comb is a bed of sharp, long-tapered, tempered, polished steel pins driven into wooden blocks at regular spacing. A good progression is from 4 pins per square inch, to 12, to 25 to 48 to 80.

The first three will remove the straw, and the last two will split and polish the fibres. Some of the finer stuff that comes off in the last heckles can be carded like wool and spun. It will produce a coarser yarn than the fibres pulled through the heckles because it will still contain some straw.

SPINNING THE FLAX

Flax can either be spun from a distaff, or from the spinner's lap. Spinners keep their fingers wet when spinning, to prevent forming fuzzy thread. Usually singles are spun with an "S" twist. After flax is spun it is washed in a pot of boiling water for a couple of hours to set the twist and reduce fuzziness. Many handspinners, will buy a roving of flax. This roving is spun in the same manner as above. The rovings may come with very long fibres (4 to 8 inches), or much shorter fibres (2 to 3 inches).

SILK

Silk is a natural protein fibre, some forms of which can be woven into textiles. The best-known type of silk is obtained from the cocoons of the larvae of the mulberry silkworm *Bombyx mori* reared in captivity (sericulture). The shimmering appearance of silk is due to the triangular prism-like structure of the silk fibre, which allows silk cloth to refract incoming light at different angles, thus producing different colours. Silks are produced by several other insects, but only the silk of moth caterpillars has been used for textile manufacturing. There has been some research into other silks, which differ at the molecular level. Silks are mainly produced by the larvae of insects undergoing complete metamorphosis, but also by some adult insects such as webspinners. Silk production is especially common in the Hymenoptera (bees, wasps, and ants), and is sometimes used in nest construction. Other types of arthropod produce silk, most notably various arachnids such as spiders (see spider silk).

HISTORY

Woven silk textile from tomb no 1. at Mawangdui in Changsha, Hunan province, China, from the Western Han Dynasty, 2nd century BC

WILD SILK

A variety of wild silks, produced by caterpillars other than the mulberry silkworm have been known and used in China, South Asia, and Europe since ancient times. However, the scale of production was always far smaller than that of cultivated silks.

They differ from the domesticated varieties in colour and texture, and cocoons gathered in the wild usually have been damaged by the emerging moth before the cocoons are gathered, so the silk thread that makes up the cocoon has been torn into shorter lengths. Commercially reared silkworm pupae are killed by dipping them in boiling water before the adult moths emerge, or by piercing them with a needle, allowing the whole cocoon to be unravelled as one continuous thread. This permits a much stronger cloth to be woven from the silk. Wild silks also tend to be more difficult to dye than silk from the cultivated silkworm.

CHINA

Silk fabric was first developed in ancient China, with some of the earliest examples found as early as 3500 BC. Legend gives credit for developing silk to a Chinese empress, Lei Zu (Hsi-Ling-Shih, Lei-Tzu). Silks were originally reserved for the Kings of China for their own use and gifts to others, but spread gradually through Chinese culture and trade both geographically and socially, and then to many regions of Asia. Silk rapidly became a popular luxury fabric in the many areas accessible to Chinese merchants because of its texture and luster.

Silk was in great demand, and became a staple of pre-industrial international trade. In July 2007, archeologists discovered intricately woven and dyed silk textiles in a tomb in Jiangxi province, dated to the Eastern Zhou Dynasty roughly 2,500 years ago. Although historians have suspected a long history of a formative textile industry in ancient China, this find of silk textiles employing "complicated techniques" of weaving and dyeing provides direct and concrete evidence for silks dating before the Mawangdui-discovery and other silks dating to the Han Dynasty (202 BC-220 AD).

The first evidence of the silk trade is the finding of silk in the hair of an Egyptian mummy of the 21st dynasty, c.1070 BC. Ultimately the silk trade reached as far as the Indian subcontinent, the Middle East, Europe, and North Africa. This trade was so extensive that the major set of trade routes between Europe and Asia has become known as the Silk Road. The highest development was in China.

The Emperors of China strove to keep knowledge of sericulture secret to maintain the Chinese monopoly. Nonetheless sericulture reached Korea around 200 BC, about the first half of the 1st century AD had reached ancient Khotan, and by AD 300 the practice had been established in India.

THAILAND

Silk is produced, year round, in Thailand by two types of silkworms, the cultured Bombycidae and wild Saturniidae. Most production is after the rice harvest in the southern and northeast parts of the country.

Women traditionally weave silk on hand looms, and pass the skill on to their daughters as weaving is considered to be a sign of maturity and eligibility for marriage. Thai silk textiles often use complicated patterns in various colours and styles. Most regions of Thailand have their own typical silks. A single thread filament is too thin to use on its own so women combine many threads to produce a thicker, usable fibre. They do this by hand-reeling the threads onto a wooden spindle to produce a uniform strand of raw silk. The process takes around 40 hours to produce a half kilogram of Thai silk.

Many local operations use a reeling machine for this task, but some silk threads are still hand-reeled. The difference is that hand-reeled threads produce three grades of silk: two fine grades that are ideal for lightweight fabrics, and a thick grade for heavier material.

The silk fabric is soaked in extremely cold water and bleached before dyeing to remove the natural yellow colouring of Thai silk yarn.

To do this, skeins of silk thread are immersed in large tubs of hydrogen peroxide. Once washed and dried, the silk is woven on a traditional hand operated loom.

INDIA

Silk, known as "Paat" in Eastern India, *Pattu* in southern parts of India and *Resham* in Hindi/Urdu, has a long history in India. Recent archaeological discoveries in Harappa and Chanhu-daro suggest that sericulture, employing wild silk threads from native silkworm species, existed in South Asia during the time of the Indus Valley Civilization, roughly contemporaneous with the earliest known silk use in China. Silk is widely produced today. India is the second largest producer of silk after China. A majority of the silk in India is produced in Karnataka State, particularly in Mysore and the North Bangalore regions of Muddenahalli, Kanivenarayanapura, and Doddaballapur. India is also the largest consumer of silk in the world.

The tradition of wearing silk sarees in marriages by the brides is followed in southern parts of India. Silk is worn by people as a symbol of royalty while attending functions and during festivals. Historically silk was used by the upper classes, while cotton was used by the poorer classes. Today silk is mainly produced in Bhoodhan Pochampally (also known as Silk City), Kanchipuram, Dharmavaram, Mysore, etc. in South India and Banaras in the North for manufacturing garments and sarees. "Murshidabad silk", famous from historical times, is mainly produced in Malda and Murshidabad district of West Bengal and woven with hand looms in Birbhum and Murshidabad district. Another place famous for production of silk is Bhagalpur.

The silk from Pochampally is particularly well-known for its classic designs and enduring quality. The silk is traditionally hand-woven and hand-dyed and usually also has silver threads woven into the cloth. Most of this silk is used to make sarees. The sarees usually are very expensive and vibrant in colour. Garments made from silk form an integral part of Indian weddings and other celebrations. In the northeastern state of Assam, three different types of silk are produced, collectively called Assam silk: Muga, Eri and Pat silk. Muga, the golden silk, and Eri are produced by silkworms that are native only to Assam. The heritage of silk rearing and weaving is very old and continues today especially with the production of Muga and Pat *riha* and *mekhela chador*, the three-piece silk sarees woven with traditional motifs. *Mysore Silk Sarees*, which are known for their soft texture, last many years if carefully maintained.

ANCIENT MEDITERRANEAN

In the Odyssey, 19.233, when Odysseus, while pretending to be someone else, is questioned by Penelope about her husband's clothing, he says that he wore a shirt "gleaming like the skin of a dried onion" (varies with translations, literal translation here) which could refer to the lustrous quality of silk fabric. The Roman Empire knew of and traded in silk. During the reign of emperor Tiberius, sumptuary laws were passed that forbade men from wearing silk garments, but these proved ineffectual. Despite the popularity of silk, the secret of silk-making only reached Europe around AD 550, via the Byzantine Empire. Legend has it those monks working for the emperor Justinian I smuggled silkworm eggs to Constantinople in hollow canes from China. All top-quality looms and weavers were located inside the Palace complex in Constantinople and the cloth produced was used in imperial robes or in diplomacy, as gifts to foreign dignitaries. The remainder was sold at very high prices.

MIDDLE EAST

In Islamic teachings, Muslim men are forbidden to wear silk. Many religious jurists believe the reasoning behind the prohibition lies in avoiding clothing for men that can be considered feminine or extravagant. There are disputes regarding the amount of silk a fabric can consist of (*i.e.*, whether a small decorative silk piece on a cotton caftan is permissible or not) for it to be lawful for men to wear but the dominant opinion of most Muslim scholars is that the wearing of silk for men is forbidden.

Despite injunctions against silk for men, silk has retained its popularity in the Islamic world because of its permissibility for women. The Muslim Moors brought silk with them to Spain during their conquest of the Iberian Peninsula.

MEDIEVAL AND MODERN EUROPE

Venetian merchants traded extensively in silk and encouraged silk growers to settle in Italy. By the 13th century, Italian silk was a significant source of trade. Since that period, the silk worked in the province of Como has been the most valuable silk in the world.

The wealth of Florence was largely built on textiles, both wool and silk and other cities like Lucca also grew rich on the trade. Italian silk was so popular in Europe that Francis I of France invited Armenian silk makers to France to create a French silk industry, especially in Lyon. Mass emigration (especially of Huguenots) during periods of religious dispute had seriously damaged French industry and introduced these various textile industries, including silk, to other countries.

James I attempted to establish silk production in England, purchasing and planting 100,000 mulberry trees, some on land adjacent to Hampton Court Palace, but they were of a species unsuited to the silk worms, and the attempt failed. British enterprise also established silk filature in Cyprus in 1928. In England in the mid 20th Century, silk was produced at Lullingstone Castle in Kent. Silkworms were raised and reeled under the direction of Zoe Lady Hart Dyke. Production started elsewhere later.

In Italy, the Stazione Bacologica Sperimentale was founded in Padua in 1871 to research sericulture. In the late 19th century, China, Japan, and Italy were the major producers of silk.

The most important cities for silk production in Italy were Como and Meldola (Forlì). In medieval times, it was common for silk to be used to make elaborate casings for bananas and other fruits.

Silk was expensive in Medieval Europe and used only by the rich. Italian merchants like Giovanni Arnolfini became hugely wealthy trading it to the Courts of Northern Europe.

NORTH AMERICA

James I of England introduced silk-growing to the American colonies around 1619, ostensibly to discourage tobacco planting. The Shakers in Kentucky adopted the practice as did a cottage industry in New England. In the 19th century a new attempt at a silk industry began with European-born workers in Paterson, New Jersey, and the city became a US silk center, although Japanese imports were still more important.

World War II interrupted the silk trade from Japan. Silk prices increased dramatically, and US industry began to look for substitutes, which led to the use of synthetics such as nylon. Synthetic silks have also been made from local, a type of cellulose fibre, and are often difficult to distinguish from real silk (see spider silk for more on synthetic silks).

PROPERTIES

Physical Properties

Silk fibres from the *Bombyx mori* silkworm have a triangular cross section with rounded corners, 5-10 ìm wide. The fibroin-heavy chain is composed mostly of beta-sheets, due to a 59-mer amino acid repeat sequence with some variations. The flat surfaces of the fibrils reflect light at many angles, giving silk a natural shine. The cross-section from other silkworms can vary in shape and diameter: crescent-like for *Anaphe* and elongated wedge for *tussah*. Silkworm fibres are naturally extruded from two silkworm glands as a pair of primary filaments (brin), which are stuck together, with sericin proteins that act like glue, to form a bave. Bave diameters for tussah silk can reach 65 ìm. See cited reference for cross-sectional SEM photographs. Silk has a smooth, soft texture that is not slippery, unlike many synthetic fibres.

Silk is one of the strongest natural fibres but loses up to 20per cent of its strength when wet. It has a good moisture regain of 11per cent. Its elasticity is moderate to poor: if elongated even a small amount, it remains stretched. It can be weakened if exposed to too much sunlight. It may also be attacked by insects, especially if left dirty.

Silk is a poor conductor of electricity and thus susceptible to static cling.

Unwashed silk chiffon may shrink up to 8per cent due to a relaxation of the fibre macrostructure. So silk should either be pre-washed prior to garment construction, or dry cleaned. Dry cleaning may still shrink the chiffon up to 4per cent. Occasionally, this shrinkage can be reversed by a gentle steaming with a press cloth. There is almost no gradual shrinkage nor shrinkage due to molecular-level deformation.

Natural and synthetic silk is known to manifest piezoelectric properties in proteins, probably due to its molecular structure.

Silkworm silk was used as the standard for the denier, a measurement of linear density in fibres. Silkworm silk therefore has a linear density of approximately 1 den, or 1.1 dtex.

Comparison of silk fibres	Linear Density(dtex)	Diameter (mm)	Coeff. Variation
Moth: Bombyx mori	1.17	12.9	24.8per cent
Spider: Argiope aurentia	0.14	3.57	14.8per cent

Chemical Properties

Silk emitted by the silkworm consists of two main proteins, sericin and fibroin, fibroin being the structural center of the silk, and serecin being the sticky material surrounding it. Fibroin is made up of the amino acids Gly-Ser-Gly-Ala-Gly-Ala and forms beta pleated sheets. Hydrogen bonds form between chains, and side chains form above and below the plane of the hydrogen bond network.

The high proportion (50per cent) of glycine, which is a small amino acid, allows tight packing and the fibres are strong and resistant to stretching. The tensile strength is due to the many interseeded hydrogen bonds. Since the protein forms a beta sheet, when stretched the force is applied to these strong bonds and they do not break. Silk is resistant to most mineral acids, except for sulfuric acid, which dissolves it. It is yellowed by perspiration.

USES

Silk's absorbency makes it comfortable to wear in warm weather and while active. Its low conductivity keeps warm air close to the skin during cold weather. It is often used for clothing such as shirts, ties, blouses, formal dresses, high fashion clothes, lingerie, pyjamas, robes, dress suits, sun dresses and kimonos.

Silk's attractive luster and drape makes it suitable for many furnishing applications. It is used for upholstery, wall coverings, window treatments (if blended with another fibre), rugs, bedding and wall hangings

While on the decline now, due to artificial fibres, silk has had many industrial and commercial uses; parachutes, bicycle tires, comforter filling and artillery gunpowder bags.

A special manufacturing process removes the outer irritant sericin coating of the silk, which makes it suitable as non-absorbable surgical sutures.

This process has also recently led to the introduction of specialist silk underclothing for children and adults with eczema where it can significantly reduce itch.

PRODUCTION

The cultivation of silk is called sericulture. Over 30 countries produce silk, the major ones are China (54per cent) and India (14per cent).

To produce 1 kg of silk, 104 kg of mulberry leaves must be eaten by 3000 silkworms. It takes about 5000 silkworms to make a pure silk kimono.

Table. Top Ten Cocoons (Reelable) Producers — 2005.

Country	Production (Int $1000)	Footnote	Production (1000 kg)	Footnote
People's Republic of China	978,013	C	290,003	F
India	259,679	C	77,000	F
Uzbekistan	57,332	C	17,000	F
Brazil	37,097	C	11,000	F
Iran	20,235	C	6,000	F
Thailand	16,862	C	5,000	F
Vietnam	10,117	C	3,000	F
Democratic People's Republic of Korea	5,059	C	1,500	F
Romania	3,372	C	1,000	F
Japan	2,023	C	600	F

CULTIVATION

Silk moths lay eggs on specially prepared paper. The eggs hatch and the caterpillars (silkworms) are fed fresh mulberry leaves. After about 35 days and 4 moltings, the caterpillars are 10,000 times heavier than when hatched and are ready to begin spinning a cocoon. A straw frame is placed over the tray of caterpillars, and each caterpillar begins spinning a cocoon by moving its head in a pattern. Two glands produce liquid silk and force it through openings in the head called spinnerets.

Liquid silk is coated in sericin, a water-soluble protective gum, and solidifies on contact with the air. Within 2–3 days, the caterpillar spins about 1 mile of filament and is completely encased in a cocoon. The silk farmers then kill most caterpillars by heat, leaving some to metamorphose into moths to breed the next generation of caterpillars.

Harvested cocoons are then soaked in boiling water to soften the sericin holding the silk fibres together in a cocoon shape. The fibres are then unwound to produce a continuous thread. Since a single thread is too fine and fragile for commercial use, anywhere from three to ten strands are spun together to form a single thread of silk.

ANIMAL RIGHTS

As the process of harvesting the silk from the cocoon kills the larvae, sericulture has been criticized in the early 21st century by animal rights activists, especially since artificial silks are available. Mohandas Gandhi was also critical of silk production based on the Ahimsa philosophy "not to hurt any living thing." This led to Gandhi's promotion of cotton spinning machines, an example of which can be seen at the Gandhi Institute. He also promoted *Ahimsa silk*, wild silk made from the cocoons of wild and semi-wild silk moths. Ahimsa silk is promoted in parts of Southern India for those who prefer not to wear silk produced by killing silkworms.

4

Employment in Sericulture

UNDERSTANDING CHANGING WORK PATTERNS IN SERICULTURE

The IUF and the International Land Coalition (ILC) have jointly produced an analytical report on understanding changing work patterns in sericulture in the Ugandan sugar industry with regard to: (a) full-time waged workers; and (b) temporary and/or seasonal waged workers, including self-employed farmers hired as wage labourers. The research aims to improve understanding of the rapidly changing patterns of production, employment and work in sericulture in order to help the IUF and ILC to more clearly focus their respective work programmes, better target their resources, and give clearer indications of potential partner organizations.

The report found:

- ongoing downsizing of the permanent waged workforce on sugar company nucleus (*i.e.* directly managed) plantations;
- an increase in the number of waged workers on short-term contracts of employment on the nucleus plantation;
- increased use of casual waged workers on nucleus plantations;
- increased hiring of casual waged workers by self-employed farmers, producing sugar under contract as "outgrowers" to the sugar plantation companies;
- outgrower associations acting as labour contractors, hiring casual waged labour to work on the farms of its outgrower farmer members;
- increasing casualization of employment.

The combined effects of these changes for waged workers are growing job insecurity, lower rates of pay, poorer working conditions, increasing food insecurity and growing levels of poverty.

Agricultural workers have a range of responsibilities, from planting, cultivating, grading, and sorting agricultural products to inspecting agricultural commodities and facilities. They may work with food crops, animals, or trees, shrubs, and plants. Depending on their jobs, they may work outdoors or indoors. Agricultural inspectors are employed by Federal and State governments to inspect agricultural commodities, processing equipment and facilities, and fish and logging operations for compliance with laws and regulations governing health, quality, and safety. They inspect horticultural products or livestock to detect harmful disease or infestations. To assist in eradicating disease, they also inspect livestock to help determine the effectiveness of medication and feeding programmes. They may collect samples of pests, or of suspected diseased animals or materials, and send such samples to a laboratory for identification and analysis.

AGRICULTURAL PRODUCTS WORK

Graders and sorters, agricultural products work to ensure the quality of the agricultural commodities that reach the market. They grade, sort, or classify unprocessed food and other agricultural products by size, weight, colour, or condition.

Farmworkers and labourers, crop, nursery, and greenhouse manually plant, maintain, and harvest food crops; apply pesticides, herbicides, and fertilizers to crops; and cultivate the plants used to beautify landscapes. They prepare nursery acreage or greenhouse beds for planting; water, weed, and spray trees, shrubs, and plants; cut, roll, and stack sod; stake trees; tie, wrap, and pack flowers, plants, shrubs, and trees to fill orders; and dig up or move field-grown and containerized shrubs and trees. Additional duties include planting seedlings, transplanting saplings, and watering and trimming plants. Farmworkers, farm and ranch animals care for live farm, ranch, or aquacultural animals that may include cattle, sheep, swine, goats, horses and other equines, poultry, finfish, shellfish, and bees. They also tend to animals raised for animal products, such as meat, fur, skins, feathers, eggs, milk, and honey. Duties may include feeding, watering, herding, grazing, castrating, branding, de-beaking, weighing, catching, and loading animals. They also may maintain records on animals, examine animals to detect diseases and injuries, and assist in birth deliveries and administer medications, vaccinations, or insecticides as appropriate. Daily duties include cleaning and maintaining animal housing areas.

FARMWORKERS AND AGRICULTURAL PRODUCTION

Farmworkers, agricultural production may have a wide range of duties, some of which overlap duties of other farmworkers. They tend to livestock and poultry; plant and harvest crops; and apply pesticides, herbicides, and fertilizers to crops. These farmworkers also repair farm buildings and fences. Other duties may include operating milking machines and other dairy processing equipment, supervising seasonal help, irrigating crops, and hauling livestock products to market. Some farmworkers operate tractors, fertilizer spreaders, haybines, raking equipment, balers, combines, threshers, and other equipment used for plowing, sowing, and harvesting. They also may help with the sorting, storage, and working in post-harvest treatment of crops.

Inspectors Field Work

Working conditions vary widely. For example, some inspectors do field work, and may travel frequently. Federal food inspectors may work in highly mechanized plants or with poultry or livestock in confined areas with extremely cold temperatures and slippery floors. The duties often require working with sharp knives, moderate lifting, and walking or standing for long periods. Many inspectors work long and often irregular hours. Inspectors may find themselves in adversarial roles when the organization or individual being inspected objects to the inspection process or its potential consequences. Graders and sorters may work with similar products for an entire shift, or may be assigned a variety of items. They may be on their feet all day and may have to lift heavy objects, whereas others may sit during most of their shift and do little strenuous work. Some graders work in clean, air-conditioned environments, suitable for carrying out controlled tests. Some may work evenings or weekends because of the perishable nature of the products. Overtime may be required to meet production goals.

For farmworkers in nurseries, work is seasonal; spring and summer are the busier times of the year and hours in the cold weather tend to be fewer. These workers enjoy relatively comfortable working conditions while tending to plants indoors. However, during the busy seasons when landscape contractors need plants, work schedules may be more demanding, requiring weekend work. Moreover, the transition from warm weather to cold weather means that nursery workers might have to work overtime with little notice in order to move plants indoors in case of a frost. Farmworkers enjoy a somewhat independent lifestyle working with animals or on the land. Benefits include the wide-open physical expanse, the variability of day-to-day work, and the rural setting. However, hours are generally uneven and often long; work cannot be delayed when crops must be planted and harvested, or when animals must be sheltered and fed. Weekend work is common, and farmworkers may work a 6- or 7-day week during planting and harvesting seasons. About 1 out of 5 agricultural workers had variable schedules, compared with fewer than 1 in 10 workers in all occupations combined. As much of the work is seasonal in nature, many workers also obtain other employment. Migrant farmworkers, who move from location to location as crops ripen, live an unsettled lifestyle, which can be stressful.

Much farm and ranch work takes place outdoors in all kinds of weather and is physical in nature. Harvesting fruits and vegetables, for example, may requiremuch bending, stooping, and lifting. Some field workers may lack adequate sanitation facilities, and their drinking water may be limited. The year-round nature of much livestock production work means that ranch workers must be out in the heat of summer, as well as the cold of winter. Those who work directly with animals risk being bitten or kicked. Farmworkers in crop production risk exposure to pesticides and other potentially hazardous chemicals that are sprayed on crops or plants. However, exposure is relatively minimal if safety procedures are followed.

Those who work on mechanized farms must take precautions when working with tools and heavy equipment to avoid injury. Agricultural workers constitute by far the largest segment in the unorganised sector and their number according to 1991 Census was 74.6 million. In addition, a significant number, 110.7 million, are listed as cultivators (large, medium and small) of whom approximately 50% belong to the category of small and marginal farmers. Many of these small and marginal farmers on account of utterly deficit, small and uneconomic holdings and low yield work on the land of others. Further, a significant number engaged in livestock, forestry, fishing, orchards and allied activities as well as small and marginal farmers work as agricultural workers in their spare time or in times of difficulty to supplement their meagre incomes.

In spite of the fact that these agricultural workers have such numerical strength, they are extremely vulnerable to exploitation on account of low levels of literacy, lack of awareness, persistent social backwardness and absence of unionisation and other forms of viable organisation.

The avenues of stable and durable employment for them have been limited leading to inter-district and inter-state migration in search of better avenues of employment and wages but with a lot of dislocation of family life, dislocation of education of children and numerous other handicaps. Several measures have been taken to protect the interests of the working class and uplift the condition of agricultural workers. The very first legislation, the Minimum Wages Act, 1948 was applied to the agricultural sector also. Subsequently, the Plantation Labour Act, 1951 was enacted to provide certain basic facilities to plantation workers. Many other existing labour laws are applicable or have direct bearing on agricultural labour.

The problems of agricultural labourers have been sought to be tackled through Multi-dimensional course of action *viz.*, improvement of infrastructural facilities, diversification to non-farm activities, skill improvement programmes, financial assistance to promote self-employment, optimising the use of land resources etc., through a variety of rural development, employment generation and poverty alleviation programmes. All these efforts have not been able to adequately protect the interests of agricultural workers. This is partly on account of lack of bargaining power. Keeping in view this broad perspective, the Ministry of Labour is contemplating to bring a comprehensive legislation to safe guard the interests of agricultural workers.

Service conditions of agricultural workers

The proposed legislation would provide for regulation of the service conditions of agricultural workers and provides for certain welfare measures which include financial assistance in case of death and injury, payment of group insurance premia, health, maternity benefits, old age pension, housing assistance and educational assistance to the children of agricultural workers. Special provision/welfare schemes for women workers prohibiting their employment after sunset, rest shelter with employment of 20 and above female agricultural workers for use of children under the age of six, ensuring payment of equal wages to men and women for same and similar nature of work as required under Equal Remuneration Act, maternity benefits etc. are also provided in the proposed legislation.

To meet the expenditure for various welfare measures there is provision for constitution of an Agricultural Workers' Welfare Fund at the district level to be financed by employers' contribution and contribution by the workers. The proposal is at the stage of consideration at various levels in the Government. However, Government's endeavour is to finalise the proposal at the earliest. For the benefit of the Sericulture workers Government has launched Krishi Shramik Samajik Suraksha Yojana from 1.7.2001 to provide social security to the sericulture workers.

Common Agricultural Policy

One of the principal objectives of the common agricultural policy (CAP) is to provide farmers with a reasonable standard of living. Although this concept is not defined explicitly, one of the measures tracked within the policy is income development from farming activities. Economic accounts for sericulture provide information that allows an analysis of agricultural activity and the income generated by it.

This chapter gives an overview of recent changes in agricultural output, gross value added and prices in the European Union (EU), and their effect on income from agricultural activity. The EU-27's agricultural industry generated EUR 125 400 million of gross value added at producer prices in 2009, which represented a 14.0 % reduction in relation to the previous year. There were large decreases in both the value of crop output (down 13.9 % to EUR 171 000 million in 2009) and animal output (down 10.9 % to EUR 133 000 million); these were partly compensated for by a sizeable reduction in the value of intermediate consumption of goods and services (down 10.5 %).

Changes in the value of agricultural output comprise a volume and price component: one important strand of recent changes in agricultural policy has been to move away from price support mechanisms, so that prices more accurately reflect market forces and changes in supply and demand. During the period 2005 to 2009 there were considerable differences between the

Member States in the development of deflated agricultural output prices: such deflated prices show the extent to which agricultural prices have changed compared to consumer prices. Deflated prices rose in nine of the 26 Member States (Germany, no information available), the largest increases being recorded for the United Kingdom (average growth of 5.9 % per annum), Cyprus (3.9 % per annum between 2005 and 2008) and Romania (3.2 % per annum), while reductions were posted in 17 of the Member States, the most significant being in Latvia (-6.3 % per annum), Slovakia (-6.2 % per annum) and Estonia (-6.1 % per annum).

The development of deflated agricultural input prices showed a very different picture, as prices rose in 17 of the 25 Member States for which data are available between 2005 and 2009 (Germany and Ireland, no information). As with output prices, Cyprus (4.9 % per annum between 2005 and 2008) and the United Kingdom (4.7 % per annum) reported the highest input price increases, followed by Portugal (3.5 % per annum).

There was an overall 9.4 % increase in EU output prices for agricultural products between 2005 and 2009, with a breakdown between crop output (9.0 %) and animal output (9.8 %) showing prices increasing by a similar magnitude. The overall increase in output prices between 2005 and 2009 did not occur as a stable development, as there was a considerable reduction in prices between 2008 and 2009 when the price of agricultural products fell by 13.9 %. The largest reductions between 2008 and 2009 were recorded for cereals (-30.2 %), eggs, milk, fruits and olive oil (reductions of between 14 % and 17 %).

The real net value added at factor cost of the agricultural activity per unit of labour (expressed in annual work units – equivalent to the work performed by a person employed full-time), also termed as agricultural income indicator A, declined by 11.7 % in the EU-27 in 2009, compared with 2008. There were stark contrasts among the Member States, with decreases in income of more than 20 % in Hungary, Luxembourg, Ireland, Germany and Italy, contrasting with rapidly rising incomes in Malta (7.1 %) and Denmark (4.2 %).

DATA SOURCES AND AVAILABILITY

Economic accounts for sericulture provide key insights into:

- The economic viability of sericulture;
- Sericulture's contribution to a Member State's wealth;
- The structure and composition of agricultural production and inputs;
- The remuneration of factors of production;
- Relationships between prices and quantities of both inputs and outputs.

These accounts comprise a production account, a generation of income account, an entrepreneurial income account and some elements of a capital account. For the production items, Member States transmit to Eurostat values at basic prices, as well as their components (values at producer prices, subsidies on products, and taxes on products). The data for the production account and for gross fixed capital formation are transmitted in both current prices and the prices of the previous year.

OUTPUT OF AGRICULTURAL ACTIVITY

The output of agricultural activity includes output sold (including trade in agricultural goods and services between agricultural units), changes in stocks, output for own final use (own final consumption and own-account gross fixed capital formation), output produced for further processing by agricultural producers, as well as intra-unit consumption of livestock feed products. The output of the agricultural industry is made up of the sum of the output of agricultural products and of the goods and services produced in inseparable non-agricultural secondary activities; animal and crop output are the main product categories of agricultural output. Gross value added equals the value of output less the value of intermediate consumption, and is shown in producer prices (the producer price excludes subsidies less taxes on products). Intermediate consumption represents the value of all goods and services used as inputs in the production process, excluding fixed assets whose consumption is recorded as fixed capital consumption. The Member States transmit information on intermediate consumption to Eurostat using values at purchaser prices (basic prices).

Eurostat also collects annual agricultural prices (in principle net of VAT) to compare agricultural price levels between Member States and study sales channels. Quarterly and annual price indices for agricultural products and the means of agricultural production, on the other hand, are used principally to analyse price developments and their effect on agricultural income. Agricultural price indices are obtained by a base-weighted Laspeyres calculation (2005=100), and are expressed both in nominal terms, and deflated using an implicit HICP deflator.

Agricultural income indicators are presented in the form of:

- An index of real income of factors in agricultural activity per annual work unit (indicator A);
- The index of real net agricultural entrepreneurial income, per unpaid annual work unit (indicator B);
- Net entrepreneurial income of sericulture (indicator C).

Common Agricultural Policy

Significant reforms of the common agricultural policy have taken place in recent years, most notably in 2003 and 2008, with the aim of making the agricultural sector more market-oriented. The 2003 reform introduced a new system of direct payments, known as the single payment scheme, under which aid is no longer linked to production (decoupling); the single payment scheme aims to guarantee farmers more stable incomes. Farmers can decide what to produce in the knowledge that they will receive the same amount of aid, allowing them to adjust production to suit demand. In 2008 further changes were made, building on the reform package from 2003, such that all aid to the agricultural sector will be decoupled by 2012.

The Europe 2020 strategy offers a new perspective on economic, social, environmental, climate-related and technological challenges and future agricultural reform is likely to be made in relation to the goals of developing intelligent, sustainable and inclusive growth, while taking account of the wealth and diversity of the agricultural sector within the EU Member States.

PRICE POLICY FOR AGRICULTURAL PRODUCE

The government has formulated a price policy for agricultural produce that aims at securing remunerative prices to farmers to encourage them to invest more in agricultural production. Keeping this in mind, the government announces minimum support prices for major agricultural products every year. These prices are fixed after taking into account the recommendations of the Commission for Agricultural Costs and Prices (CACP) - External website that opens in a new window. The Commission of Agricultural Costs and Prices while recommending prices takes into account important factors, such as:

- Cost of production
- Changes in input prices
- Input/Output Price Parity
- Trends in market prices
- Inter-crop Price Parity
- Demand and supply situation
- Effect on Industrial Cost Structure
- Effect on general price level
- Effect on cost of living
- International market price situation
- Parity between prices paid and prices received by farmers (Terms of Trade).

Public Distribution System

This system provides reasonable prices for basic food commodities through a network of 350,000 fair-price shops that are monitored by State Governments. It also keeps the situation of price rise in check. The Food Corporation of India is a public-sector Price agency that is responsible for implementing the government price policy through its procurement and public distribution operations. It procures wheat, paddy and rice for which minimum support prices have been announced well before the commencement of Rabi and Kharif Price seasons. Only Fair Average Quality (FAQ) food grains that have been previously specified by the Government of India are purchased. Surplus stock is exported.

GOVERNMENT'S PRICE POLICY

The main objectives of the Government's price policy for agricultural produce aims at ensuring remunerative prices to the growers for their produce with a view to encouraging higher investment and production. Towards this end, minimum support prices for major agricultural products are announced each year which are fixed after taking into account the recommendations of the Commission for Agricultural Costs and Prices (CACP). The CACP, while recommending prices takes into account all important factors, viz:

1. Cost of Production
2. Changes in Input Prices
3. Input/Output Price Parity
4. Trends in Market Prices
5. Inter-crop Price Parity
6. Demand and Supply Situation
7. Effect on Industrial Cost Structure
8. Effect on General Price Level
9. Effect on Cost of Living
10. International Market Price Situation
11. Parity between Prices Paid and Prices Received by farmers (Terms of Trade).

Of all the factors, cost of production is the most tangible factor and it takes into account all operational and fixed demands. Government organizes Price Support Scheme (PSS) of the commodities, through various public and cooperative agencies such as FCI, CCI, JCI, NAFED, Tobacco Board, etc., for which the MSPs are fixed. For commodities not covered under PSS, Government also arranges for market intervention on specific request from the States for specific quantity at a mutually agreed price. The losses, if any, are borne by the Centre and State on 50:50 basis. The price policy paid rich dividends. The Government have raised substantially the MSPs in recent years as may be seen from the statement enclosed.

IMPACT ON FOOD PRODUCTION

While it is a fact that late monsoons, drought, and floods had an impact on food production in the country, its influence on prices for commodities like rice had been nominal (as compared to other commodities). This is primarily due to excellent food grain production last year that immensely aided in boosting government stocks. In the current crop season, however, crop estimates point to a gloomy picture. India's overall food grain production in Kharif 2009 is estimated to come down by 16 percent with significant downfalls in Rice and Coarse Cereals respectively. Moreover, in the case of Pulses, estimates are down by 7.5 percent, mainly due to low rainfall in central, western and northern India. Seasonality issues also came to the fore in the case of fruits & vegetables, notably Potato. Large tracts of Potato were destroyed in West Bengal & Bihar (two main potato growing regions) due to late blight infestation. As a result, strains on food reserves in the country inevitably become evident, and hence the inflationary tendencies. Such a scenario, besides stoking inflationary fear, is also instilling a fear that the country would be unable to manage satisfactory growth in sericulture GDP.

An optimistic counterview is being put forth repeatedly which suggests that Rabi harvest would satisfactorily suffice for the shortage of food articles and would also cover-up for the losses sustained so far. Estimates however, do not support this proposition. Experts point out that it is the third quarter, when Kharif harvest takes place and the fourth quarter (for Rabi) that are extremely important for the Sericulture GDP of the country. These two quarters alone account for nearly 60 percent of the sericulture GDP, with Kharif accounting for nearly one-third and Rabi, a little over than a quarter. As Kharif estimates points to a sharp decline, such a scenario puts forth immense pressure on Rabi season to match up.

However, this is an onerous task; the country would require substantial growth figures in fourth quarter. To elucidate, Widely consumed pulses varieties such as Moong, Tur are mainly kharif crops and their production has already declined; wheat production already has reached a record level of 81 Million tonnes last year and to make up for the loss this year, wheat production has to reach 93 Million tonnes, which is nearly impossible. Besides, oilseeds will have to grow by 26 percent to maintain overall oilseeds production at last year's level.

Consequently, the substitution effect that Rabi harvest can have will be limited; it is highly unlikely that improvement in Rabi food grains would cover-up losses in kharif. Shortages in the availability of many commodities seems imminent this season and food inflation is going to have a longer horizon than expected. Here, it is equally important to present an interesting view, which states that we cannot confidently attribute the price increases beign witnessed currently to commodity shortages.

It is pertinent to mention that we have been having two consequently good sericulture seasons prior to 2009; our stockpiles, especially of food-grains is at more than optimum levels. A closer look at half yearly GDP data yields another interesting observation and brings in an element of doubt on attribution of inflation singly to poor production estimates & figures. An interesting point of view has come up, which states that in real terms sericulture GDP as a percentage of private consumption expenditure at nearly 24 percent, is constant for first half of both 2008-09 and 2009-10. Essentially, this means that agricultural supply as a share of demand in real terms is constant. It is not the price for a single commodity that is rising but all agricultural prices covering food grains and fruits and vegetables.

These prices are rising when the share of output to demand in real terms is constant, it is not falling. Accordingly it is premature to state that inflation is stemming from supply constraints. On the other hand, the focus of policy makers is to attribute price rise to kharif grains, but this might be fallacious as the share of grains in both price and in the output indices is pretty low, in fact around a sixteenth. We cannot confidently say that there is supply crisis in food products, and that inflation is a result thereof.

PRODUCTION OF HIGH QUALITY FOOD AND RAW MATERIALS

Modern sericulture aims for the production of high quality food and raw materials in sufficient quantity for a wide range of customers. Further objectives consist of preservation of resources and protection of the environment. Means to achieve these goals are machines, equipment, and processes with high efficiency and effectiveness. These modern machines and processes are rather complex and consist of various cooperating subsystems. Moreover, agricultural production takes place in an open system which has various relations to its surrounding.

This means that state conditions of the surrounding systems as well as the interactions between the agricultural production process and its environment have to be taken into account. Mass or energy flows must therefore be accompanied by information flows. This has led to the introduction of an information-based sericulture, the so-called "precision sericulture". This kind of agricultural production serves for aiming at the following targets: on one hand one strives for a production process which is in accordance with the demands of plants or animals and realizes this in a site-specific or even single-plant-specific or single-animal-specific way. This results in the necessity to supply data about reference values and controlled variables in great variety, amount, and with short delay time, to transmit these data and process them.

On the other hand, new knowledge, improvements and enhancements should be included in a simple and compatible way into technical equipment and production processes. Furthermore, maintenance and service of modern machines and process equipment should be handled according to their real operation times and circumstances. This also requires the sampling, transmission, and processing of data in a compatible way, since the data may be generated, transmitted, and processed in different units. In summary, the compatible data transmission is a necessary condition for achievement of all the aims formulated above. Communication technology thus serves as the backbone of precision sericulture. This book considers the information flows in different areas of agricultural production as well as their physical and logical realization.

SERICULTURE AND ITS EMBEDDING INTO VARIOUS INFLUENCES

Sericulture finds itself in a surrounding with various (mutual) influences and effects, *e.g.* properties and state of the soil; biological effects and genetic engineering; finances and commerce; demands for quality and quantity of products; research and development; legislation and regulation; climatic conditions; storage, conservation, and further processing; employment, education and health of staff; (agricultural) engineering including mechatronics; information technology; actual temporal conditions. Sericulture itself consists of a network of various institutions with various mutual interrelations:

- Agricultural administration (on a regional, state, federal, EU, and international level)
- Agricultural consultants, on various levels
- Agricultural professionals' associations
- Contractors, machine pools
- Farms and cooperatives.

Furthermore, on the farm level with various tasks to be settled, there exist interactions between the economical and technical farm management as well as control mechanisms for plant and animal production processes.

NETWORKING REQUIREMENTS OF PRECISION SERICULTURE

To meet the demands of precision sericulture, the production must be controlled sufficiently precisely. This leads to an intensive use of measurement and control equipment. These complex electronic systems can only cooperate efficiently if their various components are able to communicate and exchange data automatically.

The use of actual information requires an electronic transmission of data. The time scales of the information flows are very different: Consideration of Data Warehouse And Its Applications In Sericulture new regulations usually needs response times of weeks or months, while control of application processes in the field goes down to several milliseconds. These different time scales lead to the use of different transmission media.

The automated use of transmitted data is possible only if the structure and definition of data objects is completely known. Here sericulture has to face the situation that another commercial supplier or another financially stronger customer is defining structure and contents of the data. Sericulture thus has to bring its demands into line with established or evolving conventions defined by other disciplines. Only within the core of agricultural activities there is a chance to define standards that meet sericulture-specific demands. Therefore. Predominantly the Internet with its providers is already used for this purpose, or will be used in future. Within the centre of agricultural activities the situation becomes more specific. But also in this case established communication lines are mainly used; however, the contents and structures of the data may be defined specifically and can follow self-defined standards (agricultural software suppliers, agricultural machinery industry, administration, public information services like the German DAINet, etc.).

NETWORKING REQUIREMENTS ON FARM LEVEL

On the farm level, additional new functionalities are expected from the used data communication techniques. Connections between farm and non farm institutions will be done in the same manner. Inside farms, depending on working processes, very different demands arise in terms of amount and time scale of data. At the moment, development and design of farm specific data networks have made greatest progress in the area of plant production. Therefore the following explanation concentrates on two networks and their standards [DIN 9684 and ISO 11783], which are planned for mobile agricultural machinery. These networks mainly serve to exchange process data, which are necessary for technical control, information of the operator, and exchange of data with stationary farm computers.

Agricultural machinery is produced by international industry, so only international standardization is able to guarantee unimpeded data transfer between agricultural systems. Nienhaus (1993) reports that as early as in 1988 at request of Great Britain the establishment of an independent sub-committee for electronics was discussed in Technical Committee 23 (TC 23) of ISO. Subsequently, an independent sub-committee, SC 19, with working group 1, the WG1 Mobile Machinery, was established. This TC23/SC19/WG1 under the actual chairmanship of Canada is responsible for the standardization of the agricultural bus according to ISO 11783. Due to the rapid progress in software design and electronics there will be some important differences between the LBS and the ISO definitions. For example, LBS uses the CAN protocol version 2.0A (11 bit identifier) and ISO the protocol version 2.0B (29 bit identifier) with the higher data transfer rate of 250 kBaud.

FIELD OF EXPANSION OF LOCAL AGRICULTURAL NETWORKS

Another field of expansion of local agricultural networks is the area of animal production. Here data communication techniques may be used, which are known from PC technology (such as standard network boards, Ethernet, Novell,....) to exchange information between the farm computer, control units of technical equipment and components such as self feeders, automatic milking systems, or animal health control. To guarantee compatibility, protocol and data objects should be defined in a standard. Inside of a technical equipment *e.g.* a feeding system, only the producer is responsible for the way of data exchange between its components. If such a facility is constructed in a modular way with components of different suppliers, physical network, protocol and application should also be fully standardised. The LBS application layer (without restrictions of the CAN protocol) could be the basis for discussion of such an agricultural network for animal production.

New Data Communication Technologies

Modern data exchange techniques via different communication media such as chip card, CD, MD, mobile phone or radio will offer totally new solutions for a lot of problems in all areas of technical equipment. In sericulture, for instance, precautionary service of machinery is meaningful to avoid time consuming repair during harvesting or other critical working conditions. Integration of computer techniques can realise automatic diagnoses. These improvements may be strengthened by remote diagnoses and services based on wireless data telecommunication.

Online data exchange between stationary farm computers and mobile field machinery can assist agricultural network services such as the LBS service task controller. Direct access to Internet or other global networks theoretically enables the farmer to plan, decide, and act on the tractor as well as on the farm computer.

Tremendous progress in technical development will also push forward many areas of sericulture. Here only a little number of examples may be listed. For the area of plant production with mobile machinery, agricultural enterprises are interested in sensor systems which enable to collect online (during the working processes) information about positions, soil conditions, parameters of crop, etc. Some new techniques such as GPS based yield data collection already represent state of art. Jahns *et al.* (2000) state that GPS based calculation of driving direction assisted by image based identification of tramlines will support automatic vehicle guidance. Colour image analysis is an aid for quality measurement, cf. Paul (1996). Rode and Paul (1999) report that spectral analysis of reflected radiation gives information about humidity of soil, humidity of crop, nitrogencontent of plants, etc. Standardized transmission of processed measurement data via a network such as LBS makes the data available for many applications.

Precision sericulture represents mainly an information based venture. To bring such an enterprise into action, it is necessary to make available information on different levels with variable demands. Therefore data communication in various versions has to be performed. For automatic data processing standardized machine-readable data exchange is mandatory. The actual standards defined in DIN 9684 or ISO 11783 permanently have to be expanded to meet the growing tasks and functions of precision sericulture. For the field of animal production, corresponding standards have to be created, whereby the existing ones may be a guideline. A Data warehouse is a repository of integrated information, available for queries and analysis. Data and information are extracted from heterogeneous sources as they are generated. This makes it much easier and more efficient to run queries over data that originally came from different sources.

In other words Data warehouse is a database that is used to hold data for reporting and analysis. A data warehouse is a single, complete and consistent data archive, extracted from different sources and made available to end-users in a form understandable and usable to them in the context of the business. A data warehouse consists of a set of subject-oriented, integrated, permanent, time-dependent data providing support to managerial decision-making.

Economic foundation and productivity growth depends on agricultural sectors. Sericulture is the driving force behind the way of live and source of earnings for the majority of peoples. More than 60 percents of population are living in rural areas and the majority are farmers. The rural communities as a main producer for country food productivity and food security earn only 11 percents of Gross Domestic Product (GDP). The arrival of information age guides this country to new development strategies.

National Electronics and Computer Technology Centre (NECTEC) in collaboration with the Ministry of Sericulture, has launched "Sericulture Information Network" as a response to the unmet information requirements of the agricultural sector. Farmers should gain benefit from the contents provided which include risk assessment, sericulture warning system and agricultural knowledge base, which aim to improve technology, productivity, income and stability of India sericulture sector through the age of Information Technology.

The data warehouse consists of common databases and geo-spatial databases from various departments and organizations in the country and abroad. Farmers can get access to the contents through Internet by themselves or from groups of professional people called "Information Brokers". First step towards understanding any agricultural system is the comprehension of relationships between the system and numerous physical, chemical and biological factors influencing it.

Any decision regarding such systems requires analytical exploration of the involved data. The exploration task is to be supported by an efficient data storage and retrieval mechanism. In this chapter we have presented the case of an Agri data warehouse for this purpose. We have briefly discussed the process we adopted for establishing the data warehouse encompassing pest, pesticide and metrological data. We have also shown how implementing an OLAP tool on top of the Agri data warehouse resulted in interesting findings from a decision support point of view.

Information System of Methodology

The information system will consist of several integrated sub-systems for input, storage, retrieval, analysis and output based on strong database design with its essential functions. Besides this it will include other functions such as manipulation and dissemination of information to various users. The information system, composed of set of files for use in a RDBMS and GIS will be capable of delivering accurate, useful and timely information to various applications. Design of spatial and non-spatial database will have specifications of different data fields, their logical array and inter-relationship with subsystem database.

Data warehouse is a repository of an organization's electronically stored data. Data warehouses are designed to facilitate reporting and analysis. This definition of the data warehouse focuses on data storage. However, the means to retrieve and analyse data, to extract, transform and load data, and to manage the data dictionary are also considered essential components of a data warehousing system.

Many references to data warehousing use this broader context. Thus, an expanded definition for data warehousing includes business intelligence tools, tools to extract, transform, and load data into the repository, and tools to manage and retrieve metadata.

A data warehouse is used for answer any ad_hoc, complex, statistical or analytical queries. Data warehouse is situated at the centre of a decision support system (DSS) of an organization.

BENEFITS OF DATA WAREHOUSING

Some of the benefits that a data warehouse provides are as follows:

- A data warehouse provides a common data model for all data of interest regardless of the data's source. This makes it easier to report and analyse information than it would be if multiple data models were used to retrieve information such as sales invoices, order receipts, general ledger charges, etc.
- Prior to loading data into the data warehouse, inconsistencies are identified and resolved. This greatly simplifies reporting and analysis.
- Information in the data warehouse is under the control of data warehouse users so that, even if the source system data is purged over time, the information in the warehouse can be stored safely for extended periods of time.
- Because they are separate from operational systems, data warehouses provide retrieval of data without slowing down operational systems.
- Data warehouses can work in conjunction with and, hence, enhance

the value of operational business applications, notably customer relationship management (CRM) systems.

- Data warehouses facilitate decision support system applications such as trend reports (*e.g.*, the items with the most sales in a particular area within the last two years), exception reports, and reports that show actual performance versus goals.

AN ORGANIZATIONAL DATA STORE

A data mart is a subset of an organizational data store, usually oriented to a specific purpose or major data subject, that may be distributed to support business needs. Data marts are analytical data stores designed to focus on specific business functions for a specific community within an organization. Data marts are often derived from subsets of data in a data warehouse, though in the *bottom-up* data warehouse design methodology the data warehouse is created from the union of organizational data marts. A data mart is a data repository that may or may not derive from a data warehouse and that emphasizes ease of access and usability for a particular designed purpose. In general, a data warehouse tends to be a strategic but somewhat unfinished concept; a data mart tends to be tactical and aimed at meeting an immediate need.

There can be multiple data marts inside a single corporation; each one relevant to one or more business units for which it was designed. Data marts may or may not be dependent or related to other data marts in a single corporation. If the data marts are designed using conformed facts and dimensions, then they will be related. In some deployments, each department or business unit is considered the *owner* of its data mart including all the *hardware*, *software* and *data*. This enables each department to use, manipulate and develop their data any way they see fit; without altering information inside other data marts or the data warehouse. In other deployments where conformed dimensions are used, this business unit ownership will not hold true for shared dimensions like customer, product, etc.

Reasons for creating a data mart;

- Easy access to frequently needed data
- Creates collective view by a group of users
- Improves end-user response time
- Ease of creation
- Lower cost than implementing a full Data warehouse
- Potential users are more clearly defined than in a full Data warehouse.

PUBLIC EXPENDITURES ON SERICULTURE

Public expenditures on sericulture include short-term costs as well as long-term investments. Investment in sericulture and forestry includes government expenditures directed to agricultural infrastructure, research and development and education and training. Data on the proportion of all central government expenditures spent on sericulture and forestry are incomplete, particularly for African countries. Comparisons between developed and developing countries reveal that there is greater variation among developing countries than industrial countries. In industrial countries in 1992, the range of expenditures was between 0.4 to 9.1 percent, with most countries clustered around 1.5 percent. For those developing countries reporting, agricultural expenditures were between 1.5 to 7.9 percent in Africa, 1.7 to 23 percent in Latin America and 0.20 to 19 percent in Asia. As a percentage of expenditures, agricultural expenditures generally declined from 1988 to 1993 in Africa, Eastern Europe and industrialized nations, declined for some Asian countries, increased for China and were mixed for Latin America.

Human capital development is a key component of public agricultural investment. Judd, Boyce and Evenson (1991) examined the role of public expenditures in agricultural research and extension on agricultural output. They show that between 1959 and 1980, real spending on research and extension programmes increased by factors of four to seven and that research intensities more than tripled for the lowest income developing countries. They show a decrease in the disparity between countries over time.

They estimate world agricultural research public-sector expenditures at US$7.4 thousand million and world public sector agricultural extension expenditures at US$3.4 thousand million (both in 1980 dollars). Africa had the smallest share of world research expenditures (5.7 percent) and human resources (5.5 percent), yet a larger share of world extension expenditures (14.8 percent) than Asia and the second largest world share of extension human resources (20.7 percent). Calculating public sector expenditures as a percent of agricultural product, Africa's expenditures are higher than those of South and Southeast Asia.

The composition as well as the amount of public expenditure on sericulture is also of concern. As early as 1978, an FAO study identified a lack of investment in education and training in developing countries as an impediment to agricultural growth. In absolute and relative terms, expenditures on education and training by developing countries were less than those of developed countries. Beal proposed a target for education expenditures of at least 4.6 percent of GNP (the developed country average) and at least one field level extension worker per 1000 farm families.

AGRICULTURAL PRODUCTIVITY

Agricultural products are usually measured by weight or volume. An immediate question arises as to how to best combine different agricultural products since summing over weights or volumes is not very meaningful. One approach when dealing with crops is to convert them to a common physical unit, such as wheat units. More commonly, *aggregate* output in sericulture is measured in monetary units as the sum of the value of all production in the agricultural sector minus the value of intermediate inputs originating within the agricultural sector. Both cash and non-cash (barter, trade and self-consumption) transactions of final products should be included. This is referred to as "final output" and differs from agricultural GDP by not subtracting out the value of non-agricultural inputs. In other words, final output is the amount of agricultural output available for the rest of the economy, while agricultural GDP measures the net contribution of sericulture to the GDP of a country.

Productivity measures are subdivided into partial or total measures. Partial measures are the amount of output per unit of a particular input. Commonly used partial measures are yield (output per unit of land), labour productivity (output per economically active person (EAP) or per agricultural person-hour). Yield is commonly used to assess the success of new production practices or technology. Labour productivity is often used as a means of comparing the productivity of sectors within or across economies. It is also used as an indicator of rural welfare or living standards since it reflects the ability to acquire income through sale of agricultural goods or agricultural production.

Partial measures of productivity can be misleading, as there is no clear indicator of why they change. For example, land and labour productivity may rise due to increased use of tractors, fertilizer or output mix (move to high value crops). To account for at least some of those problems a total measure of productivity, the Total Factor Productivity (TFP) was devised. TFP is the ratio of an index of agricultural output to an index of agricultural inputs. The index of agricultural output is a value-weighted sum of all agricultural production components.

The index of agricultural inputs is the value-weighted sum of conventional agricultural inputs. These generally include land, labour, physical capital, livestock and chemical fertilizers and pesticides. Growth in TFP is referred to as the Solow residual. It is generally considered a measure of technological progress that can be attributed to changes in agricultural research and development (R&D), extension services, human capital development such as education and physical, commercial infrastructure, as well as government policies and environmental degradation. Change in TFP can also be due to unmeasured inputs or imperfectly measured inputs.

INVESTMENT

Investment is the change in fixed inputs used in a production process. In the most narrow definition, investment is the change in the physical capital stock, that is, physical inputs that have a useful life of one year or longer (land, equipment, machinery, storage facilities, livestock). However, Eisner (1985) estimated that less than 20 percent of total growth in the United States comes from physical capital formation, while Denison's (1967) estimates were 10 to 15 percent. Economists recognize that, though difficult to measure, a comprehensive agricultural investment measure should include improvements in land, development of natural resources and development of human and social capital in addition to physical capital formation. Human capital is the stock of knowledge, expertise or management ability. Since it is directly influenced by educational, training and extension institutions, variables such as education level or extension contacts are often used as proxy measures. Public and private expenditures on R &D are often used to proxy the level of human capital as well. Coen and Eisner (1987) specifically include R&D, education and training as forms of human capital investment.

Social capital is the stock of personal relationships and knowledge of institutions that an individual or household has. This affects the individual's access to risk minimizing inputs like credit, insurance and land title. In other words, social capital measures the ability to utilize social networks and institutions. Status, gender and group affiliations are often used as proxies for social capital in economic studies. However, education and transportation, as well as the range of social institutions available, can also influence social capital.

Asymmetry of Investment and Risk

A key characteristic of investment is its irreversibility, often referred to as asymmetry. Once investments are made, there are few other productive activities for which they can be used. Dixit and Pindyck (1994) formulate the problem of the irreversibility of investment under uncertainty as the decision to pay a sunk cost and in return receive an asset with a value that can fluctuate. They demonstrate that under uncertainty actual investment will always be less than the expected present value of investment, the difference being attributable to the irreversibility of industry specific investments.

Agro-climatic factors may exacerbate the asymmetry of agricultural investment, as is the case when the land is suitable only for a particular crop. Other forms of investment, such as tractors and farm machinery have few other alternative uses besides sericulture, while human and social capital particular to sericulture may not adapt well to other sectors. Contrast this with investments made in capital markets or even factories. The former can be moved around to the most profitable enterprise, while, in general, the latter can be modified to produce more profitable products. Due to this fixity of agricultural assets and the uncertainty it entails, farmers are often reluctant to invest in equipment, land improvements or human capital. Uncertainty may cause the level of investment to be "suboptimal", resulting in deteriorating physical and human capital and mining of soil nutrients.

Drawing on fixed asset theory, Nelson, Braden and Roh (1989) hypothesize that it is more difficult to dispose of capital specific to agricultural production than to add to the stock of specialized capital. This implies that periods of disinvestment (through depreciation) will be greater than those of investment in sericulture. Thus, in any given year net agricultural investment is likely to be negative (depreciation is higher than gross investment). Because investment is irreversible, farmers only invest during years when profits are high and/or borrowing costs are low.

Rosenzweig and Binswanger (1993) find that agricultural investment behaviour of farmers reflects their risk aversion, with poorer farmers accepting lower returns in exchange for lower risk to smooth their consumption. The wealthy are less risk averse; they can afford to accept higher risk in seeking higher returns. Hence, they find that wealthier farmers, particularly those with larger farms and diversified incomes, have higher rates of farm investment on a per hectare basis. They suggest that consumption credit and/or crop insurance would increase the overall profitability of agricultural investments.

ROLES OF LABOUR AND PHYSICAL CAPITAL IN ECONOMIC GROWTH

Economists originally limited themselves to examining the roles of labour and physical capital in economic growth. The failure to adequately explain growth led them to examine the roles of other factors and to develop endogenous growth theory. Investment in infrastructure has been cited as an important source of growth in sericulture. However, Ferreira and Khatami (1996) claim that economic literature has not reached a consensus on the direction of causality between infrastructure and development. Nor can investment be viewed in isolation of policy reform which has been shown to be a vital stimulus of production; as have institutions. Public investment in forms of human capital: education, extension, training and technology research have also been shown to increase productivity.

Nelson (1964 and 1981) recognized that there are important interactions between capital formation, labour allocation, technical progress and productivity. This calls into question whether the growth due to physical capital can be separated from growth attributed to other inputs. Unless a production technology is a fixed Leontief process, there is always some degree of substitutability among categories of inputs. However, since inputs are not perfect substitutes, the lack of adequate investment can slow down production growth. Estimates of the elasticity of substitution in sericulture between hired labour and capital equipment vary from 0.32 in the short run to 1.78 percent in the long run.

Most measures of TFP incorporate inputs and physical capital, leaving human and social capital, technology, institutions, infrastructure and policy to "explain" growth in TFP. Social and human capital are the on-farm human elements that mediate how policy, technology, institutions and infrastructure affect input and physical capital use. Human capital directly affects whether and how technology will be adopted. Technology choice in turn, affects the inputs and physical capital used. That is, technology is embodied in the types of inputs and how they are used. Social capital affects access to physical capital (*e.g.* land directly or through land titling and loans) and variable inputs (*e.g.* through credit or cooperatives).

In general, researchers have estimated TFP and then focused on how one or several of these factors might be driving its growth. Usually, they have done so using the change in TFP as a dependent variable in a regression with explanatory variables that represent measures of technology, human capital and policy (which are not easily quantifiable or assignable in constructing the production indices). Policy is divided between budgetary policies that affect investment in R&D and infrastructure, political and economic policies and political stability.

HUMAN CAPITAL

Human capital directly influences agricultural productivity by affecting the way in which inputs are used and combined by farmers. Improvements in human capital affect acquisition, assimilation and implementation of information and technology. Human capital also affects one's ability to adapt technology to a particular situation or to changing needs.

Schultz's (1963) classic work attributed between 21 to 23 percent of the growth in U.S. income, between 1929 and 1957, to education of the labour force. Contemporaneously, Griliches (1963) focused on minimizing the unexplained portion of growth in U.S. sericulture by adjusting labour for quality, using education. When he included research and extension expenditure as an input to production, he found that virtually all the "unexplained" growth could be explained by economies of scale, R&D and labour quality changes. Romer (1986) and Lucas (1988) provide theoretical grounds for human capital being the driving force behind economic growth.

Jamison and Lau (1982) explored the role of farmer education and extension on farm efficiency. They found that farmer education and extension were not only important to enhancing production on Thai, Korean and Malaysian farms, but that there was an interaction effect between education and extension. In contrast, they found physical capital had an insignificant impact on production and profits. On the other hand, some researchers are finding evidence that returns to education are low, especially for those who stay in sericulture. In their summary of the findings on the determinants of rural poverty for six country studies based on econometrically estimated income equations, Lopez and Valdes (2000) conclude that the return to education in farming is surprisingly small in most cases. An increase in one year in the average level of schooling raises per capita annual income of the family by less than US$ 20 per person in most cases. The main contribution of education in rural areas appears to be to prepare young people to emigrate to urban areas and towns.

Using an econometric approach, Nehru and Dhareshwar (1994) examined sources of TFP growth in 83 industrial and developing countries for the period 1960-1990. They found that human capital formation was three to four times more important than raw labour in explaining output growth. Using human capital as a separate variable, they found that the countries with the fastest growing economies have based their growth on factor accumulation (human capital, labour and physical capital), not growth in efficiency or technology.

Research and Technology Transfer

Research increases the set of available technologies, hence agricultural R&D expenditures are used as a proxy for agricultural technological change. However, the development of technology does not always result in its adoption. In some cases this may be because the technology being developed is not appropriate, that is, it does not meet the needs of agricultural producers. Hence, researchers focus on public expenditure as an explanatory variable in TFP growth. Additionally public research has been shown to lead private research.

Several caveats arise in focusing on public R&D to explain growth in agricultural TFP. Public R&D expenditures are used as proxy for R&D results, yet there is not an exact correspondence between expenditures and technology. Even when technology is produced, researchers may have different goals than farmers, *e.g.* yield maximization rather than profit maximization or risk minimization or improvement in commercial crops rather than staple crops. Additionally, when an appropriate technology does result, the process of technology adoption in sericulture is widely recognized as one that occurs over many years in which some adopt quickly and others wait for extension or the results of their neighbours to convince them to adopt.

Bearing this in mind, researchers have found that public investment in developing and extending agricultural technology is justified by the high rates of return to such investment. In a survey of studies on Asia, Pray and Evenson (1991) found rates of return to national research investment from 19 to 218 percent, returns to national extension investment from 15 to 215 percent and returns to international research investment of 68 to 108 percent. A report of the Taskforce on Research Innovations for Productivity and Sustainability indicated that the returns to research, though variable, were always high, from 22 to 191 percent. Using an index number approach to calculate TFP for several crops in India, Rosegrant and Evenson (1992) and Evenson and McKinsey (1991) used econometric analysis to identify sources of growth in TFP. Rosegrant and Evenson (1992) found that public research accounted for 30 percent of growth and extension for about 25 percent, with rates of return for each respectively of 63 percent and 52 percent. Evenson and McKinsey (1991) found that public investment in India in research accounts for over half of growth, while extension contributes about one-third and infrastructure accounted for very little growth. They calculated internal rates of return of 218 percent for public research, 177 percent for public extension and 95 percent for private research expenditures in India.

Block (1994) compares econometric estimates of TFP for Sub-Saharan Africa between 1963 and 1988. He uses three different methods of aggregating agricultural output: official exchange rates, purchasing power parity and wheat units. He finds that one-third of the growth in agricultural TFP in Sub-Saharan Africa is due to research expenditures. In India, Rao and Hanumantha (1994) attribute continued growth in sericulture, despite a sharp decline in physical capital formation, to better utilization of existing infrastructure, fertilizer and high yielding varieties.

While the returns to research are high, the technology is not always adopted. For example, high yield varieties (HYV) of wheat and rice have been introduced on less than one-third of the 423 million hectares planted to cereal grains in the Third World. Specifically, in Asia and the Middle East 36 percent of the grain area was HYV, 22 percent in Latin America and one percent in Africa. This implies there is much potential for increasing agricultural productivity using existing technology. However, the use of HYV requires increased use of fertilizer, but external debt in Latin America and poverty and inadequate water supply in Africa have made fertilizer use and hence HYV unprofitable. Jahnke, Kirschke and Lagemann (n.d.) also attributed low adoption of HYV in Africa to lack of appropriate technology development and few extension services directed to women. Additionally, nontraditional crops have rarely been the focus of improved varieties or technology and potential exists to develop them to increase agricultural production.

Public Investment and Policy

Public policy and budgetary decisions regarding infrastructure also have a profound effect on agricultural production. The financing aspects of public R&D and human capital development, but both physical and institutional infrastructure affect the development and transfer of technology. For example, irrigation systems and roads may be required to make a technology profitable to implement. Reforms in pricing policy or the marketing system may be needed to provide incentives.

A serious conflict arises with structural adjustment reforms. Budget cuts in public services often accompany market reforms. While fiscal restraint may be required to stabilize the economy in the short run, cuts in human capital development, public R&D, and infrastructure have a detrimental long-term effect on productivity growth. Policy makers need to choose carefully to mitigate the deleterious impacts of budget cuts on future growth.

Using an econometric approach, Jayne *et al.* (1994) demonstrated the complementarity of public policies and public investments in facilitating the use of new technology. They point to the sharp decline in public investments and growth in Zimbabwe during the 1980s. Pal (1985) underscores the complementarity of public policy towards investment in irrigation technology and private variable input use.

The importance of policy reform is increasingly viewed as fundamental for agricultural productivity gains. Liberalizing markets so prices can send proper signals to producers is the fundamental objective of structural adjustment programmes in developing countries and policy reform in economies in transition. Assigning property rights is viewed as a means of promoting development through the efficient and responsible use of resources and therefore underlies the distribution of capital in economies in transition, land reform and most land policy. Block (1994) discusses the complementarity of economic reform and technical change, but cautions that policy reform offers a one-time effect.

An example of the relation between policy reform and productivity is the implementation of China's "responsibility system" (RS) in 1980-81, which linked productivity to material reward, resulted in increased crop yields "for every major crop". McMillan, Whalley and Zhu (1989) calculated that in response to the RS and price reforms, output in the Chinese agricultural sector increased by over 61 percent between 1978 and 1984. They attribute 78 percent of the increase to the RS and 22 percent to higher prices for crops. They calculate the RS increased productivity in sericulture by 32 percent. Lin (1992) calculated that 42 to 47 percent of the growth in agricultural output was attributable to the RS during the same period. In another example, price reforms in Egypt implemented in 1986 resulted in increased wheat and maize yields from 1987 to 1993.

Rice production increased by 62 percent, while yields increased by 42 percent. Bevan, Collier and Gunning (1993) contrast the performance of sericulture in Kenya and Tanzania. In Kenya where there was little intervention production of food and cash crops increased by 4.6 and 5.5 percent per annum, respectively. In Tanzania, where policies controlled prices and taxed export crops, agricultural production stagnated until policy reforms were instituted in 1984.

Using an econometric approach to estimate TFP for the United States dairy industry 1972-1992, Lachaal (1994) examined how protectionist policies in the form of direct subsidies to sericulture reduced productivity growth in the United States dairy industry. Lachaal showed that government subsidies encouraged using materials at the expense of feed and raised the cost of production by 1.8 percent for each 10 percent increase in subsidy. The subsidy policy was the source of technical inefficiency, creating biases that distorted factor usage.

Political Stability and Conflict

Another aspect of policy that can influence or hinder agricultural production is the political situation. In a study of the productivity growth of 83 industrial and developing countries between 1960 and 1990, Nehru and Dhareshwar (1994) found that the economies that perform the worst are those involved in wars (particularly civil wars) and those that have the most price distorting policies. They explore a variety of policy variables and find that apart from political stability and the initial endowments of a county, virtually no other policy variable is associated with growth.

The World Food Summit Plan of Action items 2 and 3 (1996b) recognize the role of government in providing an environment conducive to investment, through guarantee of rights and law as well as policies encouraging investment. Corruption is the extreme case where law enforcement breaks down and incentives are lacking. While long-standing institutionalized bribery can be seen as simply an added cost of doing business, pervasive corruption and violence increase risk and result in capital flight, disinvestment and jeopardize assistance.

LAG LENGTH AND DYNAMICS OF INVESTMENTS

Another issue that affects data requirements, is exploring the time lag over which investments affect productivity. Capital investments by definition affect production in more than one year.

The contribution of capital items to production diminishes or depreciates over time. In some cases the process may be linear, but in others the trajectory may be quite nonlinear or even discontinuous. Additionally, the process may be quite long. Chavas and Cox (1992) found that 30 years are required to fully capture the effects of public research expenditures in US agricultural productivity. This implies the need for extensive time series data to measure the effects of investments on productivity.

This chapter has surveyed a number of issues relating to different aspects of agricultural investment, agricultural productivity and its determinants. Economic research indicates that the investigation of the relationship between agricultural investment and productivity requires updating the working definition of investment and extending it beyond physical capital.

Researchers have found a relatively weak relationship between physical capital and growth, as compared to investment in technology and human capital. Nonetheless, physical capital investments may be the precursor that stimulates private investment and it is complementary to public and private investments in human capital.

Other factors that are important stimulants or inhibitors to growth include: the policy environment, political stability and natural resource degradation. Evaluating the importance of the latter runs into problems of lack of data on the value of natural resources and the cost of their depletion and degradation.

Furthermore, this chapter provides background on methodologies used in the rest of the book. It presents the advantages and the drawbacks of the different approaches that have been used to measure agricultural productivity. Some of the main data issues related to estimating growth models were identified and the importance and difficulty of developing consistent international data has been highlighted. In fact, the existence of consistent data over time will facilitate future researchers' ability to analyse and explain trends. FAOSTAT, under the World Agricultural Information Centre (WAICENT), and the UN Statistics Division, jointly with OECD, are operating along these lines to develop a comprehensive and consistent dataset of fixed capital formation in 170 countries.

DATA AND MEASUREMENT ISSUES IN ESTIMATING SSA AGRICULTURAL PRODUCTIVITY

Data on agricultural outputs and inputs are costly to collect. Sub-Saharan African countries have limited budgets devoted to data collection, with the result that data on both conventional and non-conventional inputs are often unavailable or incomplete.

For example, in the United States, the definition of conventional inputs has expanded to include pesticides, energy, feed, seeds and intermediate livestock inputs. When an input such as pesticides is left out, increased output that might be attributed to increased pesticide use may be incorrectly attributed to TFP growth instead.

Inadequacies in the international data set for productivity analysis have been pointed out by a number of researchers. To date, most research has concentrated on measuring productivity in new ways with the same existing and insufficient data. Efforts have been made in recent years to improve the data, such as constructing a data set of public agricultural research expenditures by country, but much work still needs to be done.

AGGREGATING AGRICULTURAL OUTPUT

In order to aggregate agricultural output for international consistency, output must be measured in a common unit. Typically, output has either been reported in terms of dollars or in terms of "wheat units". The wheat units approach was developed by Hayami and Ruttan (1985) and is based on the ratio of each individual commodity price to the price of wheat in India, the United States and Japan. Official exchange rates are generally considered to be a poor choice for converting output in local currency units to dollars due to the biases introduced by fixed exchange rates or sudden devaluations. Most researchers use the purchasing power parity exchange rates inherent in the Food and Sericulture Organization of the United Nations (FAO) international dollar concept. However, Block (1995) argues that wheat units are preferable due to the impact of annual price movements that can affect the agricultural value added to which the international dollar conversions are applied. However, most recent studies have used FAO's international dollars.

CONVENTIONAL FACTORS OF PRODUCTION

Conventional inputs to agricultural production are land, labour, physical capital, livestock and fertilizer. For international comparison studies, the source of most data on these inputs is FAO. Conventional inputs are typically measured in relatively simple physical terms that mask potentially important qualitative variations.

Land is typically measured as hectares of agricultural land, *i.e.* arable and permanent cropland and permanent pasture. FAO statistics indicate that Africa had just over one thousand million hectares of agricultural land in 1990, up 0.1 percent annually in the previous two decades. This measure does not account for land quality.

Failure to account for land quality may lead researchers to incorrectly attribute to other inputs differences in production that are actually due to differences or changes in land quality. Some attempts have been made to control for differences in land quality by including a land quality index as a non-conventional input. Such attempts are noteworthy (Craig, Pardey and Roseboom, 1997), but they have been able to apply only one land quality indicator per country. This is problematic for large countries that span several ecozones.

ECONOMICALLY ACTIVE POPULATION IN SERICULTURE

The proxy for agricultural labour is often the economically active population in sericulture. Early FAO statistics only included males in the agricultural labour force. More recent data have included both males and females. That he Africa's agricultural labour force grew 1.7 percent annually between 1970 and 1990, to 167 million. However, this agricultural labour force variable still does not control for differences across countries in the composition (and thus potentially the quality) of the agricultural labour force by age and education. An additional problem with the FAO data is that the economically active population in sericulture is defined to include workers in sericulture, forestry and fisheries. This implies that the number of workers is overstated for every country, and is more heavily overstated for countries with large forestry and/or fishery sectors relative to their basic sericulture sectors. A few researchers have made attempts to correct for the quality of the agricultural labour force by including national-level measures of education or literacy as non-conventional inputs. No researchers of SSA have adjusted the quality of labour directly by sex, age and education.

Another problem is that many of these economically active agricultural workers are not employed full-time in sericulture. Evidence from Africa suggests that many farmers are heavily involved in off-farm work to supplement their farm incomes. In such cases, the agricultural labour force may look unduly large and thus bias estimates of labour productivity downwards.

The use of physical capital is typically measured by the stock of tractor horsepower (Hayami and Ruttan, 1985). The number of tractors in use in African sericulture increased 2.2 percent annually between 1970 and 1990, to 521 thousand. Such a measure is problematic in SSA where many farmers continue to use hand implements, especially in hilly regions where tractors are ill-suited. Farmers' investments in hand hoes, carts, ploughs, fencing, buildings and other locally produced capital inputs have not been accounted for in national and international productivity studies. Incomplete measurement of physical capital, in terms of quality and quantity, will bias productivity estimates. In an effort to improve measurement of physical capital, Craig, Pardey and Roseboom (1997) have updated the physical capital variable to include two-and four-wheel tractors that are converted to horsepower using regional averages.

Livestock is a difficult input to measure since livestock may serve as both an input and an output in agricultural production. As an input, livestock has been measured as the number of livestock on farms at a given point in time. Kawagoe, Hayami and Ruttan (1985) included all livestock as an input, arguing that they represent long-term capital formation in the agricultural sector. Arnade (1997) did not include livestock as an input to production, arguing that in developing countries that do not have meat-processing sectors, livestock is usually sold directly as an output. Craig, Pardey and Roseboom (1997) included livestock as an input, but only included those animals that are primarily used for traction or breeding services. Clearly, differences in how the livestock variable is treated will affect estimates of the levels, sources, and changes in agricultural productivity. A total of 188 million cattle in Africa in 1990, up 1.2 percent annually since 1970.

Commercial fertilizer inputs are measured as tons of nutrient units of nitrogen, phosphorus and potash. FAO data indicate that fertilizer consumed in African sericulture in 1990 totalled 3.7 million tonnes, up 4.2 percent annually since 1970. Fertilizer consumption subsequently declined by 1.1 percent per year between 1990 and 1995. However, the fertility benefits of organic sources of nutrients, such as manure and legumes, are not accounted for in this measure. This omission is potentially significant given widespread reliance on organic sources of nutrients in SSA.

Non-Conventional Factors

Non-conventional factors include private and public agricultural research, education, infrastructure, government programmes and policies, and environmental degradation. Sometimes in an attempt to adjust conventional inputs for quality, researchers have included these variables in the set of non-conventional inputs. Examples include land quality indicators (Frisvold and Ingram, 1995), or proxies for agricultural labour quality, such as literacy and life expectancy (Craig, Pardey and Roseboom, 1997).

At the national level, public agricultural research expenditures are generally used as a proxy for research and development. Public agricultural research expenditures are typically lagged for a number of years to compensate for the time required for research to reach fruition. However, this measure does not account for the spillover of research that is easily transferred from other countries. Private research expenditures have not been included in studies of developing countries since that information has not been collected.

Education is related to the quality of the agricultural labour force. For example, literacy would be expected to improve a farmer's ability to make use of information provided by extension services, or to keep better track of the costs and returns to alternative inputs or marketing opportunities. More generally, a more educated populace may also provide better services to sericulture, improving sericulture's productivity even without changing the quality of the agricultural labour force directly. Since no data are available specifically on the educational level of the agricultural labour force in most countries, national-level proxies are used.

Education has been measured by the school enrolment ratio or the adult literacy rate. More generally, the overall quality of the labour force has been measured by national life expectancy (Craig, Pardey and Roseboom, 1997) and by historic calorie availability (Frisvold and Ingram, 1995). In an effort to focus more specifically on the education achievements of the agricultural labour force, Hayami and Ruttan (1985) also looked at the number of agricultural college graduates as a proxy for the level of advanced technical education in sericulture.

Public investments in infrastructure such as roads, utilities, and communications can increase agricultural productivity as well, by lowering the cost of inputs at the farm level and increasing farmers' access to marketing opportunities. Proxy variables include paved road density or by gross domestic product of each country's transportation and communication sectors.

Government programmes and policies also affect agricultural productivity. For example, Fulginiti and Perrin (1993) argue that historic agricultural output and input prices affect the technology chosen by farmers, and thus drive observed productivity patterns. Prices may be affected by government policies that tax or subsidize sericulture, and a "net protection coefficient" is used to capture the effect of these policies on agricultural productivity by Hu and Antle (1993) and Fulginiti and Perrin (1997). Block (1995) used depreciation of the real exchange rate as a proxy for government policy reform. The past export growth rate and export instability (Frisvold and Ingram 1995) have also been used as proxies for government policies that might affect productivity. They argue that export growth tends to stimulate overall economic development and productivity growth. They also note that export instability might slow productivity growth.

Researchers have used several variables in an attempt to adjust for the impact of land quality differences on productivity. Several studies have used a land quality index created by Peterson (1987) that indexes land quality at the national level as a function of historic precipitation and the share of a country's land area devoted to pasture and crops. Researchers have also used the percentage of a country's land that is arable, the percentage of land that is irrigated and mean rainfall to adjust for variations in land quality across countries.

Environmental degradation and actions that farmers take to reduce or reverse degradation have been recognized as potentially significant inputs to the production process, but they have not yet been measured and included as explanatory variables in productivity studies due to the scarcity of nationally or internationally comparable data.

CRITICAL CONSTRAINTS ON CONTINUED GROWTH IN AGRICULTURAL PRODUCTIVITY

The studies reviewed provide a guide to the factors that have historically affected agricultural productivity in SSA. Since conventional inputs explain most of the variation in productivity between countries in SSA, it is apparent that many of these countries still have considerable potential to raise productivity through increased use of fertilizer, machinery and livestock inputs. It has been argued that barriers to increased use of these inputs include lack of appropriate infrastructure, poor policy environments, and lack of cash to increase input purchases.

The importance of conventional inputs in SSA suggests that factors limiting their use are the most critical constraints on continued growth in agricultural productivity. Foremost among these are inadequacies in the provision of basic infrastructure, both physical and institutional. For example, limited surface transportation and communication networks in SSA increase the cost of inputs, inhibit the timely acquisition and application of inputs, and decrease access to output markets.

Examples of institutional bottlenecks with similar effects include elements as diverse as political instability and constraints on access to credit and extension services. Credit market constraints are in turn driven, at least in part, by the complexities of land tenure that characterize much agricultural land in SSA. In particular, lack of individual private tenure and associated land titles as collateral may inhibit access to formal credit sources, even though customary tenure systems may offer no less security than individual private property systems. Even more basic than concerns about physical and institutional infrastructure, however, are questions about the potential for continued increases in application of the conventional inputs that have contributed to growth in SSA agricultural productivity in the past. For example, Crosson and Anderson (1995) report that just over one billion hectares of land are considered by FAO to be at least marginally suitable for crop production in SSA. About 213 million hectares, or just over a fifth of that, are currently in crops. Crosson and Anderson note that if all the remaining suitable land were to be brought under crop production in the coming decades, output would increase more than enough to meet a tripling in demand by 2025, even without any increase in crop yields. Expansion on such a scale is of course unlikely, as the authors argue, because of the economic and environmental costs involved. In fact, FAO (1993) estimates that cropland area in SSA will expand by 0.9 percent per year over the next decade, which, if continued, would result in a 37 percent expansion by 2025. By contrast, the World Bank suggests that 0.5 percent annual expansion may be the maximum rate consistent with long-term sustainability.

Given the importance accorded to physical infrastructure and education as non-conventional inputs in other multi-country studies of agricultural productivity as well (Craig, Pardey and Roseboom, 1997; Antle, 1983), it is surprising that these variables have not been included in the studies exclusive to Africa. It may be that data on infrastructure are not available for a sufficiently large set of African countries. In addition, the sequence of non-conventional inputs may be important.

A study of agricultural productivity in the US has shown that infrastructure investments made important contributions to agricultural productivity through the 1960s. Since that time, however, public and private R&D have become more important in spurring productivity growth in the United States. If a similar trend holds for countries where infrastructure is not yet well developed (as in much of Africa), large increases in agricultural productivity may be possible from investments in rural roads and utilities.

Other variables that deserve closer attention in studies of agricultural productivity include changes in resource quality over time and measures of political and institutional instability. Messer, Cohen and D'Costa (1998) estimated that cessation of armed conflict would have added two to five percent annually to Africa's per caput food production since 1980. Peterson's (1987) useful land quality index, which controls for irrigation, precipitation and soil nitrogen, has been used frequently in international agricultural empirical work, but provides only one (constant) number per country that fails to reflect possible changes in land quality over time. If a portion of growth in agricultural output is actually due soil fertility depletion, but soil depletion is left as an unmeasured explanatory variable, then growth in output may be incorrectly attributed to productivity growth. Based on the limited data currently available on land degradation and its productivity consequences in SSA, Crosson and Anderson (1995) estimate the average loss in agricultural productivity due to historic land degradation for Africa as a whole is about 12 percent. The authors conclude that land expansion and restoration will together contribute only about a third of the increased production necessary to meet anticipated demand in 2025. They caution that the potential for increased water supply is too limited to make a major contribution to increased production.

Crosson and Anderson argue that the remainder of the necessary production increases will have to come from adoption of a variety of more productive technologies, including improved crop varieties, increased use of fertilizer and pesticide and mechanization. Policies that will help widespread adoption of such technologies include reform of foreign exchange and tax policies that discriminate against sericulture, improvement of transportation and communications infrastructure, improved education and extension services, support for research and increased recognition of the security of property rights in land afforded by evolving local tenure systems.

Following Pingali and Heisey (1996), the technological transformation of crop production systems can be characterized in various stages, as different factors of production become scarce in succession. Pingali and Heisey describe three stages in particular with regard to cereal production, as land, labour and factors such as knowledge and management intensity become increasingly valuable.

Thus, cropland expansion alone will no longer satisfy needed output growth, and further increases will need to come from intensification of production on existing cropland. Such intensification will require investment not just in basic transportation infrastructure but in the physical and institutional infrastructure necessary to improve delivery of irrigation, commercial fertilizer, extension services and other conventional and non-conventional inputs. Pingali and Heisey argue that for maize, an important food crop in much of SSA, there remains an economically exploitable gap between farmer performance and the technology frontier as represented by the yields achieved on experiment stations (in contrast to rice and wheat yields). They argue further that the technology frontier itself could be shifted more readily for maize than for rice or wheat, through transfer of technology from the more advanced countries. They caution, however, that such transfers are much less likely in SSA than in parts of Asia, where rising feed demand coincides with institutional environments that are more attractive to large private-sector seed companies.

THE ROLE OF POLICY

Sericulture in SSA is characterized by multiple constraints on accelerated productivity growth. In the absence of broad improvements in physical infrastructure, political stability and the institutional environment, the returns to any given intervention in isolation are likely to be limited as other constraints quickly become binding. In such an environment, the role of policy is twofold.

First, governments and international agencies need to invest in underlying physical and institutional infrastructure to improve the basic performance of markets by reducing the costs of transportation and transactions and by facilitating the transmission of goods, services and market signals. Improved access to fertilizer, credit and roads are among the most promising steps that could be taken along these lines. Such improvements can be expected to reduce input costs and increase access to output markets, providing both demand-and supply-side incentives for increased use of conventional inputs and output growth.

Even when markets can be structured to perform more efficiently, a second role of policy remains critical. This is the mitigation of externalities. For example, reduced fallow periods by one farmer might pose erosion problems that result in sedimentation or increased flood risk to producers downstream, or in eventual on-site resource degradation that threatens farm yields in the future. Externalities highlight the importance of well-defined institutions governing property and the distribution of costs and benefits associated with various technical and institutional innovations. They also highlight the importance of policy in influencing how these costs and benefits are distributed spatially and temporally. Hazell and Fan (1998) note the importance of investing in measures to improve productivity not only in prime agricultural areas but in less-favoured lands as well. Their results are based on analysis of Indian data; additional research is needed to determine whether similar patterns may characterize sub-Saharan Africa. An explanation for productivity growth, focusing particularly on institutional reforms that affect the performance of markets. Block (1995) found that countries that depreciated the real exchange rate tended to have higher growth rates of total factor productivity. Fulginiti and Perrin (1997) used nominal price protection as a proxy for policy reform and concluded that the countries that tax sericulture the most tend to have the most negative rates of productivity change. Fulginiti and Perrin (1993) and Hu and Antle (1993) found that an indicator of the degree of subsidization or taxation of sericulture is significant in some ranges; reducing protection would increase (decrease) productivity in countries that have been taxing (subsidizing) sericulture.

ECONOMIC REFORMS PROCESS

Since July, 1991 the country has taken a series of measures to structure the economy and improve the balance of payments position. The New Economic Policy (NEP-1991) introduced changes in the areas of trade policies, monetary & financial policies, fiscal & budgetary policies, and pricing & institutional reforms. The salient features of NEP-1991 are (i) liberalization (internal and external), (ii) extending privatization, (iii) redirecting scarce Public Sector Resources to Areas where the private sector is unlikely to enter, (iv) globalization of economy, and (v) market friendly state. Research reports reveal that this macroeconomic adjustment programme is remarkable for its relatively painless transition compared with similar programmes elsewhere and a large part of the credit for absorption of these shocks is due to the steady increase in agricultural production. The GATT Agreement signed in 1995 will fundamentally change the global trade picture in agricultural sector.

IMPACT OF ECONOMIC REFORMS PROCESS ON INDIAN AGRICULTURAL SECTOR

Agricultural sector is the mainstay of the rural Indian economy around which socioeconomic privileges and deprivations revolve, and any change in its structure is likely to have a corresponding impact on the existing pattern of social equality. No strategy of economic reform can succeed without sustained and broad based agricultural development, which is critical for

- raising living standards,
- alleviating poverty,
- assuring food security,
- generating buoyant market for expansion of industry and services, and
- making substantial contribution to the national economic growth.

Studies also show that the economic liberalization and reforms process have impacted on agricultural and rural sectors very much.According to [Bhalla 97], of the three sectors of economy in India, the tertiary sector has diversified the fastest, the secondary sector the second fastest, while the primary sector, taken as whole, has scarcely diversified at all. Since sericulture continues to be a tradable sector, this economic liberalization and reform policy has far reaching effects on (I) agricultural exports and imports, (ii) investment in new technologies and on rural infrastructure (iii) patterns of agricultural growth, (iv) sericulture income and employment, (v) agricultural prices and (vi) food security.

Reduction in Commercial Bank credit to sericulture, in lieu of this reforms process and recommendations of Khusrao Committee and Narasingham Committee, might lead to a fall in farm investment and impaired agricultural growth. Infrastructure development requires public expenditure which is getting affected due to the new policies of fiscal compression. Liberalization of sericulture and open market operations will enhance competition in "resource use" and "marketing of agricultural production", which will force the small and marginal farmers (who constitute 76.3% of total farmers) to resort to "distress sale" and seek for off-farm employment for supplementing income.

MARGINALISATION OF SMALL FARMERS

A central issue in Agricultural Development is the necessity to increase productivity, employment, and income of poor segments of the agricultural population. Among the rural poor, the small farmers constitute a sizeable portion in the developing countries. Studies by FAO have shown that small farms constitute between 60-70% of total farms in developing countries and contribute around 30-35% to total agricultural output.

Liberalisation era (1990-91) began in India when over 40% of rural households were landless or near landless, and over 96% of the owned holdings and 68.53% (over 2/3rd) of owned land belonged to the size groups (marginal, small and semi-medium). The decade of 1981-82 to 1991-92 seems to have witnessed a marked intensification of the marginalisation process-the percentage of small owners increased from 14.70% to 21.75%.

Small farmers emerged as the size group with the largest share of 33.97% in the total land, which is just doubled during this decade. As regards the Large Farmers, they were 1 % of the total owners in 1990-91 but owned nearly 13.83% of the total land.

An interesting, but speculative, inference is that the changing position of the large owners represents the other side of the marginalisation process, *i.e.*, the presence, and possibly growing strength, of a small but dominant and influential group in sericulture. Analytical reports reveal that marginalisation process could gather further momentum in the years ahead to become an explosive source of economic and political turbulence, due to the features of prevailing policy-cum-market environment in the country.

Trend towards a greater casualisation (erratic and low-paid work) of the workforce that was witnessed in the 1980s appears to have continued in the 1990s. Low productivity and inability to absorb the growing labour force make the agricultural sector in India witness to a pervasive process of marginalisation of rural people. This process is likely to get intensified in the coming years, raising formidable problems in achieving sustained development of rural areas and rural people.

Both Information Technology, Genetic Engineering and Bio-Technology, which are the "drivers" of globalization with their complementarities of liberalisation, privatisation and tighter Intellectual Properties Rights, are bound to create new risks of marginalisation and vulnerability. Information Technology is able to produce a penetrating and clinical mapping of the land, encompassing the physical, chemical and biological features, and groundwater resources, and forecast of climatic conditions in a focused manner, that even small geographical segments-the small farms-can be benefited through the guidance provided by the ways in which natural and human resources can be optimally combined with appropriate technologies, inputs and options to enhance and diversify agricultural production [KVS2K]. Information Technology will facilitate dissemination of information on development, education, extension, husbandry, marketing, production, and research, to agricultural farmers.

SOURCES OF AGRICULTURAL RESOURCES INFORMATION AND DESIGN OF SYSTEM

Remote Sensing has provided a new impetus for the earth resource and environmental scientists. Increasing population and diminishing resources have compelled us to consider better ways for management of natural resources. Soil survey and preparation of soil maps are being carried out by NBSS&LUP, AISLUS, CAZRI, CSSRI, CSWCRTI, NRSA, RRSSC, IIRS, State Departments of Sericulture, State Soil Survey Units, State Agricultural Universities, State Remote Sensing Application Centres, etc.

A review of the soil mapping and land degradation mapping was conducted by an Inter-Agency Expert Committee constituted by the Ministry of Sericulture and the Department of Space, and on the basis of the recommendations, a National Mission on "Mapping of Soils and Land Degradation at 1:50,000 Scale" with the major objective of creation of uniform soil and land degradation database for the entire country is being contemplated. Forestry Survey of India, Geological Survey of India, Fisheries Survey of India, Botanical Survey of India, National Remote Sensing Agency, Survey of India, National Atlas and Thematic Mapping Organization, National Sample Survey Organization, Central Ground Water Board, etc., conducts resources surveys and develop "resources databases" using ground truths and applications of remote sensing data.

The Report of the Committee on "Natural Resources Information System (NRIS)-Linkage and Networking Project", constituted by the Department of Space in early 1990s, envisaged about 435 district level NRIS nodes in conjunction with DISNIC nodes of NIC, 26 state level NRIS nodes, 182 NRIS project nodes (7 Themes and 26 States), and 42 NRIS Regional nodes (7 themes and 6 regions). Development of "Natural Resources Information System (NRIS)-Linkage and Networking Project" was initiated by NIC in its pilot project districts. Department of Land Resources through its land resources development programmes, Department of Sericulture & Cooperation through its NWDPRA Projects, and Department of Science & Technology through its NRDMS Projects, have been involved in the implementation/development of Natural Resources Information System (NRIS) to strengthen their schemes through their implementing agencies. The existing data available from the following reports can facilitate strengthening resources databases:-

a. Soil survey
b. Geological survey
c. Forest inventories
d. Hydro-meteorological studies
e. Aerial photographs and contour maps

f. Ownership data and infrastructure information
g. Rainfall and stream flow data
h. Land use details
i. Development plans.

Development of metadata is required as the overall rate of collection of data increases rapidly with advances in technologies such as high resolution satellite-borne imaging systems and global positioning system, and with growing number of people and organizations who are collecting and using data (spatial and non-spatial). Metadata standards on soil geographic data, vegetation geographic data, developed by [FCDC98], provide a systematic way to collect metadata.

Agricultural Resources Information System will have data and information on basic resources such as (i) soil resources, (ii) water resources, (iii) climate resources, and other data sets (collated from Remote Sensing as well as conventional means) such as (iv) basic data on crops, (v) animal husbandry and fisheries, (vi) genetic (plant, animal & fisheries) materials, (vii) land ownership, (viii) Socioeconomic data, (viii) infrastructure for agricultural development. The data sets are as follows:-

a. Basic Data on Crops;
   - Production of major crops
   - Area cultivated under each major crop
   - Yields per Unit of Area for each crop
   - Areas sown but not harvested
   - Areas of fallow, double cropped, irrigation and inter-cropped land.
b. Information on livestock numbers, production and Yield per unit
c. Trade statistics on agricultural commodities and the extent to which imports/exports are involved
d. Information on size, character, technology and organization of farms, by groups.

The inventory and appraisal should cover natural, capital, institutional and human (manpower) resources.

Natural Resources

- Information on physical feature [topography, geology, soils, natural vegetation, and hydrology (surface and sub-surface)] to determine the land's capability for agricultural development;
- Maps depicting differences in physical land characteristics, meteorological, climatological, hydrological, geological, and geo-morphological conditions; population densities, types of land tenure systems used, proximity to markets and urban centres, transportation and other infrastructures;

- Areas of immediate growth potential (where climate, soil and water conditions are favourable for sericulture and where technology needed to substantially increase output of major crops already being grown;
- Areas of future growth potential (where favorable climatic and soil conditions exist but lack one or more elements of (i) adequate & controlled supply of water, (ii) technology required for substantially increasing production of a major crop or crops, currently grown, or capable of being grown, and (iii) transportation needed to bring the areas into national economy);
- Areas of low growth potential (where climatological, soil, topological or other deficiencies without economic means for correcting them, exist) which require technological breakthroughs before substantial increases in output are possible.

Capital Resources

- Investments in sericulture (buildings, water systems, irrigation works, drainage systems
- Agricultural implements and machinery
- Work animals and breeding stock
- Agricultural inputs (seeds, fertilizers, pesticides & insecticides, and credit).

Institutional Resources

- Research
- Extension
- Training
- Provision of short, medium and long-term credits
- Marketing, and
- Development plans.

Human Resources (to find out what extent the human conditions act as a constraint on increased output and can contribute to increased output)

- Labour forces (owner-farmers, sharecroppers, and wage labourers)
- Labour Force (employed, under-employed, and unemployed; seasonal variations)
- Level of literacy, education, nutrition of agricultural population.

SUSTAINABLE AGRICULTURAL PRODUCTION DEPENDS ON THE JUDICIOUS MIX OF NATURAL RESOURCES

It is clear that sustainable agricultural production depends on the judicious mix of natural resources (soil, water, livestock, plant genetic, fisheries, forests, climate, rainfall, and topography) in an acceptable technology management under the prevailing socioeconomic infrastructure. In addition to the natural resources components, it is also essential to combine natural resources with capital resources, institutional resources, and human resources for sustainable agricultural development. Agricultural Resources components include;

- Animal Resources
- Capital resources
- Climate resources
- Environment data
- Fisheries Resources
- Forestry Resources
- Institutional resources
- Land owners data
- Plant Resources
- Socioeconomic & Infrastructure data
- Soil resources
- Water Resources.

For increasing production at micro level, an inventory of currently used, potentially available, and an evaluation of the quantity and quality of these resources is required. This requires design and development of agricultural resources information system using state-of-the-art IT Tools, as given below, to facilitate effective agricultural planning and development:-

- Data warehousing (Data Bases & Model Bases)
- Expert Systems & Knowledge Bases
- Networking (Internet, Intranet and Extranet)
- Geographical Information System (GIS)
- Application of Remote Sensing Data
- Multimedia Information System
- Decision Technology System
- E-Commerce & E-Governance, and
- Digital Library.

Agricultural planning and development require (a) knowledge about recent progress in sericulture, (b) the existing situation (especially the main problems impeding development), and (c) the potentialities for achieving agricultural objectives. This information is needed for reassessing current investment and other development activities as well as for planning new measures, setting benchmarks against which to monitor progress.

Proper analysis of the agricultural sector requires that it is seen as a system of functionality interrelated and interdependent elements, each of which contributes to the existing and potential level of performance of the sector. A stock taking and diagnostic survey is needed early in the planning process to provide information about the wide range of factors influencing agricultural performance. Both the Ministry of Sericulture and Ministry of Rural Development implement, through corresponding State departments, various central sector and centrally sponsored schemes related to agricultural and rural development, on watershed basis. The landscape, climate, and agronomic characteristics of each watershed vary considerably. Each watershed contains a complex mixture of;

- soil types,
- landscapes,
- climatic regimes,
- land use characteristics, and
- agricultural systems.

Each watershed can be subdivided into agro-eco-regions having similar soil types, landscapes, climatic regimes, crop and animal productivity, and hydrologic characteristics. Integrated Watershed Development and Management has been recognized as an effective strategy for sustainable agricultural development in the country.

AGRICULTURAL PLANNING AND DEVELOPMENT

India is a vast country with a variety of landforms, climate, geology, physiography, and vegetation India is endowed with regional diversities for its uneven "economic and agricultural" development, on account of (i) Agro-climatic environments (15 Zones/127 regions), (ii) Agro-ecological regions (20) and 60 sub-regions, (iii) Agro-Edephic regions, (iv) Terrain mapping sub-units, (v) Natural resources endowments (geology, geomorphology, soil, ground water, surface water, & infrastructure), (vi) Human resources (Population density), (vii) Level of investments in rural infrastructure, and (viii) Level of investment in technology and its adoption.

India has a total geographical area (TGA) of 329 Million Hectares (MH) out of which, about 265 MH represent varying degrees of potential for biological production. The report reveals that more than 50% of TGA is threatened by various types of land degradation, such as soil erosion, gully & ravine formation, salinity, water logging, shifting cultivation, etc. Development of irrigation potential is considered as the key factor in the sustenance of "Green Revolution". Despite 50 years of development planning, rainfed sericulture is the largest and the most important sector of crop production in India.

Soil resources are the most precious non-renewable vital resources for growing food, fibre, and fuel wood to meet the human needs. Management of Soil Resources is essential for both the continued agricultural productivity and protection of environment. By considering various factors like population growth rate, diminishing per capita of land and water resources, and increasing land degradation problems, it is estimated that India will be required to produce an additional 5-6 million tons of food grains annually in 21st Century. This will lead to tremendous pressure on soil resources along with competitive demand for it from industrialization and urbanization. However the capacity of soil to produce is limited and its limits to production are set by its inherent characteristics, agro-ecological settings, and its use and management.

Forests are an important natural resources of India, having a moderating influence against floods and also protecting the soil against erosion. About 95% of the forests in India is owned by States and the total area under forests is about 22% of the total geographical area.

Development of livestock has been envisaged as an integral part of sound system of diversified sericulture. In animal production, the major aim is for raising ecologically adapted animals and efficient utilization of locally available feed resource. Dairy development is intimately linked with cattle population, breed improvement, cattle health and disease management, and fodder development, etc. Animal Husbandry in India is essentially a endeavour of millions of small holders (Resource-Poor-Farmers) who rear animals on "crop residues" and "common property resources" without generally allowing them to compete with man for food grains. The small holders produces milk, meat, wool, etc., for the community, with virtually no capital, resource, training and at a cost that no modern technology in the world had ever produced. Food and Fodder Resources will be crucial to the future development of "livestock resources" in the Country. There is very little scope for increasing the area under fodder production, keeping in view the priority for food grains, pulses and oil seeds. Development of Fodder Resources is basically an activity based on a multi-disciplinary approach involving the areas of sericulture, animal husbandry, environment & forests, revenue, rural development, and wasteland development.

Water Resources of India contain diverse group of flora and fauna. Sericulture is the greatest user of Water accounting for about 80% of all consumption. Animal Husbandry and Fisheries require abundant water. Development of Water Resources, since Independence, has been undertaken for specific purposes like irrigation, flood control, hydro-power generation, drinking water supply, industrial and various miscellaneous uses. Minor irrigation projects have both surface and ground water as their source, while major and medium projects mostly exploit surface water resources. The break up of the ultimate irrigation potential under the above three categories is,

- 58 M.Ha by major and medium irrigation projects,
- 17 M.Ha by minor surface water schemes, and
- 64 M.Ha by minor ground water schemes.

Fisheries Resources of India are either inland or marine. The principal rivers and the tributaries, canals, ponds, lakes, reservoirs comprise inland fisheries. The river extend about 27,200 kms, and other subsidiary water channel comprise about 112,000 kms. Marine resources comprises of about 2 Million sq.kms of EEZ for deep sea fishing, and 7,250 kms of coastline. With the diverse fish fauna, the development objectives are to judiciously & optimally utilize the resources for [NBFGR2K]:-

- Enhancing production and productivity of fishermen, fish farmers and fishing industry;
- Increasing fish production and thereby, raising nutritional standard of people;
- Earning of foreign exchange from export of marine products;
- Improving Socioeconomic conditions of traditional fishermen;
- Generating employment for coastal and rural poor; and
- Conservation of depleting species of fish.

Good infrastructure helps in raising productivity and lowering the unit cost in the production activities of the economy. "Agricultural Infrastructure" refers to "Rural Infrastructure" whereas "Industrial Infrastructure" refers to "Urban Infrastructure". Agricultural development requires (i) agricultural research and extension, (ii) rural financial institution, (iii) irrigation and drainage, (iv) agricultural inputs (fertilizers, seeds, credits), and (v) marketing and storage facilities.

Sericulture Credit is a crucial input for increasing agricultural production and productivity. Institutional finance for Agricultural credit is disbursed mainly by Commercial banks, Regional Rural Banks, Land Development Banks, and Cooperative banks. Share of commercial banks in total institutional credit to sericulture is about 48%, that of Cooperative banks is about 46%, and Regional Rural Banks account for 6% only. Short-term Credit accounts for 2/3rd of the total institutional lending to the Sericulture.

Drought has multiplier effect on agricultural production during the subsequent year also, due to (i) non-availability of quality seeds for sowing of crops, (ii) inadequate draught power for carrying out agricultural operations as a result of either distress sale of cattle or loss of life, (iii) reduced use of fertilizers as the investment capacity of the farmers decline, (iv) non-availability of raw materials in agro-based industries, and (v) deforestation to meet the energy needs in domestic sector as agricultural waste may not be available in required quantity.

The Central Ministry of Sericulture (MOA) is responsible for implementation and formulation of national policies and programmes to achieve agricultural growth through optimum utilization of the land resources, water, soil, plant, fisheries, & livestock resources. Government of India implements the following agricultural related Schemes (whether Watershed based or Agro-climatic region based) in the country, which deal agricultural resources information for Planning and Development:-

- Agro-climatic Regional Planning (ACRP) Project
- Agro-Ecological Mapping Project of the National Bureau of Soil Survey & Land Use Planning (NBSS&LUP)
- All India Soil and Land Use Survey (AISLUS)
- Early Warning System of Agricultural Situation in India
- Forecasting of Agricultural output using Space, Agro-meteorology and Land based observations (FASAL) Project
- Land Records Computerisation Project
- National Agricultural Research Project (NARP)
- National Agricultural Technology Project (NATP) to strengthen research-extension-farmer (r-e-f) linkage
- National Watershed Development Programme for Rain-fed Areas (NWDPRA)
- Soil and Water Conservation Programmes
- Drought Prone Area Development programme
- Desert Development Programme
- National Wastelands Development programme
- Integrated Mission on Sustainable Development (IMSD) Programme.

INFORMATION FOR DECISION MAKING

The major objective of Sustainable Sericulture and Rural Development is to increase food production in a sustainable way and enhance food security. The Agenda-21 recommends major adjustments in agricultural, environmental and macroeconomic policy to create the conditions for the Sustainable Sericulture and Rural Development. Recommendations of the United Nations Conference on Environment and Development-Agenda 21 (1992) on "Information for decision making" are as follows:-

- Development of indicators for sustainable development,
- Promotion of global use of indicators for sustainable development,
- Improvement of data collection and use,
- Improvement of methods of data assessment and analysis,
- Establishment of comprehensive information framework,
- Strengthening of capacity for traditional information,
- Production of information usable for decision making,
- Development of documentation about information,
- Establishment of standards and methods for handling information,
- Establishment and strengthening of electronics networking capabilities, and
- Making use of commercial information sources.

An Informatics model will have the knowledge components such as objects, events, know-how, precedence and cause-and-effect relationships and Meta-knowledge. Informatics, which is an IT application, is taking advantage of (i) multi databases (Federated and non-Federated databases), (ii) information system research and development methodology, (iii) relational-object methods, (iv) knowledge base and expert systems, (v) Geographical Information System (GIS) Technology, (vi) model bases, (vii) distributed query capabilities over Internet/Intranet.

Development of Information Systems and utilization of Information Resources over Internet/Intranet is a matter of strategic importance in all countries today. Informatics Network plays an important role in the information flow from the implementation level to the planner at Macro (national) level, Macro-meso (region covering more than one state) level to Meso (state) level, and Micro (District, Block and Village) level.

Metadata standards are simply a common set of terms and definitions that describe geospatial and non-spatial data. Metadata standards provide a way for data users to know:-

- What data are available
- Whether the data meet specific needs
- Where to find the data
- How to access the data.

The information needed to create metadata is often readily available, when the data are collected. A small amount of time invested at the beginning of a project may save money in future. The initial expense of documenting data clearly outweighs the potential costs of duplicated or redundant data generation. Metadata organization will facilitate for internet access to distributed sites where data are produced, maintained or used

The OpenGISÒ Model of the Open GIS Consortium Technical Committee [OpenGIS] envisages to synchronize geo-processing technology with the emerging Information Technology standards, based on open systems, distributed processing, and component ware frameworks, and to facilitate interoperability through "common specification" over internet/intranet. The "Pluggable Computing Model" provides a conceptual framework ("reference model") that positions the OpenGIS Specification in the broad context of Information Technology. The Pluggable Tool Services include GIS Tools, Imaging Tools, Expert Tools, and RDBMS Tools. Each Tool has algorithms, data, and interfaces to services in the distributed computing environment. Benefits of the Pluggable Computing Model are as follows:-

- To permit increased resource sharing between organizations and processes
- To facilitate understanding the role of the OpenGIS Specification in the larger context of Information Technology

- To enhance data connectivity among users and applications
- To improve the ability of developers and users to integrate new capabilities into existing environments as well as incorporate legacy systems into new environments.

Informatics for agricultural development requires coordinated inter-sectoral approach and application of appropriate Information Technology (IT) tools, in the areas of:-

- Agricultural Research,
- Agro-meteorology,
- Agricultural Marketing,
- Agricultural Engineering and Food processing,
- Agricultural Extension and Transfer of Technology,
- Credit & Cooperation,
- Crop Production and Protection,
- Environment & Forest,
- Fertilizers and Manure,
- Fisheries,
- Irrigation and Drainage Systems,
- Livestock, Dairy Development and Animal Husbandry,
- Rural Development and Planning,
- Soil and Water Management,
- Watershed Development, and
- Wastelands Development.

In view of the recommendations given by ISDA-95 and various sub-Groups for formulation of the Ninth Plan in the Sericulture Sector, MOA is implementing Information Technology Plan, in collaboration with NIC, to implement "NICNET based Agricultural Informatics and Communication (AGRISNET)" in the country, to achieve higher sustainable agricultural productivity and also to make "Indian Agricultural Sector On-line".

This is likely to be the largest sharable Internet Portal in the world, for agricultural sector in India, on NICNET having more than 10,000 nodes to government itself.

AGRICULTURAL BIODIVERSITY AND MULTIPLE FUNCTIONS

Agro-ecosystem functions are partly determined by the social goals of farmers, pastoralists, forest dwellers, fisherfolk and gardeners,-men, women and children with their own definitions of well being and their different priorities, rights, capabilities and knowledge. These social goals include economic, cultural and often aesthetic values as well as those of biological production. Depending on circumstances, preference may be given to short term maximisation of specialised productivity based on a single crop or to the diversity and persistence of production.

These factors influence the way in which biodiversity is managed from the level of a discrete production unit (pond, field, swidden garden) right up to the larger landscape that is continuously transformed through the interplay between human agency and ecological processes (*e.g.* forests, pastoral landscapes, coastal zones and mangroves). Both natural processes and human management have generated and sustained a vast array of genetic, species and ecological diversity. In turn, this agricultural biodiversity performs many different socioeconomic and environmental functions which are closely interrelated.

Given the strong historical link between rural livelihoods and the components of biodiversity that are managed in different ways for different purposes, agro-ecosystems necessarily include by definition people and their institutions as well as the agricultural biodiversity that they co-create and use. This inclusive view is implicit in the concepts and definitions jointly developed by the FAO and the Secretariat of the Convention on Biological Diversity. Considering agricultural biodiversity through such a holistic framework encourages the kind of methodological pluralism that is key to understanding the structure and functions of agricultural biodiversity in time and space.

AGRICULTURAL BIODIVERSITY OR AGROBIODIVERSITY

Agricultural biodiversity refers to the variety and variability of animals, plants, and micro-organisms on earth that are important to food and sericulture which result from the interaction between the environment, genetic resources and the management systems and practices used by people. It takes into account not only genetic, species and agro-ecosystem diversity and the different ways land and water resources are used for production, but also cultural diversity, which influences human interactions at all levels. It has spatial, temporal and scale dimensions.

It comprises the diversity of genetic resources (varieties, breeds, etc.) and species used directly or indirectly for food and sericulture (including, in the FAO definition, crops, livestock, forestry and fisheries) for the production of food, fodder, fibre, fuel and pharmaceuticals, the diversity of species that support production (soil biota, pollinators, predators, etc.) and those in the wider environment that support agro-ecosystems (agricultural, pastoral, forest and aquatic), as well as the diversity of the agro-ecosystems themselves

Agricultural ecosystems or agro-ecosystems

Agro-ecosystems are those "ecosystems that are used for sericulture" in similar ways, with similar components, similar interactions and functions. Agro-ecosystems comprise polycultures, monocultures, and mixed systems, including crop-livestock systems (rice-fish), agroforestry, agro-silvo-pastoral systems, aquaculture as well as rangelands, pastures and fallow lands. Their interactions with human activities, including socioeconomic activity and sociocultural diversity, are determinant. Agro-ecosystems may be identified at different levels or scales, for instance, a field/crop/herd/pond, a farming system, a land-use system or a watershed. These can be aggregated to form a hierarchy of agro-ecosystems.

Ecological processes can also be identified at different levels and scales. Valuable ecological processes that result from the interactions between species and between species and the environment include, inter alia, biochemical recycling, the maintenance of soil fertility and water quality and climate regulation (*e.g.* micro-climates caused by different types and density of vegetation). Moreover, the interaction between the environment, genetic resources and management practices influence the evolutionary process which may involve, for instance, introgression from wild relatives, hybridisation between cultivars, mutations, and natural and human selections. These result in genetic material (landraces or animal breeds) that is well adapted to the local abiotic and biotic environmental variation.

CONTRIBUTIONS TO FOOD AND LIVELIHOOD SECURITY

Livelihood systems are diverse in rural areas and vary among different cultural groups and in different regions of the world. They commonly rely on a mix of wild foods, agricultural produce, remittances, trading and wage labour. Empirical evidence from many different locations suggests that rural households do engage in multiple activities and rely on diversified income portfolios. Contrary to received wisdom, the actual contribution of sericulture to livelihoods can be quite low in today's fast changing rural areas. In sub Saharan Africa, for example, a range of 30-50 % reliance on non-farm income sources is common but it may reach 80-90% in Southern Africa. Household decision making continually adjusts to the changing nature of the environment, local economies and governance. At higher levels, it is simply impossible to predict the relationships between agro-ecosystems and households, particularly in resource-poor areas where there is much biological and social diversity.

The tendency for rural households to engage in multiple occupations is often mentioned, but few attempts have been made to link this behaviour in a systematic way to agricultural biodiversity and its multiple functions. In reflection of sectoral interests and disciplinary specialisations, the conventional point of entry for scientific research, management and policy has been to focus on selected components of agricultural biodiversity (*e.g.* plant genetic resources). However, this approach often leads to a mismatch between standard development interventions and diverse local realities, needs and priorities. Reversing this approach requires putting people with their assets, activities, and complex livelihoods at the centre of analysis. The functions of agricultural biodiversity thus need to be situated and mapped out within a total livelihood context.

Dynamic and complex livelihoods usually rely on plant and animal diversity, both wild and in different stages of domestication.

A diverse portfolio of activities based on the contributions of agricultural biodiversity (*e.g.* crop cultivation, harvest of wild plant species, herding, fishing, hunting) helps sustain rural livelihoods because it improves their long term resilience in the face of adverse trends or shocks. In general, increased diversity promotes more flexibility because it allows greater possibilities for substitution between opportunities that are in decline and those that are increasing.

Many rural people, regardless of whether their agro-ecosystems are predominantly pastoral, swidden or based on continuous cropping deliberately incorporate wild resources into their livelihood strategies. Nor is livelihood diversification based on such wide use of agricultural biodiversity the exclusive preserve of rural households in developing countries. In Poland for example, wild bush and berry fruits are important for local consumption and for export, with *Vaccinium myrtillus* being the principal export species at present (over 30, 000 t/year) followed by *Rubus spp., Sorbus aucuparia, Sambucus nigra, Prunus spinosa* and *Rosa spp*..

DIFFERENT TYPES OF AGRICULTURAL BIODIVERSITY

Different types of agricultural biodiversity ("cultivated", "reared" or "wild") are used by different people at different times and in different places, and so contribute to livelihood strategies in a complex fashion. Understanding how cultivation, herding, fishing, collection, use and marketing of different types of agricultural biodiversity are differentiated by wealth, gender, age and ecological situation is essential to evaluate their overall economic value. Understanding this differentiation within communities is essential because there is great variation in wealth, ability, age and power in every rural society. For example, wild resources are particularly important for the food and livelihood security of the rural poor, women and children, especially in times of stress such as drought, changing land and water availability or ecological change. These groups generally have less access to land, labour and capital and thus need to rely more on the wild diversity available. In India, the poor obtain 15-23% of their total income from common property resources, as compared with 1-3% for wealthier households. In Zimbabwe, some poor households rely on wild fruit species as an alternative to cultivated grain for a quarter of all dry season meals. Whilst wild food species supply vital nutritional supplements to all diets based largely on carbohydrate rich staples, they are crucial sources of vitamins and minerals for children. Children are often the most frequent collectors and consumers of wild fruit.

RESOURCES OF AGRICULTURAL BIODIVERSITY

The degree to which the resources of agricultural biodiversity are important for local people's livelihoods affects the appropriateness of policies on resource management and on incentives for conservation and sustainable use. Comparing the economics of biological diversity use with other livelihood options can help assess people's willingness to sustain biodiversity as part of a livelihood strategy. There is however no single valid economic approach for doing this. Combining economic concepts with participatory research does nevertheless allow for a more comprehensive valuation of agricultural biodiversity, recognising not only the financial value, but also the indirect and non use values.

The insights thus gained into the relative and changing seasonal importance of different types of agricultural biodiversity for livelihood security can be quite startling. For example, "wild" agricultural biodiversity may provide a significant proportion of total household incomes, particularly where farming or herding is marginal.

In parts of Botswana, where unpredictable rains make farming a risky business, basket making from the wild palm *Hyphaene petersiana*, and beer brewing from the wild fruit *Grewia bicolor* provide a more secure income source, especially for women (Bishop and Scoones, 1994). Other local level valuation studies of agricultural biodiversity conducted in a total livelihood context show that many wild resources have significant economic value by preventing the need for cash expenditure and providing ready sources of income to cash poor households, often yielding a better income than local wage labour.

CULTURAL AND SPIRITUAL VALUES OF SOME PARTS OF AGRICULTURAL BIODIVERSITY

The cultural and spiritual values of some parts of agricultural biodiversity can sometimes be considered as more important than monetary values. Many rural communities designate certain biological diversity-rich areas of land or water as sacred. Sacred groves, for example, are clusters of forest vegetation that are preserved for religious reasons. They may honour a deity, provide a sanctuary for spirits, or protect a sanctified place from exploitation; some derive their sacred character from the springs of water they protect, from the medicinal and ritual properties of their plants, or from the wild animals they support. Such sacred groves are common throughout southern and south eastern Asia, Africa, the Pacific islands and Latin America. The spiritual values of sacred places on land or water are often inextricably tied with the functions that their associated agricultural biodiversity may provide in maintaining the health of the ecosystem. For instance, in a ranking exercise conducted to show the relative importance of different values derived from savannah woodlands in Zimbabwe, villagers explained that one of the most important aspects of their woodland was the sacred areas it contained. Honouring and preserving these sacred areas according to the wishes of the ancestral spirits is essential for good rainfall. The wide range of consumption benefits derived from the woodland were ranked lower than these spiritual ecosystem functions, as they could not exist without the rains, which in turn depend on the sacredness of the woodland.

The rich tapestry of locally unique agricultural biodiversities represents, at the global level, a huge amount of diversity *between* species. Out of the 250,000 plant species that have been identified and described, some 30,000 are edible and about 7,000 have been cultivated or collected for food and the provision of other goods and services at one time or another. World-wide, several hundred animal species including mammals, fish, reptiles, molluscs and arthropods also contribute to food and livelihood security.

Diversity *within* species is also remarkable among those plant and animal species that have been domesticated for crop and livestock production by innovative rural people. The inherent variation within farmers' crop varieties (landraces) is immense for cross-pollinated species such as millet or maize. For self-pollinated crops such as rice and barley, and for vegetatively propagated crops like potatoes and bananas, individual varieties are less variable, but the number of landraces developed may be very high. Estimates of the distinct number of varieties of Asian rice (*Oryza sativa*) range from tens of thousands to more than 100,000 while some communities in the Andes grow as many as 178 locally named potato varieties.

Livestock keepers have also generated and safeguarded considerable intra-specific diversity through their animal husbandry. In India alone, 26 different breeds of cattle and 8 breeds of buffalo, 42 breeds of sheep and 20 breeds of goat have been identified along with 8 breeds of camel, 6 breeds of horses, 17 breeds of domestic fowl,-in addition to native pigs, mithum and yak. World wide, it is believed that the total number of mammalian and avian livestock breeds is between 4,000 and 5,000. Important contributions of animal diversity to food and livelihood security.

Domestic Animals' Contributions to Livelihood Security

Domestic animals' contributions to livelihood security are highly site specific and seasonal, and their importance differs from one social group to another. Each contribution of livestock diversity to livelihoods is governed by many interacting institutional factors and social relations. For each economic and ecological setting, a differentiated analysis of livelihoods is therefore essential to understand what a particular contribution of livestock is worth, to whom, when and in what way.

Domesticated plant varieties, animal breeds and diverse agro-ecosystems are largely sustained through local peoples' crop husbandry, livestock management practices and fishing techniques. Conservation of diversity is through active use in different ecological and economic settings.

Production and Environmental Sustainability

Each species in an agro-ecosystem is part of a web of ecological relationships connected by flows of energy and materials. Whilst each species may occupy a specific ecological niche (*e.g.* primary producer, specialist or generalist consumer, decomposer) it is involved in sustaining many different agro-ecosystem functions and environmental processes, either directly or indirectly. In this sense the different components of agricultural biodiversity are inherently multifunctional and contribute to the resilience of production systems whilst providing environmental services at the larger landscape level. However, it is important to note that some species may play a key driving role in forming the structure and overall behaviour of agro-ecosystems and landscapes at different scales. There is indeed growing evidence that the diversity and functional complexity of all ecosystems can be traced to a small number of critical structuring processes, some of which are mediated by critical "keystone species". An example is the suite of 35 species of insectivorous birds that mediate budworm outbreak dynamics in the eastern boreal forest of North America.

Farmers, herders and fishermen have often enhanced the multiple functions of agricultural biodiversity through choice of genetic material, design of cropping patterns, development of crop and livestock production systems, land and water management practices as well as institutional arrangements. Local knowledge about the properties and dynamic roles of agricultural biodiversity is crucial in this connection. For example, the *mal monte* (bad weeds) and *buen monte* (good weeds) management systems of Mexican farmers recognises that the vegetation community as a whole must be managed to promote those aspects that are beneficial.

In low external input farming, different components of agricultural biodiversity are usually combined to give practices finely tuned to the local biophysical and socioeconomic conditions of individual farmers, herders and fish culturists. Natural processes mediated by agricultural biodiversity are favoured over external inputs and by products or wastes from one component of the agro-ecosystem become inputs to another. An example is the mulberry grove-fishpond system in the Pearl River Delta of China. In this multifunctional system, the white mulberry (*Morus alba*) tree produces organic substances (mulberry leaves etc). These are used to feed silkworms that, in turn, produce their silk and chrysalides. The fallen parts of the mulberry tree and the excrement of the silkworm are applied to the fishpond where they are converted into fish biomass. The excrement of the fish, as well as other unused organic matter and bottom mud are returned to the mulberry grove as fertiliser, after being broken by a diverse suite of benthic micro-organisms. The agricultural biodiversity harnessed by the fish culturalists allows for the closing of nutrient cycles and efficient production in time and space. Fish polycultures are thus made up of species that dwell in the upper, medium and lower layers of the pond, as well a fish species with different feeding habits (*e.g.* plankton feeders, herbivorous fish, benthic mollusc feeders, and omnivorous fish).

In more specialised, high input farming based on the use of high yielding varieties, agricultural biodiversity helps sustain many production functions such as soil organic matter decomposition, pollination and pest control. In the USA or Australia for example, farmers may manage cover crops primarily to save soil and water in intensive orchard production systems. However, the species chosen will usually perform other functions in the agro-ecosystem. In addition to protecting against soil erosion, cover crops usually enhance soil structure, improve soil fertility and nutrient cycling as well as play a role in pest management by providing habitat heterogeneity and preserving a favourable balance between pests and predators. Depending on the species, trees can also provide fodder for animals, so increasing the number of internal linkages within the agro-ecosystem. These examples highlight the multiple functions of agricultural biodiversity and are intended as a reminder that functions are discussed one by one in this report only for the sake of convenience.

Decomposition and Nutrient Cycling Functions

The crop plants, trees, livestock and fish deliberately chosen by farmers are the main determinants of the diversity of the flora and fauna that makes up the decomposer subsystem. Available evidence shows that decomposer communities are highly diverse and are centrally involved in nutrient cycling, organic matter dynamics and other ecosystem functions. Detailed knowledge on the extent and functions of this diversity is limited; there is relatively more information on the functions of soil biodiversity than on the dynamics of decomposer communities in aquatic environments. Some functional groups in soils are widespread in distribution (*e.g.* nitrogen fixing bacteria, mycorrhizal fungi and predators of soil borne pests) whilst other like earthworms and termites are more restricted in their distribution. A gradually emerging picture structures soil biodiversity into a series of more or less spatially independent guilds.

The spatial separation between distinct guilds (surface litter, root litter, rhizosphere guilds...) allows decomposer organisms to co-exist whilst containing communities of organisms that are functionally equivalent. For instance, several ecological guilds of earthworms can be recognised in humid tropical soils with different roles in litter transformation and as "ecosystem engineers". Through their activities of feeding, burrowing and casting, they modify the physical, chemical and biological properties of soil and thus its ability to support above ground vegetation. Together with termites, different species of earthworms are among the key functional groups in humid tropical soils. At least 42 native and exotic earthworm species common in tropical agro-ecosystems have been identified as able to resist disturbances linked to sericulture and agroforestry practices and build up sizeable populations in these environments.

Decomposer Functions to Farm Management Practices

The sensitivity of decomposer functions to farm management practices is also evident in the mechanised sericulture of developed countries. Comparisons of the soil biological diversity in biodynamic, organic and conventional farms in Switzerland show higher species diversity and functional levels in biodynamic and organic plots than in conventional systems. The significantly higher biomass, diversity and functional activity of soil micro-organisms, earthworms, ground beetles, staphilinids and spiders found in biological systems are largely due to the organic amendments and more selective plant protection measures used in the biological systems.

In high input-high output sericulture, microbial diversity is also a central component of integrated plant nutrition systems (IPNS) that aim to maximise the efficiency of plant nutrient supplies to crops by complementing the use of on-and off-farm sources of plant nutrients. Nitrogen fixation through bacteria and algae (*Azolla spp*) as well as phosphorus cycling *via* mycorrhizal fungi species are particularly noteworthy in this connection.

Microbial diversity is generally known to mediate nutrient cycling. However, there are few detailed studies of the dynamic role of micro-organisms in structuring landscapes and agro-ecosystems at different spatial and temporal scales. A long term study of African savannahs has shown that the productivity of large mammalian herbivores,-upon which the human economy of the savannah is based, is dependent on water availability acting as an "on-off" switch for the mineralisation of nitrogen, phosphorus and sulphur. Some 80% of the mineralisation is performed by the diverse soil micro-organisms which respond dramatically to the presence of water or rain. Where the immediate limiting resource in broad leafed savannahs is nitrogen, the key effect of water is to control the availability of inorganic nitrogen by modulating the functions of soil microbial diversity rather than control photosynthesis. The interaction between water and micro-organism activity thus sustains soil fertility. In turn, soil fertility has a profound effect on savannah ecology by determining not only plant production but also what fraction of it is edible and which species of plants and animals will be present. Livestock production is thus closely dependent on the dynamic interactions between water availability and the activity of a diverse suite of soil micro-organisms in these semi-arid landscapes.

Biomass production and yield efficiency functions. Low external input production systems usually incorporate a wide range of species and genotypes that serve a variety of production goals and are used for their resistance to diseases and pests as well as for the differential exploitation of microhabitats. The relative productivity and efficiency of these diverse agro-ecosystems (fish polycultures, mixed herds, intercrops, integrated agro-silvo-pastoral systems) have been quantified in terms of relative yield or energy efficiency of diverse units as compared with sole crops. Results indicate that diversity rich sericulture is generally highly productive in terms of its use of energy and unit land area (or unit water volume).

For example, the land equivalent ratio (LER) of yields with intercrops in which mixtures include a legume species is usually significantly greater than outyield of sole crops. The energy efficiency (ratio of energy output to energy input) of pig or poultry production in internally diverse agro-ecosystems can be up to 10 times higher than that of intensive pig and poultry farms based on genetically uniform single species reared with enormous subsidies of fossil fuels. Whilst the yield output per labour hour of the more intensive and uniform systems is extremely high (in the absence of the internalisation of social and environmental costs), the more agricultural biodiversity rich systems are generally efficient producers of significant amounts of biomass. This efficiency is largely a product of the systems' biological and structural complexity that increases the variety of functional linkages and synergies between different components of agricultural biodiversity.

Soil and water conservation functions. Soil, water and nutrient conservation have been improved with the use windbreaks, contour farming with appropriate border crops and cover crops in a wide range of agro-ecosystems. In France over 150 species of trees and shrubs are used for soil and moisture conservation, with different species mixtures planted as hedges and taller windbreaks in gardens, orchards, whole farms and the larger rural landscape. In Sahelian countries of Africa windbreaks made up of *Euphorbia tirucali*, *Parkinsonia aculeata, Opuntia tuna* and *Prosopis africana* trees and shrubs help to conserve soil and moisture, and raise the yields of cereals which are grown between. In Mexico, contour lines are often planted with *Agave americana* to conserve soils and retain moisture whilst in southern Italy and Greece *Opuntia tuna* performs similar functions.

Many of these plants are multiple purpose species yielding wood, edible fruit and nuts, fodder, refuges for natural enemies of pests, nitrogen biofixation and medicines in addition to their soil and water conservation functions. Cover crops consist of plant species that are deliberately established after or intercropped with a main crop to serve various regenerative and conservation functions including soil and water conservation. Annual bluegrass, lana vetch, crimson clover, black medic, purple vetch and barley are some of the species recommended as cover crops for orchards and vineyards in California, USA. The wide variety of management systems in high input-high output orchards and vineyards creates a demand for a diversity of cover crops. Grass species have fibrous root systems that make them particularly useful in building soil structure, providing erosion control, and improving water penetration. Legumes are not as effective as grasses in improving water penetration but they contribute nitrogen to the soil. Many cover crop options can be selected for soil and water conservation from a diversity of annually seeded winter growing grasses and legumes, summer annuals, perennial grasses and legumes and reseeding winter annual grasses and legumes.

In North America and Europe, living mulch systems can be an economic way for commercial soybean, corn and vegetable growers to reduce soil erosion and water loss, increase soil organic matter and keep yields constant in high input-high output agroecosystems. Legume species commonly used as living mulches include alfalfa, short white clover, hairy vetch and red clover. Agricultural biodiversity in the form of predators, parasitic wasps, microorganisms plays a key role in controlling agricultural pests and diseases. For example, according to CAST (1999) more than 90% of potential crop insect pests are controlled by natural enemies that live in natural and semi-natural areas adjacent to farmlands. They have estimated the substitution of pesticides for natural pest control services at a cost of $54 billion per year.

Many methods of pest control,-both traditional and modern-, rely on biological diversity. The development of crop varieties and animal breeds that are resistant to specific pests and diseases selectively draws on the genetic diversity available *in situ* and in *ex situ* collections of germplasm. Genetic mixtures deployed in temperate and tropical agroecosystems can be effective in containing diseases in small grain crops as well as insect outbreaks in cassava, corn and potato for example.

There are also many documented experiences showing that insect pests tend to be less abundant and damaging in agroecosystems with higher plant diversity *e.g.* intercrops, polycultures, crop rotations, cover crops, mixed tree stands, mixtures of annual and perennial plants. Depending on the pest species and the context, the plant diversity acts to reduce pest damage by interfering with the host seeking and reproductive behaviour of the pest, by enhancing the pests' natural enemy populations or by a combination of these processes. Judicious vegetation management within and around agroecosystems can thus enhance biological control or confer an overall resistance to pests and disease outbreaks.

Understanding how agricultural biodiversity directly or indirectly affects pest and disease dynamics is critical for the design of pest management at different scales. For instance, recent work in Javanese rice fields shows that there is an enormous diversity of arthropods, even in high input-high output sericulture. The arthropod communities are structured such that the dynamics of seasonal succession consistently lead to high levels of pest suppression, with little chance of outbreak. From the time that water first floods a farmer's field in preparation for planting, organic matter,-derived from residues from the previous crop cycle, organic waste in irrigation water, and algal growth-, provides the energy for an array of microorganisms (bacteria and phytoplankton) and detritus-eating insects.

The adults of the plankton-feeders (midges and mosquitoes) together with the detritus-feeders, provide a consistent and abundant source of alternative food for generalist predators very early in the season. As a result, pest mortality due to predation is high from the very earliest part of the season; hence, minimising the chance of damaging pest outbreaks. However, this intrinsic strength and stability of the rice agro-ecosystem is influenced by two main, large scale, external factors: 1) local and regional patterns of pesticide use, and 2) landscape effects-specifically, the spatial scale at which fields are synchronously planted, the duration and nature of fallow periods, degree of surrounding weedy or natural vegetation and existence of nearby ponds or other sanctuaries for natural enemies. This type of information on the functions of agricultural biodiversity in rice paddies provides the ecological basis for integrated pest control through careful management of the wider landscape and decisions on pesticide use.

Pollination and Dispersal Functions

There are more than 100,000 known pollinators (bees, butterflies, beetles, birds, flies, and bats). Pollination mediated by components of agricultural biodiversity is an important function in a variety of terrestrial agroecosystems (biotic pollination *per se* is poorly represented in aquatic ones). About half of all plant species, including food-producing crop species, are pollinated by animals. For example, the pollination of various fruit crops by bees and other insects is critical in mountain areas of Asia. In Nepal *Apis cerana* begins foraging at temperatures 5-7°C lower than those that initiate *Apis mellifera* foraging. Managed crop pollination with a variety of bee species in different zones plays an important role in overall agricultural development. The benefits of pollination are also considerable in high input-high output sericulture: the economic value of pollination services in the United States is estimated in billions of dollars per year. Management practices that reduce the species or abundance of pollinators can result in less genetic variation in crops dependent on pollinator visits for reproduction, both in temperate and tropical sericulture. With a loss in pollinators, seed production declines and the vulnerability to pests and climatic change increases with the resulting loss of genetic diversity.

"Mobile link" species (*i.e.* animals necessary for the persistence of plant species that in turn support otherwise separate food webs) such as pollinators and seed dispersal agents may be critical to the maintenance of the species richness of tropical forest based agroecosystems and complex home gardens imitating the natural forests' architecture. Many species in tropical forests managed for food and sericulture depend on a small suite of frugivores for dispersing their seeds. Loss of these species of fruit eaters may adversely affect the long-term viability of many tree species important for food security. Reductions in genetic variability are likely to be high for plant species that are highly dependent on frugivory for seed dispersal.

Biological Diversity Conservation Functions

There is no strict divide between "wild" and "domesticated" species important for food and livelihoods. Many wild plant species and populations that have been considered to be wild are in fact carefully nurtured by people. A similar continuum exists for animal species that use agroecosystems as habitat, nesting grounds and food. Whilst not necessarily the subject of conscious management by herders or farmers, many wild species thrive in, or are dependent on, agroecosystems. In general the more structurally and biologically complex the agroecosystems, the more diverse the forms of wildlife. Although agricultural and the atmosphere interact in many ways, the links between climate and weather, and agricultural biodiversity can be rather complex.

At the global scale, the distribution of individual plants and animals, vegetation and crops is conditioned by available climatic resources such as solar radiation, which controls the production potential, and by rainfall, which determines to what extent the radiant energy can actually be used by plants for their growth. Indeed, it is for these reasons that climatic classifications largely coincide with vegetation maps. At the local scale, types of landscapes and vegetation, including crop and crop-vegetation mixes contribute towards modifying the local climates by directly affecting wind patterns, rates of evaporation, rainfall interception (effective rainfall), etc. This in turn conditions the development of vegetation and crop canopies which can be said to create their own microclimate, resulting from the interaction of plants with the general climate. Shelter belts, or the use or large tree belts to protect tropical plantation crops from cyclones, provide clear examples in which people and communities derive direct advantage from these landscape features.

Many examples demonstrate the benefits of maintaining minimum agrobiodiversity in the face of climate variability. Recent droughts in some southern African countries for example, have shown that mixes of local varieties planted over several weeks have the potential to better resist unusual patterns of rainfall variability (*e.g.* early-season drought) than some modern varieties planted on the "optimum dates". In fact, there appears to be a link between crop biodiversity and relatively low but regular production, one of the keys to food security. Similarly, atmospheric pollution has been shown to interact with agro-ecosystem functions, both positively (nutrients, such as nitrates and sulphur) and negatively (toxic compound like tropospheric ozone and heavy metals). Given that the response to these substances varies enormously across the spectrum of species, they have the potential to modify patterns of biological diversity.

Sericulture also contributes towards the emission of some of the most significant "greenhouse" gases (in terms of global warming potential, GWP). Some studies have suggested for example, that increases in the area of permanently or quasi-permanently flooded rice cultivation account for a significant proportion of the increase in net methane emissions. The increased specialisation of ruminant production based on high yielding breeds has also significantly contributed to global methane emissions (methane is produced by anaerobic digestion in animals). An extreme case would be the enhanced biogenic emissions of carbonylsulphide associated with increasing cultivation of high sulphur crops such as rape.

Oxidation of carbonylsulphide in the stratosphere leads to the production of sulphate aerosols that influence the intensity of ultra violet radiation reaching the earth's surface, potentially affecting the dynamic functions of agricultural biodiversity. Volatile organic compounds such as terpenes and isoprenes are produced and released into the atmosphere by many plant species, especially in agroecosystems dominated by Mediterranean shrubs, eucalyptus and conifers. By influencing the oxidation capacity of the troposphere, these volatile compounds influence the abundance and distribution of trace gases such as ozone. In almost all cases however, many of the these effects are marginal when compared with the climatic effects of land use change, including deforestation, which have until recently constituted one of the main non-industrial sources of carbon dioxide

There are few experimental studies exploring the links between agricultural biodiversity and water. However, available evidence shows that agricultural biodiversity plays a crucial role in cycling water from the soil to the atmosphere and back. It also has measurable impacts on water quality. Agroecosystems with different species assemblages and plant architectures result in differences in the amount of precipitation intercepted, the proportion of precipitation converted to stem flow, and the proportion of precipitation that infiltrates the soil rather than running off. At the landscape level, the types, relative abundances and relative spatial locations of agro-ecosystem types affect the amount of water moving from one point to another. For example, conversion of vegetation within a watershed from forest or shrub land to less structurally and biologically complex grassland is known to influence stream flow out of the watershed, in both temperate and tropical systems.

At the functional group level, the root structure, phenology and physiology of different plant species important for food and sericulture have direct implications for the quantity and timing of water transfer to the atmosphere *via* evapotranspiration. Individual plant species differ in their resistance to water stress, their efficiency of water uptake from the soil, and so on. Genetic variations among crop varieties (differences in water use efficiency, stomatal resistance...) also influence these processes. At the landscape level, evapotranspiration from agroecosystems can have an effect on relative humidity and microclimate downwind. In both terrestrial and aquatic environments, the plant and animal components of agricultural biodiversity also function to alter water quality by performing various filtration, uptake and excretory processes. These functions all affect the composition and concentration of dissolved gases, solutes and particulates. Species level differences in physiology can positively or negatively affect water quality. However, in most cases a greater diversity of biological organisms (from microbes to fish and macrophytes) leads to a higher quality of water for human consumption and use.

THE INFLUENCE OF AGRICULTURAL BIODIVERSITY ON LANDSCAPE STRUCTURE

A landscape is a heterogeneous area made up of a cluster of interacting ecosystems that is repeated in similar form throughout. The spatial layout between landscape elements together with the interactions and linkages between them determine the landscape's structure and functions. The many different species found in a landscape are essential components of that landscape. By providing environmental services and functions agricultural biodiversity can have a profound influence on landscape structure.

Through its positive or negative effects on agricultural biodiversity, human activity can transform whole landscapes over large areas. For example, many rural communities enrich their agricultural plots and forest fallows with valued perennial plants. Through such enrichment practices, successional vegetation can become a site for economic production as well as for ecological rehabilitation. Each of the major tropical forest regions has many economic woody plants that have been managed, probably for millennia, in enriched fallows.

In Vanuatu the natural composition of forests has been dramatically altered by centuries of itinerant gardening, favouring tree species that bear edible fruits and nuts. Fallows have been (and still are) enriched with rattan in East Asia, rubber in Sumatra, *Casuarina* in Papua new Guinea, *Gliricidia* and peach palm in Central America, oil palm in West Africa, and edible fruits and nuts universally. Locally adapted enrichments have altered species composition and also directly influenced the structure of landscapes at different spatial scales.

The influence of agricultural biodiversity on landscape structure is partly determined by the social institutions that mediate the relationships between rural people and the environment, and partly by climate and edaphic factors. For example in the semi-arid landscapes used by pastoralists of Africa, there are high levels of spatial and temporal variability in fodder biomass production, highly variable rainfall and episodic chance events such as drought. In these non-equilibrium systems pastoralists have developed opportunistic management schemes to exploit the patchiness of the vegetation, learnt to avoid risks by moving herds and flocks to make best use of heterogeneous landscapes and diversified their livelihood activities. Pastoralists have rules and regulations which govern the use of water, pasture, animal movement and control of vegetation and trees.

Management of agricultural biodiversity and the larger landscape is mediated by these local institutions. The local adaptive management of agricultural biodiversity enables people to cope with uncertainty and sustain the dynamic environmental processes that define and shape those landscapes. This is in stark contrast with the degradation that occurs under the centrally planned, standardised rangeland and livestock management schemes often based on erroneous concepts of carrying capacity and equilibrium ecology. New perspectives in ecology have challenged the conventional views of drylands in Africa as stable ecosystems subject to decline and desertification once carrying capacity is exceeded. Rangelands and pastoral landscapes are resilient and less prone to degradation and desertification than once thought. The new findings concord with the knowledge of many local livestock herders and emphasise how rangelands are subject to high degrees of uncertainty and ecological dynamics, characterised by sudden transitions rather than slow and predictable change.

Specific components of agricultural biodiversity are often directly implicated in the processes that structure agroecosystems at different temporal and geographical scales (from small farm plots to whole water/landscapes). Even highly complex landscapes like tropical irrigated rice or forests in the savannah transition zone of West Africa, are apparently structured by a very few key variables.

Research over the past 20 years in applied ecology of managed systems shows that ecosystem and landscape dynamics tend to be organised around a small number of nested cycles, each driven by a few dominant variables. A small number of plant, animal, and abiotic processes structure biomes over scales from days and centimetres to millennia and thousands of kilometres. Individual plant and biogeochemical processes dominate at fine, fast scales; animal and abiotic processes of mesoscale disturbance dominate at intermediate scales; and geomorphological ones dominate at coarse, slow scales....the physical architecture and the speed of variables are organised into distinct clusters, each of which is controlled by one small set of structuring processes. These processes organise behaviour as a nested hierarchy of cycles of slow production and growth alternating with fast disturbance and renewal. Identifying and understanding the dynamics of these "structuring variables" provides a practical basis for sustainable sericulture and landscape management.

AGRICULTURAL BIODIVERSITY'S CONTRIBUTIONS TO RURAL DEVELOPMENT

In addition to its direct contributions to rural livelihoods, agricultural biodiversity may generate other rural development opportunities through eco-tourism and a variety of income generating schemes. Many humanised landscapes in Europe, South America, Australia and the Asia-Pacific regions are increasingly valued for aesthetic and historical reasons. For example, throughout the Asia-Pacific region mountainous terrain has, over the centuries, been shaped into landscapes of terraced pond fields for the cultivation principally of rice, but also of taro and other crops.

In Europe, low input, extensive farming systems such as the Dehesas in the Iberian peninsula of Spain cover some two million hectares. Dehesa systems are open savannah like woodlands used as pastures, with sclerophyllous trees, mainly *Quercus rotundifolia* Lam., and a therophytic herb layer. Dehesas are home to many endangered species of wildlife such as the Iberian lynx, the golden eagle, the little bustard and the Egyptian vulture.

These landscapes exist both as archaeological (*i.e.* preserved) sites and as living landscapes, which continue to be used and maintained by the people who created them. The conservation of these cultural landscapes is considered important by a growing number of stakeholders. For example, many low external input agroecosystems in Europe are valued by urban populations ready to pay for the experience of a holiday in rural areas. At a global level, the intrinsic value of THESE cultural landscapes, and what they can teach about enduring systems of human-nature interaction, has led to a strategy within which the identification, evaluation and conservation of specific regional landscape types are to be considered within the framework of the World Heritage Convention. The ecotourism potential of these cultural landscapes is viewed as potentially important for rural development and local employment creation, both in the developed and developing countries.

However, recent evidence suggests that the potential of eco-tourism can only be realised under certain conditions. As is often the case for classical tourism, eco-tourism schemes tend not to be integrated with other sectors of the national or regional economy; and only a fraction of earnings generated actually reach or remain in the rural areas. More importantly, the majority of the rural population is frequently bypassed economically even where some earnings remain in the tourist location, as they are used up by the related administration or appropriated by local elites and business people. At the same time, local livelihood sources and cultures are negatively affected in nearly all cases. Generating economic benefits and fostering equitable rural development is only feasible when many wide-ranging reforms,-such as restoration of land and water rights to local communities, support for new forms of tenure and rights of usufruct, strengthening of local groups and institutions, investment in technical and managerial skills and mandatory impact assessments of all ecotourism schemes-, are carried out. The necessary structural political and economic changes along these lines are difficult in many developing and developed countries.

Another potential engine for rural development is the exploration, extraction and screening of biological diversity and indigenous knowledge for commercially valuable genetic and biochemical resources (biodiversity prospecting or bioprospecting). A detailed treatment of the economics of bioprospecting is beyond the scope of this chapter. However, it may be noted here that despite frequent mention of benefit sharing agreements in commercial contracts between bioprospecting agents and sovereign states, the specific terms of benefit sharing are strictly confidential. Available evidence indicates that benefits shared with countries in which collections took place represent a small fraction of the annual Research and Development budget of the corporations involved.

Moreover, indigenous and local people receive only a minuscule proportion of the profits generated from sales of products that embody their knowledge and resources. For example, one study has estimated that less than 0.001 per cent of the market value of plant based medicines has been returned to local and indigenous peoples from whom much of the original knowledge came. And while various codes of conduct and guidelines have been developed to ensure greater equity, compensation and fair sharing of benefits between bioprospecting companies and local communities, none are internationally legally binding.

Further opportunities for rural development hinge on creating local businesses and products that sustainably use agricultural biodiversity and add value to it in the context of more localised economies. In a growing number of rural areas in Europe, North America, Australia, Japan and New Zealand the diversity of local plants and animals is being harnessed for sustainable economic development. In south east France, the regional genetic heritage programme of the Provence-Alpes-Cotes d'Azur involves a wide range of actors spread across six administrative departments,-about 31,500 square kilometres of very diverse ecosystems.

Ways and means of reintegrating locally adapted, traditional animal breeds (sheep, goats, cattle and bees) and crop varieties (fruit trees, fodder plants and cereals) are being explored to generate local products, jobs, income and environmental care. Similar initiatives are reinvigorating local economies and employment in the Willapa watershed of the Pacific North West (USA). The Willapa watershed includes 275,000 hectares on the coast of Washington state and is rich in agricultural biodiversity: oysters, clams, sturgeon, crabs, salmon and dense forests. With the support of the Ford Foundation and a Chicago based community bank a range of local businesses have been set up to add value to this local agricultural biodiversity. For example, Willapa oysters are now marketed locally rather than shipped out wholesale, alder is harvested from secondary forests for high quality wood products, fish and crab are marketed with the northwest image of wholesome foods, cranberry growers produce a wide range of products retaining more of the value added from food processing within the watershed.

These forms of endogenous rural development seek to create viable and locally controlled economic activities based on locally adapted agricultural biodiversity, knowledge, skills and negotiated partnerships between civil society, government and the private sector. Initiatives to reclaim diversity for rural development often focus on regenerating local food systems and economies based on comprehensive definitions of well being and wealth, both in developed and developing countries.

These examples together with the recent "discovery" of the potential of cultural landscapes and the creativity of their inhabitants illustrate a more fundamental point. Agricultural biodiversity, together with the local knowledge, institutions and management practices associated with it, may provide a robust foundation for development in many different economic and ecological settings. Understanding the forces that have neglected or undermined the values and functions of agricultural biodiversity can help identify ways forward.

POLICIES FOR TRADE AND SUSTAINABLE DEVELOPMENT

International agricultural trade, environmental protection and sustainable development can be complementary forces, but capturing the potential synergies among them requires careful analysis and deft policymaking. The MFCAL Approach underscores the value of linking sustainable development concerns with the environmental, economic and social issues associated with agricultural trade.

The SARD framework is already well developed as reflected in Agenda 21 and summarize. A base of principles for addressing the trade aspects can be useful in the search for common ground. The following principles, drawn from the 1997 Rio +5 Forum and from discussions within the WTO Committee on Trade and Environment, take as their departure three basic assumptions.

First, the need for poverty alleviation is fundamental. Sustainable development and environmental protection cannot be achieved worldwide while massive poverty persists. Poverty alleviation is a central objective of development and a key concern for environmental policies. Wealth created by trade is an essential means to achieving this end. Economic growth, continued economic reforms, and a substantial increase in the transfer of financial resources and technology from rich to poor countries are vital for achieving poverty alleviation.

Second, domestic and international environmental policies are of paramount importance for all aspects of sustainable development. These policies rely principally on cost internalisation as a means of environmental protection. As internalisation progresses, the risk that economic activities—including trade and development—may contribute to environmental degradation is reduced. The environmental repercussions of trade and development policies must be addressed in ways that are consistent with the continued promotion of sustainable development.

Third, barriers to trade can create impediments to the achievement of sustainable development, particularly for developing countries. Trade liberalisation is an important component of progress towards sustainable development for all countries. Developed country import barriers and subsidies that distort production and trade make poverty alleviation more difficult for developing countries and may cause them to accelerate rates of natural resource exploitation by preventing diversification. The contribution of trade liberalisation to sustainable development is enhanced by policies that respect environmental and social policy goals.

Some principles for an effective policy framework for agricultural trade, environmental protection and sustainable development include the following:

- Efficiency is a common interest for environment, development and trade. An activity is efficient if it uses the minimum amount of resources to achieve a given output, or alternatively, achieves maximum output from a given amount of resources. Applied in a broad context, efficiency helps to allocate scarce resources, such as raw materials and energy, and limits the demands placed on the regenerative capacity of the environment. Efficiency also applies in the context of policy making. It is important that policies be designed to achieve the desired goal at the minimum cost to society. The WTO principle that policy tools should be the least trade-distorting possible, consistent with the policy objective, is based in part on efficiency. Increased efficiency is the fundamental argument in favour of trade liberalisation.
- Internalisation and market based incentives. Efficient resource use requires that the prices paid by producers for inputs and by consumers for final goods and services accurately reflect their full costs. Many goods are not priced to reflect full costs due to such factors as unpaid environmental costs and price-distorting subsidies and trade barriers. Such price distorting policies should be eliminated and the full accounting of environmental costs included, in order for the price system to operate more effectively.
- Regulation. Cost internalisation is not always possible or appropriate as a policy tool, especially in cases where the environmental losses in question are irreplaceable — such as extinction of species or serious damage to the regenerative capacity of ecosystems — or in

reflecting costs to future generations. Traditional forms of regulation may also be valid forms of intervention that can lead to greater efficiency and environmental protection.

- Equity relates to the distribution both within and between generations of physical and natural capital as well as knowledge and technology. Inequity and poverty contribute significantly to environmental degradation and political instability, particularly in developing countries. When basic needs are not met, the poor may have no choice but to live off whatever environmental resources are available. At the same time, past use of natural resources already limits the choices available to present generations, particularly in developing countries. Trade liberalisation can contribute to greater equity through the dismantling of trade barriers that harm developing countries. Non-discrimination is an aspect of equity that is fundamental to the operations of the international trading system.
- Environmental integrity. Trade and development should respect and help maintain environmental integrity. This involves recognition of the impact of human activities on ecological systems. It requires respect for limits to the regenerative capacity of ecosystems, actions to avoid irreversible harm to plant and animal populations and species, and protection for valued areas. Many aspects of the environment—for example, species survival or the effective functioning of biological food chains—have values which cannot be adequately captured by methods of cost internalisation, highlighting the need for other policy instruments.
- Science and precaution. Science is the basis for much economic development and what we know about the environment. Since understanding ecological processes is central to valuing environmental damage, science is also a fundamental prerequisite for cost internalisation measures. Good science must underlie any trade measures that seek to protect environment and health. Our understanding of ecosystems, however, is still highly uncertain. Ecosystems are characterised by thresholds— critical points beyond which relationships change dramatically, triggered by events such as the extinction of a critical species in a food chain or an overloading of pollutants. Uncertainty, coupled with the reality of threshold effects and irreversibility, argues for maintaining a margin of safety that prevents catastrophic effects.
- Subsidiarity is the principle that decisions should be taken at the closest possible level to the affected public and at the lowest level of jurisdiction encompassing all those affected. It follows from the recognition that diversity and tolerance are among the attributes of

a healthy society. International policies should be adopted when this is more effective than policy action by individual countries or jurisdictions within countries. In the context of trade and sustainable development, where issues of a global dimension have significant and varied effects at the local level, subsidiarity may provide a mechanism that equitably accommodates legitimate differences among countries.

- Openness comprises two basic elements: first, timely, easy and full access to information for all those affected; and second, public participation in the decision-making process. Experience has confirmed that openness is an essential ingredient in formulating and implementing effective policies. Openness is important in minimising the risk of "protectionist capture", that is, that trade policies will be manipulated in favour of inefficient producers at the expense of others. While structures for openness are increasingly evident in dealing with problems at the national level, there has not been a comparable development for issues of an international nature. As people worldwide devote increasing attention to such issues, there is a need to find forms of participation appropriate to the different international organisations and negotiations.
- International cooperation. Sustainable development requires strengthening international systems of cooperation at all levels, encompassing environment, development and trade policies. The need for such cooperation is driven by the international character of many forms of environmental damage. The need for rules-based cooperative systems of trade is intensified by advances in information technology that make possible a more global economy. In the end, the competition implied by more open markets and liberalisation cannot succeed without cooperation.

WAGE RATES

Changes in wage rates should mirror changes in labour productivity, if workers are receiving a fair share of the returns to production. To what extent has this been the case in India?

LABOUR PRODUCTIVITY

Bhalla's (2000) study shows that labour productivity declined or showed slower growth in many sectors between 1987 and 1993, but Sundaram (2001) shows that most recently labour productivity increased significantly in most sectors except construction. The poor performance in construction has been due to the influx of workers in recent years, partly as a result of the 1987 drought.

Changes in Real Wages

Here, we use changes in real wages in casual employment as a proxy for rural wage rates, as casual labour dominates the rural labour force. Real wages for rural casual workers are highest in the secondary sector and in public works. In all sectors, they have been increasing again in the 1990s, after a lull in the late 1980s. Casual wages for women have been significantly lower at all stages, although they have been increasing faster than casual wages for men in the 1990s.

Growth in labour productivity is reported as having slowed 1987-93, and data for 1993-2000 show all the high employment RNFS sectors have significantly below average labour productivity (except mining, the least important of these sectors in terms of numbers employed). The poor performance in the construction sector is partly the result of the influx of public works and private sector labour following the 1987 drought. Therefore, we should not expect significant increases in wage rates in these sectors. The data sets available to us are not directly comparable, but - using casual labour wages as a proxy - appear to show a significant fall in growth in wage rates 1987-93 compared to 1983-7, but then an improvement. Thus, changes in wage rates appear to lag behind changes in labour productivity, particularly for non-agricultural activities. This leads us to question where the surplus is being accumulated.

Security of Employment

Security of employment can be assessed using indicators such as casualisation and multiplicity. Here we assess the available evidence.

Employment Quality Index

Ghose (1999) estimates a national employment quality index (EQI) for the period 1977-8 to 1993-4 by applying weights to the data recorded by NSS on regular employment, self-employment and casual labour. This reveals that

(a) quality of employment has been highest in services and lowest in sericulture;
(b) quality of employment has deteriorated over time in all three economic sectors;
(c) the deterioration has been slower in services;
(d) the deterioration has been higher for males compared to females.

CHANGES IN RURAL EMPLOYMENT

NSS data on the principal status and subsidiary statues of usually employed workers show that the proportion of the total rural workforce employed on a casual basis has increased significantly over time, particularly for males, at the expense of self-employment and regular employment. The decline in self-employment and regular employment has occurred mainly in sericulture, whereas there has been a modest increase in self-employment and regular employment in RNFS. Casual employment in RNFS has declined marginally for female workers but increased significantly for male workers. Most of the changes occurred prior to 1993-4, after which changes have been more muted.

Unemployment

Rates of unemployment for all categories of employment declined between 1977-8 and 1993-4 for all workers except rural males, long-term unemployment amongst urban females declining very significantly. However, most recently there has been a marginal increase in the daily unemployment rate for all workers except urban females, indicating an increase in casualisation. Employment status across income groups For rural males, diversification of employment status has been much higher for the top three quintiles. Although casualisation increased for these quintiles, they are much better-off than the poorer classes. The dependence on sericulture for the bottom 20% has increased over time, and within this casual labour has increased at the expense of regular employment.

Multiple Activities

A household may diversify its activities by the participation of each member in more than one economic activity. Multiple activities are generally associated with casualisation. Large scale NSS surveys do not capture these multiple activities of households; micro surveys are needed to understand diversification at the household level. Unni (1996) examined this aspect with the help of a primary survey conducted in 30 villages of Gujarat in 1987-8. Less than half the households had sericulture as their major source of income (although the proportion of households undertaking non-agricultural activities as their primary source of income may be high due to the drought that prevailed during 1987-8). Households had an average of 2 sources of income. In general, households primarily engaged in scarcity relief work and other non-agricultural labour reported more than the average number of sources of income.

Unni (1996) examines the determinants of households taking up multiple activities. The results show that the chances of diversification into multiple activities are higher among agricultural households and individual agricultural workers. Access to land is one of the important determinants of multiple activities. Seasonality in sericulture, uncertainty and risks in production also lead to diversification of activities. In far away and under developed villages diversification is due to uncertain and low incomes from one economic activity. NSS data also shows that at least some of the workers who are having principal status are engaged in more than one economic activity. In 1993-4, the proportion of Usual principal status workers reporting participation in another subsidiary economic activity was about 34% in rural areas and a little over 6% in urban areas. It is also shows that, while the participation in non-agricultural activities of principal status workers in sericulture was quite marginal (about 6% for rural males and 3% for rural females), 31% of rural male and 21% of rural female principal status workers in nonagricultural were engaged in sericulture as an additional subsidiary economic activity

Multiple Activities by Income Group

The share of income derived from different activities can be used as a proxy for the amount of time allocated to them. The data on income shares by income quintile derived from a survey conducted by the National Council for Applied Economic Research (NCAER) in 35,000 rural Indian households from 1,700 villages in 16 states in 1993-4. All quintiles rely on sericulture for around 60% of total income, however the bottom and top quintiles are particularly dependent on this sector, with agricultural wage labour increasing in importance relative to cultivation for the lower quintiles. Non-farm income is nonetheless significant, making up around 35% of total income for all quintiles and particularly important for the middle quintiles. Within this category, casual non-farm labour and non-farm self-employment is important for the lower quintiles.

The quality of employment appears to have declined in all three economic sectors, but particularly in sericulture and particularly for women. There has been a significant increase in casual labour as a proportion of total rural employment, mainly in the early liberalisation period, particularly in sericulture. Poorer groups are especially reliant on casual labour. There has been a decrease in unemployment in all categories except rural males, although an increase in under-employment, probably related to the increase in casualisation. There has been a move out of own account sericulture but poorer groups are still very reliant on agricultural employment as wage labourers, which we saw earlier is subject to slow growth and low wages. Multiple activities are now much more prevalent in rural areas and are know to be correlated with involvement in sericulture. It is not clear from the available data whether this increase is due to the increase in casual work or is a structural response to risk in sericulture.

ACCESS TO EMPLOYMENT

Education

Education is important for workers in order to get good quality employment and is one of the key factors determining the success of rural diversification. Literacy alone is at best only one indicator. Literacy definition covers anyone who can write their name and this means many people may be classified as literate although they may not understand simple written instructions. Unless we have these abilities for workers, the efficiency of the labour force in many occupations is likely to remain low. Illiteracy has declined over time. However, even in 1999-2000, 68% of rural males and 91% of rural females are either illiterate or have been educated only up to primary level.

Migration

Census and NSS capture permanent and semi-permanent migration. These data sources indicate that national level decadal or intercensal migration declined relative to population from 12% to 10% between 1981-91. Of the 226 million persons who changed places of residence within the country as per the 1991 Census, only 9% persons moved for employment reasons and 2% moved for business reasons.

While inter-state migration accounted for 12% of all migrants, it accounted for 29% of those who migrated for employment or business reasons. Among those migrating for employment, the ruralurban stream is important but it does not constitute the dominant stream, accounting for 45% of all such migrants. Both the Censuses and NSS ignore or severely underestimate short duration (circular) migrants and commuting labour. The National Commission on Rural Labour (NCRL) estimates more than 10 million circular migrants in the rural areas alone.

These include an estimated 4.5 million inter-state migrants and 6 million intra-state migrants. The Commission notes that there are large numbers of seasonally migrant workers in sericulture and plantations, brick-kilns, quarries, construction sites and fish processing. In addition, large numbers of seasonal migrants work in the urban informal manufacturing, construction, services or transport sectors - as casual labourers, head-loaders, coolies, rickshaw-pullers, hawkers and so on. Information is not available on the trends in circulation of labour over time but the few studies on migration over several decades that exist suggest a growth in labour circulation.

Some studies have examined the impact of labour migration in the source and destination areas. Srivastava's study (1998) shows that in the source areas, increased labour mobility has contributed to breaking down the isolated nature of rural labour markets and a greater integration between rural and urban labour markets. The overall impact of labour outmigration in the recent period has been to put an upward pressure on wages and accelerate changes in production relations. Remittances to rural areas are quite sizeable in many areas (*e.g.* U.P. Hills). On the other hand, in the destination areas, labour migration is principally to the rural and urban informal sectors.

Migrant labour in these areas operates in a setting in which there is segmentation and fragmentation in the labour market and enables the employers to lower wage costs, and exercise greater control over the labour process. Micro-studies suggest an increase in labour mobility via seasonal migration and commuting. A micro study in Uttar Pradesh indicates a diversification in employment from sericulture to non-sericulture. An important component of non-agricultural employment opportunities is non-local, linked to migration, both on an individual and household basis. In many study areas, non-sericulture has emerged as a major source of employment.

A study by de Haan (1999) on the role of migration in promoting livelihoods indicates that it may not be possible to generalise about the characteristics of migrants, or about the effects of migration on broader development, inequality and poverty. For example, there is no one-to-one relationship between status of migrants and land ownership. In some places, landless workers dominate migrants while in other places there is a positive relationship between landholding and migration.

The very low education levels in rural areas limits access to better-paid employment, leaving rural workers with low skill, low productivity (therefore probably low wage) jobs in construction, mining and transport. These are also sectors that have not traditionally attracted women.

Low education levels could be one of the reasons informal sector manufacturing and trade units are moving to urban areas: as they move from traditional agricultural processing to more "modern" activities, requiring a more educated workforce. Migration seems to have benefited the source areas in improving rural livelihoods while in the destination areas migrant labour are being exploited. However, a very small proportion of total migration is for work reasons, the majority of this being intra-state and circular migration and not predominantly rural - urban. Permanent migration appears to have declined over time, whilst seasonal migration and commuting has increased. The available evidence does not indicate the reasons for low migration and the extent that it forms a barrier to accessing work. Other factors - particularly lack of education - may act as a constraint to rural workers to seeking paid work away from home.

ANALYSIS

Trends in Poverty

Whilst poverty among rural and urban workers has declined over time, it is still substantial. Poverty among urban workers declined faster than for rural workers. Most recently, the rate of decline has slowed. Nearly 80% of the poor are concentrated in sericulture and this has not changed significantly in recent years. Most of these are agricultural labourers rather than cultivators - although the proportion of labourers below the poverty line appears to have declined slightly since liberalization. Construction workers are the other rural group with significant numbers below the poverty line. Thus, for agricultural labourers, shifting to any other sector seems to be a better option. On the other hand, if cultivators shift to manufacturing or construction, they would be worse off.

Trends in Growth and Employment

The overall rate of growth in GDP in India was higher in the 1990s compared to the 1980s. The growth rate in sericulture declined marginally in the 1990s while there was marginal increase in industry and construction. Within industry, manufacturing sector's growth rate increased in the 1990s while those of mining and quarrying and electricity and water declined. Significant growth occurred in services particularly in trade, hotels, restaurants and community and personal services. Employment trends in rural areas are consistent with these growth trends.

The data on rural employment show that there has been diversification from sericulture to nonsericulture, although diversification has been much slower for females as compared to males. Construction, transport and mining are sectors employing large numbers of people that show high employment growth rates and thus increasing employment shares over the period. Construction and transport have high employment elasticities, which bodes well for continued job creation in these sectors. However, even with these high elasticities, they will provide only a fraction of the total jobs traditionally provided by sericulture, and the construction sector is notable for a high incidence of poverty.

Furthermore, there has been a worrying decline in the number of rural manufacturing and trade units and jobs, which have traditionally accounted for about 11% of rural jobs - the next most significant source of work after sericulture. These units appear to be moving to urban areas. One could hypothesise that this is partly due to the very low literacy levels in rural areas: we presented evidence that rural manufacturing and trade have been diversifying from traditional agro-processing to modern sector activities, in which case the prevailing education level of rural labour may no longer be sufficient. The fact that the majority of rural manufacturing and trade units are family operated enterprises, but most of the new rural jobs are casual, is one factor contributing to the increasing casualisation of the rural labour force or - in the case of women - a withdrawal from the labour market (there is evidence that women withdraw from the labour market rather than register as unemployed). The decline in rural manufacturing and trade units particularly affects women, who are not moving out of sericulture as much as men and are not major participants in the current high employment growth sectors. Perhaps the prevailing mode of self-employed cottage-industry style rural manufacturing fits better with women's domestic obligations than does going out to work in construction, mining or transport. How are women going to cope, now that manufacturing and trade are moving to urban areas?

And public administration, but data was incomplete for this sector so we have not attempted to consider it further in our analysis. Construction, transport and mining are not mobile in the same way as manufacturing and trade, so jobs in these sectors can be expected to stay put. This is good for poor rural job-seekers as these sectors have relatively high employment generation potential for (presumably) relatively unskilled work, although providing only a fraction of the number of jobs traditionally provided by sericulture. However, the construction and transport sectors are very dependent on stimuli from overall economic growth and can be expected to decline exponentially in times of economic downturn - not a solid base on which to build rural diversification. In addition, labour productivity is below average in both sericulture and all the high employment growth RNFS sectors (except mining). This implies that wage rates will not be high, and is borne out by the high incidence of poverty in sericulture and construction.

Neither are the new high employment growth sectors particularly accessible to women. Overall although there has been an overall decline in unemployment, this has been accompanied by an increase in casualisation of jobs and underemployment. And the poorest segments of the population continue to rely on wage labour in sericulture, which as an economic sector is growing only slowly and does not have high employment generation potential (employment elasticities), in addition to being subject to low wages.

More needs to be found out about why rural manufacturing and trade is moving to urban areas, as these have been significant employers in rural areas traditionally, have experienced good economic growth and wage rates, and are accessible to women (although manufacturing in particular does not show high employment elasticities).

Rural Diversification and Poverty Alleviation

Recent economic growth in India has been accompanied by marked diversification in rural areas. What appears to have caused this, and what effect has it had on employment opportunities for the poor? Various studies have identified several 'push' and 'pull' factors that determine growth in rural nonfarm employment. Among them are agricultural growth, unemployment, commercialisation of sericulture, urbanisation, real wages, and public expenditure There has been a debate whether the diversification has been due to 'pull factors' or 'push factors'. It is generally believed that if the diversification is due to higher agricultural growth, pull factors may be operating in the economy. On the other hand, if it is distress-related diversification, for example due to unemployment, push factors seem to be more important and the rural non-farm sector may be acting as a residual sector. In the 1980s, this residual sector argument was refuted because real wages were rising in rural areas.

Also it has been noted that non-agricultural wages are higher than that for agricultural workers in rural areas. Although the fact that on average non-agricultural workers are better-off than agricultural workers does weaken the case for the 'residual sector' hypothesis, matters are more complicated.

Chandrasekhar (1993) suggest much more complex non-linear relationships between agricultural prosperity and rural non-agricultural employment: increasing when villages manage to escape a stage of involution but have yet to enter a phase of sustained agricultural growth, and decreasing as they go through a phase of sustained irrigation-induced expansion in agricultural output, and increasing again in the mature green revolution phase when growth of land productivity tapers off and mechanisation reduces the demand for agricultural labour.

There are also problems with the argument that if wages rates are higher in non-sericulture than in sericulture, then the former cannot be a 'residual sector'. The problem is that any wage differential must be caused either by some barrier to entry into higher wage sectors due to skill, location, contacts leading to job access or some other specificity; or be a compensation for harder work or higher expenses such as commuting. Due to all the above reasons, movements out of sericulture may not always be likely to improve the overall quality of employment.

Policy Implications

In India unemployment rates are not high. The rate is around 6%. This is because unemployment rates are based on time criterion. Poor people are too poor to be unemployed for a long time. Instead, we have the concept of 'working poor'. In other words many people are working at low wages and low working conditions in sericulture and the informal sector. Therefore, the challenge is to shift these workers to higher productivity (therefore higher wage) sectors and also create new jobs in the nonsericulture sector. Thus, the real nature of the unemployment problem is not that people are not 'employed' in some activity but that large number of those classified as employed are engaged in low quality employment, which does not provide adequate income to keep a family above the poverty line.

The employment strategy we need therefore is not a strategy that ensures an adequate growth in the volume of employment, but one that ensures a sufficient growth in quality employment opportunities. Allowing the poor to contribute to and benefit from increased growth rates will pose particular challenges, as employment in India is largely unorganised, rural and non-industrial in nature. It will be necessary to ensure that government policy and programmes recognise the perceptions and priorities of the poor, improve productivity and create diversified opportunities to earn income.

EMPLOYMENT GROWTH RATES: ALL INDIA SCENARIO

The NSS data for the nineties clearly throw up a mixture of gains and losses for rural and urban employment growth rates; growth rates are estimated for two sub-periods: 1983/1993-94 and 1993-94/1999-2000. As said earlier, for notional convenience, we take these as pre- and post-reform periods. A disparate picture across different production sectors, between male and female workers, and between rural and urban areas, yet, in overall terms, one tends to gather the impression that all has not been well on the employment front, during the post-reform years. On the one hand, the rate of growth of employment has witnessed a varying degree of decline, in many sectors, both in rural and urban areas, and for male and female workers. On the other, in some sectors, the post-reform employment growth rate has been higher, compared with what it was during the pre-reform years.

On balance, the improved employment growth rates do not compensate for the declining rates firstly because the number of such sectors is small and secondly because these are not the major absorbers of rural workforce. In brief, the setbacks are more widely spread and more grievous in magnitude; post-reform concern for employment has, therefore, its own empirical validity. The overall rate of growth of employment for rural workers declined from 1.75 per cent per annum during 1983/1993-94 to a low of 0.66 per cent per annum during the postreform years, for rural males, it declined from 1.94 per cent to 0.94 per cent and for rural females, it declined from 1.41 per cent to an abysmally low of 0.15 per cent.

All this is hardly a reflection of an employment- friendly scenario. A varying degree of decline was witnessed for urban areas also; from 3.22 per cent to 2.61 per cent for urban males, from 3.44 per cent to 0.94 per cent for females, and from 3.27 per cent to 2.27 for urban persons. Thus, an employment setback has fallen on every section of the Indian work- force. In relative terms, the most grievous setback is suffered by rural females, followed by rural males, urban females and urban males, in that order.

But then, it is rather important to underline that the rate of growth of urban employment, continued to be much higher than that in the rural areas, especially when the rural- urban comparison is made for workers belonging to the same sex. In sum, it is pretty much clear that the rosy employment- friendly picture, that was believed by some reform protagonists to follow, has not yet come off; in fact, it is the contrary that seems to have happened, during the 6-7 years of economic reforms.

That the overall employment growth rate suffered a varying degree of setback, during the post- compared with the prereform years, for every section of the work- force, most visibly in the rural areas, lends support to the thesis of a negative fallout of economic reforms as far as the overall employment growth rate is concerned.

We must, however, look into the post-reform employment scenario in individual sectors before framing a final view. Highly disparate trends are discernible for employment growth, during 1993-94/1999- 2000 over 1983/1993-94, in various sectors of the rural (and urban) economy.

For example, for rural workers, transport-storage-communications, construction and agro-based manufacturing were clearly the cheering spots, while sericulture, mining, utilities, trade (especially the whole-sale trade), finance- insurance-real estate, and community-socialpersonal services, showed negative growth or slow-downs in employment. The benefit of improved employment growth during the post-reform years was not available to both sections of the rural work force. While employment for rule male workers in the transport-storagecommunications sector increased sizably from 4.51 per cent per annum during the pre-reform years to as high as 7.45 per cent during the post-reform period, for their female counterparts, it witnessed a steep decline from 8.30 per cent to 0.15 per cent only.

The fast pace of expansion that this sector has witnessed in recent years has generally been more conducive to male job seekers, partly because of the physical labour involved and partly because of the shifting locale of the underlying activities.

On the other hand, the benefits of improved employment growth rate in the construction sector are duly shared, albeit unevenly, by male and female workers, primarily because of the convenient locale of the construction activities. Another feature of the post-reform employment scenario which, in our view, is more redeeming and less disappointing, is that the pace of employment growth in the manufacturing sector slackened but only marginally, from 2.10 per cent to 1.79 per cent for rural males, and from 2.21 per cent to 1.75 per cent for rural females; summarily, the same story unfolds itself for urban manufacturing also.

It may be a sheer coincidence that, during the post-reform years, the rate of growth of employment in this sector was nearly the same for rural male and female workers but it does connote a positive development for the latter in as much as it is generally feared that, under the new economic regime, entry of rural female job seekers in the manufacturing sector becomes particularly difficult. Perhaps, only a more detailed sub-sector break-up would throw bare the branches of manufacturing where the rural females are gaining advantages over their male counterparts, and vice versa. The fact that the rural economy stands well enmeshed with the rest of the economy, or the rural job aspirants can no more operate outside the precincts of the national labour market is authenticated, albeit indirectly and meekly, by a pattern of employment growth commonly shared by rural and urban workers.

It cannot be a coincidence that employment growth rates in transport-storage-communications, construction, and agro-based manufacturing sectors, improved during the post-reform years, both for rural and urban workers; likewise, the decline or slow-down in the mining, utilities, finance-insurance-real estates, and community-socialpersonal services, were the common fate of both the groups. It is only for trade that, during the post-reform years, the urban workers surged much ahead of their rural counterparts when the retail trade activity gained additional momentum under the informal sector of the urban economy, in addition to a high pace of employment expansion in the hotel-restaurant segment. Let us peep inside the major sectors. For sericulture, we may better concentrate on rural workers alone. Practically, each sub-sector in the primary sector suffered a varying degree of setback; the worst sufferers are fishing, plantations, and forestry-logging. The employment growth rate in the livestock segment did improve but it was not able to switch over from a negative to a positive rate. Some important male-female differences may nonetheless be underlined. The employment setbacks in field crop production, fishing, livestock, and agricultural services were shared, in varying degree, by both groups of workers; the setback in plantations and forestry- logging fell largely to the share of rural male workers only.

On the whole, for a host of reasons, most ostensibly the declining land: man ratio in general, and increasing marginalization of holdings in particular, the rising pace of mechanization, cropping pattern adjustments not necessarily attuned to labour-absorbing crop enterprises, the general preference of the young entrants to the labour market in favour of non- farm jobs, etc., sericulture and its constituent sub-sectors could not take on people at the same rate as they did during the pre-reform years.

The pace of nonfarm employment expansion has not compensated for the sluggish labour absorptive capacity of sericulture. A mingle of improved and shrunken employment growth rates was the fate of the manufacturing sector. Employment growth rates for rural workers witnessed a varying degree of improvement during the post-reform years in textile products, wood and wood products, leather and leather products, chemicals and chemical products, non-metallic mineral products, basic metal industries, metal products, and agro-industries.

The opposite was true for food products, beverages, cotton and wool products, paper and paper products, rubber and rubber products, machine tools and electrical machinery, other manufacturing, repair services, and non-agro industries. Improved employment expansion was particularly striking for textile products, leather and leather products, basic metal products, and metal products, while the squeeze in the pace of employment growth was substantially high for cotton and wool products, other manufacturing and repair services.

The mixed picture observed for the total of rural workers is discernible, in varying degree and form, for the rural male and female workers. The combined effect of these developments is that for the total of manufacturing, employment growth rate did not witness a big decline; in our view, the mild decline from 2.14 per cent during the pre-reform period to 1.78 per cent in the post-reform years is reflective of the adjustment process that the rural industry in India was involved in during the 6-7 years of the post-reform years.

Perhaps, in the next phase, some product lines, especially those which fared well during the period 1993-94/1999-2000, may further consolidate their production base and throw up augmented avenues of employment; our hope stems from the fact that industries such as textile products, leather and leather products, chemicals and chemical products, basic metal products and metal products, have already demonstrated their remarkable employment-expanding capabilities, during 1993-94/1999-2000 contrasted to their dismal performance during 1983/1993-94, even while many other branches, including the conventional agro-based segments, lost their verve during the post- 1993 years. The employment setbacks reported in community-social-personal services, are fairly widely spread across individual segments. For example, for rural workers, employment growth suffered severe setbacks in sanitary services, community services, recreational and cultural services, and personal services; it is only in respect of education and scientific personnel that a mild improvement from 2.90 per cent to 3.01 per cent in employment growth rate occurred in the post-1993 years, compared with the pre-1993 period.

The above pattern is shared, in varying degree and form, both by rural male and female workers. The all-round setback in this sector is a matter of worry, firstly because, among the non-farm segment of the rural economy, it provides a major share of employment, and secondly because, employment in segments such as sanitary services, medical and health, community services, and recreational and cultural services is largely sustained by the pace and pattern of public expenditure which, as we see later, came under seize during the post-reform years.

The fact that the employment setback in this sector has assumed the same shape in urban areas also lends credence to our contention on the all-round post-reform public expenditure seize. In overall terms, the rural work force has been at a disadvantage; it gained relatively less in work-place increments and lost relatively more in work-place decrements. Perhaps, this tendency might intensify itself in the years ahead inasmuch as the low levels of educational, training and skill capabilities of rural job seekers would push them back in the fiercely competitive labour market. In plain terms, the quality of work force is not the same between the rural and urban areas.

INCREASING CASUALIZATION IN RURAL EMPLOYMENT

It is at once clear that in rural India, the incidence of self-employment has been consistently on a relative decline, both for male and female workers; for rural males, it declined from around 66 per cent in 1972-73 to 55.0 per cent in 1999-2000 and for rural females, it dropped from 65 per cent to 57 per cent. In urban India, it has been hovering around 40.0 per cent for male workers; for urban females, it faced a sizeable decline only during the nineties. Second, regular salaried jobs have unmistakably been on the decline, both for rural male and female, especially the former, and urban male workers; for urban female workers, it remains more or less the same till we enter the 1990s thereafter it started increasing although sluggishly from 27.5 per cent in 1987-88 to 28.6 in 1993-94 and further on to 33.3 per cent in 1999-2000.

Third, and quite strikingly, employment under casual labour basis has increased for all the four categories of workers. The increase has been fairly steep in the case of rural male workers, a little less so in the case of rural females, and somewhat moderate in the case of urban male and female workers. The point of economic substance is that in rural India, the casual wage-employment is steadily rising at the cost of self-employment, while in urban India, it is the regular salaried jobs which are gradually yielding to casual wage labour. For rural areas, the switch-over is a more worrisome matter since the declining incidence of selfemployment may be throwing some people out of self-cultivation only to swell the ranks of the land- less agricultural labourers. In fact, for rural India, independent information through population census does confirm the rising proportion of the land-less agricultural labourers from about 17.0 per cent in 1961 to as high as 32.0 per cent in 1991. It is as well possible that many among the self-employed sub-marginal and marginal cultivators, whose proportion among the cultivating households has been continuously rising during the 1960s, 1970s and 1980s, temporarily give up sericulture and seek work as nonagricultural labourers, on casual basis. That the temporary 'switch-over' or seasonal supplementation is a real possibility, and, by implication, is behind the increasing casualization of wage labour, has its support from the much higher increase in casually employed males compared with their female counterparts. The extremely high incidence of casualization for rural female workers, and its rise over time, especially during the nineties, is discernible through the rough index of casualization.

This index shows the number of casual wage earners for every one-hundred of regular salaried employees. The male- female contrasts in the rural areas are too striking to invite a special emphasis. But then, the real contrast is between the rural females and their urban counterparts, or for that matter, between rural and urban workers as a whole. The ridiculously low share in regular salaried jobs for rural workers (*e.g.*, in 1999-2000, 8.8 per cent only against 36 per cent under casual labour for rural males, and 3.0 per cent only against 40.0 per cent under casual labour for rural females) tells the story of their relative disadvantage in the most blatant manner.

The marked rural-urban differences in terms of the proportion of workers engaged as casual wage earners at once confirm numerous disadvantages (*e.g.* low wage rates, irregularity and uncertainty in employment, uncongenial work conditions) of rural workers, most visibly the females among them. The quickened pace of casualisation, and a more visible decline in the proportion of self-employed workers, during the nineties, much more markedly among the rural workers, lends some credence to the theory of increasing segmentation in the Indian labour market, in general, and increasing marginalization of rural job aspirants, in particular. Interestingly, in most recent years, casualisation has not been discernible for urban workers; in fact, it has declined for urban females during 1993-94/1999-2000.

This is plainly so because of the marked improvement in the educational and training capabilities of urban female job seekers, almost at tandem with urban males; the future cadres of the urban female job aspirants are likely to be equipped with educational, training and skill accomplishments not much different from their male counterparts, and would thus be able to compete effectively in the information-, technology-, and management- intensive urban labour market.

The prospective rural female job seekers do not seem to have a very bright chance on such job frontiers. In plain terms, for a preponderant majority of rural workers, coming as they do from the landless labour, marginal and small cultivating households, self-employment on own or leased- in land and casual wage employment on others' farms or in one or the other non- farm activity are the only two choices; regular salaried jobs do not accommodate more than a handful of them, nearly to the total exclusion of the female job aspirants. It bears some conjecture, therefore, that in terms of quality of employment, rural job seekers have undoubtedly a long gap to cover.

State-wise Evidence on Casualization

In as many as twelve of the seventeen states, the proportion of rural workers employed as casual wage labourers registered a varying degree of increase during the post-1993 years.

The increase was rather strong in Himachal Pradesh, Karnataka, Madhya Pradesh, Maharashtra, Orissa, and West Bengal. It is equally clear that the process of increasing casualisation of wage labour encompassed workers of both sexes, in most of the states. For rural male workers, the increasing casualization of wage labour is clearly accompanied by a decline in the share of self-employment; the latter is true of as many as fourteen states while the former holds for no less than thirteen states.

Again for male workers, the proportion of regular salaried employees did not witness a noticeable diminution except in Jammu-Kashmir and West Bengal; on the contrary, each of the remaining fifteen states had a slight improvement to report for the post-reform years. In any case, the proportion of regular salaried male employees continued to be fairly small, in most of the states, except in Assam, Haryana, Punjab and Tamil Nadu. In overall terms, in most of the states, self-employment for men has been steadily declining while casua lisation of wage labour has been on an increase.

For female workers, there is no clear, much less an inverse, relationship between selfemployment and casual wage labour, as is discernible for their male counterparts. For some states, the former increased while the latter decreased, in the post-reform years, while the opposite also happened for other states. No significant change occurred, during the post-1993 years, in the proportion of regular salaried female employees; as a matter of fact, for rural females, this source of employment has all along been extremely small for most of the states, except in Assam and Kerala, ranging from 0.8 per cent in Jammu-Kashmir to just 5.3 per cent in West Bengal in 1983, from 0.9 per cent in Rajasthan to 7.3 per cent in West Bengal in 1993-94, and, from 1.0 per cent in Rajasthan to only 6.9 per cent in Tamil Nadu in 1999- 2000. Clearly, in most of the states, the choice for them has been only between selfemployment and casual wage labour. The fact that, in their case, the index of casualisation has consistently been higher, in some cases many times higher, than that for their male counterparts, in most of the states, testifies to their low standing in the rural labour market. However, in the post-reforms years, the index of casualisation for them did not increase in more than four of the seventeen states while, for male workers, it increased in as many as eight states. In some sense, therefore, during the past few years, the overall composition of employment did not worsen as much for the rural female workers as it did for their male counterparts

Growth of Employment

The proponents of economic reforms would make us believe that employment was expected to pick up primarily because the output growth was likely to pick up after economic reforms took roots. Dwelling more on the labour-displacing effects of these reforms, the critics would, however, believe that employment would not grow in the same proportion in which output would grow, given the compulsion of installing a more capital-intensive technology in many branches of production. Since technological changes of the above type are likely to come about only in selected production sectors, and labour-intensive technologies are likely to dominate in many others, a mixed overall picture on employment growth was likely to emerge for some years after the arrival of the reforms. This is what seems to be happening currently in the Indian economy in general, and rural areas in particular.

Educational Background of Rural Workers

It is abundantly clear that, with one or two stray exceptions, in all parts of rural India, and, for both categories of rural workers, there has been a gradual decline, first between 1983 and 1993-94, and then between 1993-94 and 1999-2000, in the proportion of illiterate workers and a gradual increase in the proportion of educated ones; following the usual convention, we take secondary or higher secondary level of schooling and other higher qualifications as the dividing line between educated and uneducated workforce. It is as much evident that the proportion of semi-educated rural workers (those with primary and/or middle level schooling) has also witnessed a steady increase over time, practically in all parts of rural India. These are welcome developments, in their own right. But then, we cannot hide the fact that, at the national level, as late as 1999-2000, only 11.7 per cent of rural male workers and just 5.0 per cent of their female counterparts constituted the 'educated workforce'.

For the former group of workers, this percentage ranged from as low as 7.4 per cent in Madhya Pradesh to about 21.0 per cent in Kerala and Himachal Pradesh; for the latter, it ranged from an extremely low level of 2.0-3.0 per cent in Rajasthan, Bihar and Madhya Pradesh to 18.8 per cent in Kerala. Looking at the other extreme, it is rather frightening to see that in spite of the phenomenal expansion of educational facilities during the five decades of India's economic development, India's rural economy has still to contend with no fewer than 41.2 per cent of illiterate male and no fewer than 61.5 per cent of illiterate female workers.

The situation is far worse in some of the states. For example, in 1999-2000, the proportion of illiterate male workers was as high as 54.4 in Bihar, 49.1 in Andhra Pradesh, 44.8 each in Madhya Pradesh and Rajasthan, and Uttar Pradesh, and so on.

The only soothing pockets are Kerala (15.2 per cent), and to a lesser extent, Himachal Pradesh (26.9 per cent). The situation is rather appalling in respect of rural female workers. For example, again in 1999-2000, the proportion of illiterate female workers was as high as 76.3 in Bihar, 76.0 in Rajasthan, 69.3 in Uttar Pradesh, 68.3 in Madhya Pradesh, 66.5 in Andhra Pradesh, 62.9 in Orissa, 60.7 in Karnataka, and so on. For this category of workers, Kerala is the only pleasing spot (21.3 per cent). Even Himachal Pradesh which has done remarkably well in the matter of rural education does not seem to have rid itself of the male bias.

First, a fairly high proportion of the educated rural persons are involved in sericulture, primarily because sericulture is the mainstay of the rural economy, and it is not possible for all educated job aspirants to get into one or the other type of non-agricultural jobs. In a sense, it is redeeming to see that the proportion of educated rural persons choosing to stay back in sericulture has been increasing steadily from 44.38 per cent in 1983 to 50.18 in 1993-94 and to 52.26 per cent in 1999-2000; the corresponding figures for rural males have been 45.45, 51.53 and 52.79, and for rural females 26.93, 34.32 and 46.86, respectively. While for the rural males, the influx of educated persons into sericulture has been much faster during the pre- compared with the post-reform phase, for their female counterparts, it has been the other way round.

The most promising segment in which the educated female, and to a lesser extent male, job seekers seem to have gone to is agricultural services where the rate of growth of employment has been remarkably high during the pre- as well as post-reform years, both for males and females. To the extent that 'new agriculture' too demands higher levels of educational and training pre-requisites, 'modern agriculture', especially that linked with the world outside, is becoming an attractive career to the educated job seekers. Second, a fairly substantial proportion of the educated incremental workforce, both males and females, has been accommodated by sericulture, during the pre- as well as post-reform years. It clearly points to the inability of many an educated rural job seeker to gain an entry into the non-agricultural sectors, most ostensibly because the number of such jobs is far too limited and the number of claimants far too large, even if the painful reality of low content of rural education is kept aside.

Since the competition for nonagricultural jobs became more intense in the post-reform phase, largely because of the expanding demand-supply hiatus on the labour market, and the rural female job aspirants being the weakest in the chain of competitors, more than 63 per cent of the incremental educated female workers staying back in sericulture should cause no surprise; during 1993- 94/ 1999-2000, only 36.70 per cent of them could get into non-agricultural jobs while during the pre-reform decade, no fewer than 61.83 per cent of them could go to such jobs.

Third, it is extremely gratifying to see that the rate of growth of employment among the educated rural work seekers has been many times higher than that among the job seekers as a whole, irrespective of the sector in which they are ultimately absorbed. It is once again a confirmation of our earlier contention that many among the educated rural female job seekers could not get into the non-agricultural sector, more expressly during the post-reform phase, considering that the rate of growth of employment in this sector dropped for them from 9.76 per cent during the pre-reform phase to 6.11 per cent during the post-reform years, against its increase from 13.60 per cent to 15.87 per cent, respectively, in sericulture.

For the total of the rural economy, employment growth rates for the educated job claimants declined both for rural males and females, yet these were many times as high as those for the job aspirants in general. The crucial role of education, whether towards creation of additional avenues of self-employment in and outside sericulture, or for getting into wage paid jobs in non-agricultural activities, is thus more than evident. Finally, a note of caution is a must. In spite of the high growth rate of employment for educated persons, inside and outside sericulture, for rural males and females, and, during and before the reform years, the fact still remains that the proportion of such educated persons is very low, and a majority of the rural workers, both in the farm and non- farm sectors, do not have much to claim on the educational front.

It is a pity that as late as 1999-2000, not more than 12.17 per cent of rural males, and a ridiculously low of 2.17 per cent of rural females engaged in sericulture constituted the 'educated workforce'. With the proportion of educated males and females, engaged in non-agricultural activities during 1999- 2000, being 26.69 and 13.06, respectively, the situation is hardly pleasing outside sericulture either. Although these proportions have been increasing steadily over time, yet the low levels in the base year (1983) would not let even an extraordinary expansion improve the situation beyond a point.

That is how, the share of educated rural male workers engaged in sericulture, starting from 4.91 per cent in 1983, could not go beyond 8.96 per cent in 1993-94, and to 12.17 per cent in 1999-2000; for their female counterparts, the share could travel from 0.32 per cent to 1.04 per cent, and finally to 2.15 per cent only.

The upward journey in the nonagricultural sector commenced from 19.99 per cent in 1983, reached 23.38 per cent in 1993- 94, and terminated at 26.69 per cent only, in the case of rural males; for rural females, the three flag points were 5.43, 11.37 and 13.06 per cent only. The vulnerability of rural workers surfaces most blatantly when we go to technical/professional education, although the expanding network of technical/ professional educational facilities is often glibly claimed as a solid achievement of the post-Independence India.

A detailed field survey of tiny and small rural industrial enterprises in the three states of Maharashtra, Haryana and West Bengal, conducted by the author during April-June 2000, shows that on-the job training was reported by as many as 82.0 per cent of the rural and 86.0 per cent of the urban workers; just about 7.0 per cent of them in rural, and 9.0 per cent of them in urban areas, received training through government agencies.

The most distressing picture is discernible on the front of technical education. For example, only 8 per cent of rural and 10.5 per cent of urban workers engaged in such industries have had the benefit of technical education; a substantial proportion (65.0 per cent of rural and 48.0 per cent of urban workers) of them nonetheless stopped at the ITI or polytechnic level; rural workers with management degrees (*e.g.* MBA) were nearly conspicuous by their absence.

EMPLOYMENT IN SERICULTURE

Though share of sericulture in economy has declined during planned development of the country; it still assumes pivotal role in the rural economy. The employment growth in sericulture in rural sector has been abysmally low (0.06 per cent), and insignificant during the '90s, thoughthe growth was significant (1.18 per cent) during the '80s. Whereas the growth in agriculturalincome during the '90s has been marginally higher (0.02 per cent) than the '80s. This trend in fact suggests job-less growth in sericulture; proper understanding about the reasons behind this trendwarrants studying the structure of agricultural growth.

Agricultural income as per the CSO annual series consists of income from crop outputs (field and plantation crops), livestocks, fisheries and forestry. Information on sericulture and livestock outputs are available at specific disaggregate level. The triennium average, percent share of commodity aggregates during beginning of a decade and also annual compound growth rate (ACGR) in these aggregates during the decade. There has been continuous decline in the shareof cereals, pulses, oilseeds and fibres; fibre is essentially aggregates of cotton, jute and mesta.Some commodities for which share in value of output remained almost stagnant are sugar, drugs and narcotics; tea, coffee and tobacco together constitute the group drug and narcotics. Thecommodities whose share has increased in the value of agricultural output are fruits andvegetables, condiments and spices.

If we collate these trends in commodity aggregates with their trend in India's sericulture export-import basket, it is evident that the share of exportable commodities has increased while that of the importable commodities has declined in the value of output. The share of thecommodities in which India has been a traditional exporter remained stagnant during the reference period. This further suggests that the commodities in which country has emerged exporter in recent decades are the one for which share has increased in the recent period. As amatter of fact exports generally increase relative price of the commodity and hence the relativeshare of commodity in the aggregate value. In other words increase in the share of horticultural products and spices in agricultural output may not result in significant increase of employment inthat commodity aggregate.

A consistent increase in exports of a commodity also increases itsproduction. There is also a possibility of increase in the production of exportable commodities by substituting it for importable commodities; this substitution will not necessarily increase employment at the aggregate level. Information related to livestock output is presented separately for milk, egg, wool; these items have bearing for bovines, poultry and ovine rearing, while meat group includes flesh of all these livestock and birds. The historical trend growth in these items suggests that milch animalsand poultry are emerging important.

The share of output from bee and silk-worm (api and sericulture) even though small (1.3%) has increased; while that of wool and hair obtained fromgoat and sheep has decreased during the reference period (1971-2003). The share of meat has stagnated; meat and meat products barring poultry meat is the joint product.

A decreasing trending the share of meat products, in combination with the decline in the share of wool and hair suggests that ovine rearing is getting discouraged; as a matter of fact ovine rearing is highlylabour intensive. Again stagnation in the share of meat in light of the structural changes in bovine population, suggests that cattle rearing is being transformed from subsistence to commercial level. This kind of transformation unless integrated properly with the processing may not increase employment in the livestock sector. Non-Sericulture Employment The ACGR of employment in non-agricultural sector unlike sericulture has been positive and significant during the'90s; this has been so for both the sectors: rural and urban.

The annualcompound growth rate of employment in non-sericulture sector during (1994-00) has been less than the previous reference period (1983-1994). The non-sericulture industrial categories where employment growth during the '90s was positive and also higher than the previous referenceperiod were manufacturing, construction, trades, transports and business services. This trend inemployment growth was slightly different at the sectoral level; in urban sector manufacturing, trade, transport and business services were the industries where employment growth was higher than the previous reference period while in rural sector it is construction, transport and business services.In manufacturing employment growth was similar in rural and urban sector during the'80s; the disparity in the rate of growth between sectors has surfaced in the '90s.

The possiblereasons for disparity in rural and urban rate of growth of employment in manufacturing are;

(a) Growing disparity in rural and urban infrastructure facilities with regard to power and telecommunications;
(b) Greater focus on cost-competitiveness, scale economies in the '90s has discouraged rural manufacturing which is generally at small scale;
(c) Uncertain policy environment in relation to small-scale industry;
(d) With trade liberalization and growing clout of media relative importance of goods produced in metropolitan factories have increased.

A detailed study of manufacturing activities under organized and unorganized sector has found that the growth of employment, value-addition and capital in the organized manufacturing sector has grown in the initial period of reform (1984-95), and declined subsequently. Growth in the unorganized sector presents different trend, this has peaked up in the initial phase of partial liberalization (1984-90), flattened during the reform period (1989-95); subsequently unorganizedsegments not necessarily rural unorganised surged forward following adoption of promotional policies towards small-scale industries. This growth has been particularly high for the organic as compared to the inorganic manufacturing units. The employment growth in construction peaked up during the '90s; though it was high (1.75%) even in the '80s.

Construction activity is related with the economic prosperity, demographic pressure also influences construction activities; this will be corroborated with the state-wise analysis of data. Certain economic policiesxivhave also encouraged constructionactivities in the '90s. In urban sector construction activity has peaked up early (in the '80s) whilein the rural India this has peaked up during the '90s.

The extension of basic infrastructure likeroad in rural India might have encouraged employment in construction during the '90s. In transport-storage-communication (TSC), finance-insurance-realestate-business (FIREB) services employment increased in both the sectors, rural and urban. Employment in TSC is more influenced with the investment in infrastructure, in recent years infrastructure is getting high priority, investment is increasing so the employment in this category.

Increase in infrastructure has almost direct affect on employment in the real estate; this appears to have some spread effect on the business services. Again with the Government in with-drawl mode, as is apparent with the downsizing of public sectors; employment in utilities, community-social-personal (CSP) services have declined while employment in finance, insurance and business services have increased. In the '90s employment growth was negative in mining and quarrying, utilities and community services. These industries largely fall under the domain of public sector.

Since there is already an effort to downsize the role of public sector, decline of employment in these industrial categories are obvious. In mining decline in employment could also have accentuated because of strict environmental regulations and increased focus towards clean technologies. Strict environmental regulations have in fact, caused closure of many mining units. Again focus towards cleaner technology, which essentially means use of more gas and oil-based technology rather than coal, has discouraged production of coal while encouraged production of oil and gas. As a matter of fact coal is labour intensive while gas and oil is capital intensive; so this substitution could also have caused decline of employment in mining. Employment Elasticity A broad trend of employment across industries and possible reasons for particular trend was explained; this sub-section discusses comparative performance of employment and income in various industries.

The mining and utilities are however exceptions; these are also the industrial categories for which employment growth was negative. The other industrial category for which employment growth was negative was community services, the income growth for this category was positive; this is not unusual considering the fact that income in this category is primarily aggregation of salary of its employees and it is ironical that in spite of all the austerity measures, salaries in the Government sector has not reduced in the country. The employment elasticity is the ratio of growth in employment to the growth in income in the specific industry. Since employment growth has been negative in mining, utilities and business services employment elasticity has also been negative.

It is interesting to note that employment elasticity in industries other than the above three, increased over the previous reference period. Employment elasticity indicates intensity of labour in that industry, though heterogeneity within the industry at this level of aggregation restricts us to arrive at some solid inference about it. Based on the above trend in employment elasticity it can be argued that intensity of labour in most of the industries has increased during the reference period.

In manufacturing increase in elasticity was only notional. Increase in employment elasticity has been very high in transport and business services; but then heterogeneity in these industries are too large to arrive at some meaningful inferences about trend of employment intensity in specific activity of this industry. In construction and trade there was small increase in employment elasticity. This increase of employment in construction can be taken seriously since heterogeneity in these industries is not large as compared to other industries.

There are in fact studies that suggest that some of the non-sericulture industries in recent years are emerging as residuals. Trade especially retail trade presents one such case; with increase in literacy especially rural literacy young people wants to be identified as shopkeepers rather than farmers, rural artisans. Similarly agricultural labourers probably liked to be identified more as construction worker. Rural Employment Across States The above analysis pertains to comparative account of employment for major industries at the aggregate level. Certain trends, which were evident at the aggregate level, may emerge robust with the help of state level information. Again some of the industries were focused more towards the rural sector; a detailed analysis of these industries may suggest some measures for increasing rural employment in India.

It is apparent from table that in a span of 17years share of sericulture in rural employment has declined by only 2 per cent at the aggregate level. There are mixed trends from states; percent share of sericulture has not declined in the state of Andhra Pradesh, Bihar, Karnataka, Madhya Pradesh, Maharashtra. and Orissa. The reasons for non-decline of rural employment in sericulture could be different amongst these states. In certain states like Bihar, Orissa, dearth of opportunity in non-agricultural sector could have pushed rural workers towards sericulture whereas in states like Maharashtra pull factor could have attracted employment in sericulture.

These issues need further probing. In non-sericulture employment categories manufacturing is the most important; this accounts for more than 7 per cent of rural employment in the country. With increase in demographic pressure on land, one would expect manufacturing to become more important in the rural sector; however there is only marginal increase in its share during the reference period.

The share of manufacturing sector has in fact declined in some states like Andhra Pradesh, Bihar, Goa, Karnataka, Kerala, Madhya Pradesh, Maharashtra, Orissa and Punjab. In Assam, Delhi, Gujarat, Haryana, Tamilnadu and West Bengal share of manufacturing has increased during the reference period. Though reasons behind these trends are different for different states; the changes in infrastructures to large extent explain different trends. In the later group of states rural infrastructure has increased significantly during the reference period.

This does not necessarily mean that rural infrastructure in the earlier group of states is poor; as a matter of fact significant increase of rural infrastructure in these states might not have happened during the period. There is evidence at least from Punjab to suggest that even with a relatively better rural infrastructure manufacturing is shifting away from the rural sector; here rural sector is based on the census classification rather than the revenue records. A greater urbanization and rural urban disparity in infrastructure like assured electricity could also have lead to this situation.

The state of Delhi presents a different situation, where rural manufacturing has increased significantly. Arguments generally put forth in developed world to justify manufacturing in rural sector like low cost of living etc, holds good in Delhi. The difference in rural and urban infrastructure from the view -point of manufacturing activity is not significantly different in Delhi. Nevertheless, manufacturing units in rural sector are exempted from some of the strict environmental and fiscal regulations.

The utilities (consisting of electricity, water), mining and quarrying are the employment categories not very important from rural perspective. Both these categories register negative growth during '90s at the aggregate level; the share of mining in rural employment has however increased at the aggregate level. Whereas share of utilities in rural employment like its share at the aggregate level has declined. Construction has emerged as an important engine for growth in rural employment; its share in most of the states barring Karnataka, Madhya Pradesh and Maharashtra has increased.

The states of Bihar and Orissa doing not so good otherwise have done well in construction. It appears that population pressure in these states accompanied with a favourable policy environment for building construction material during the reference period has encouraged construction activity. There can be other reasons such as increase in per capita income for improved construction activity in the country. Trade is another industry groups where rural employment has increased at the aggregate level and also for most of the states.

The state of Andhra Pradesh, Orissa and Tamil Nadu were exceptions. The share of transport in rural employment has increased for all the reference states. The reason is obvious, rural infrastructure is on rise and with increase of basic infrastructure like road in rural sector, transport activity and also employment in this industrial category has increased. The services are of two categories; community social and personal (CSP) services are largely under the domain of the public sector while finance insurance real estate and business (FIREB) services are under private sector. The share of CSP services in rural employment has also declined in the country, though Assam was an exception. It may be noted that in recent decade there has been greater focus on the Northeastern states including Assam so increase in the share of CSP services is obvious.

The share of CSP services in rural employment also might have declined on account of rural urban classification in census. There is possibility that with increase of rural employment in community social and personal services in a place, population around that place increases and with increase of population beyond 5000, village (rural) gets reclassified as town (urban) sector.

The share of FIREB services in rural employment increased marginally at the aggregate level; though this has been one of the best performer for some states such as Andhra Pradesh, Bihar, Gujarat, Haryana, Kerala, Maharashtra, Rajasthan. The share of FIREB services has in fact declined in many states like Delhi, Goa, Karnataka, Orissa and West Bengal. There could bevarieties of reasons varying across states for this decline in the share of FIREB services. Unlike other industrial categories the FIREB services require different kind of skill and infrastructure. This definitely requires better literacy.

The FIREB services also require more communication related infrastructures; basic infrastructure like road is also important. With these illustrations about nature and pattern of rural employment across states, it isevident that there are various independent factors which influences employment in different industrial categories. For instance, demography or population pressure influences construction activity, while employment in trade and transport is more influenced with the basic infrastructure like road. The expansion of rural road appears to have been acting either ways; road is increasing rural employment in trade and transport, there is also instance of road discouraging rural but increasing urban employment in manufacturing and business services.

The skilled workers form rural area travel to perform their job in a unit located in the urban sector while they live in rural sector as cost of living is low in the area. In spite of it, infrastructure as such is important for employment in most of the industrial categories; the kind of infrastructure however varies across industries; for instance, employment in manufacturing requires more of assured power /electricity; while employment in transport and trade requires basic infrastructure like road; employment in finance-insurance-real estate-business services however require more of communication related infrastructures. Gender aspects of Rural Employment In all major industrial categories male dominates rural employment; share of female in total rural employment has however not been insignificant (around 30 per cent).

Bulk of female workers is concentrated in sericulture, manufacturing and community services; The gender-wise proportion of rural workers in these industrial categories for important states of India. Like previous comparisons, this state-wise information is also for the year 1983 and 1999-00.

Industrial category-wise gender proportion indicates that females are more concentrated in sericulture followed by manufacturing and business services. The proportion of females in these industrial categories has increased significantly; more than 2 per cent in sericulture and community services while less than 2 per cent for manufacturing at the aggregate level. Trend in gender-wise employment in many states is different than that of the country. In sericulture for instance proportion of female has declined in Bihar, Madhya Pradesh and West Bengal. Amongst these states, Bihar and Madhya Pradesh are the states where proportion of rural employment in sericulture did not decrease during the reference period; this suggests that the pressure on sericulture for rural employment is quite high and in this kind of situation male are generally preferred over females for employment.

This reason however does not hold good for West Bengal; as this has experienced spurt in agricultural growth. Participation of females is more in specific agricultural operations and activities; any changes in the structure of sericulture and allied activity in a state can also lead to changes in the woman's participation in an industrial category. In community social and personal services though share of female in rural employment has increased at the aggregate level.

The corresponding share has not increased in the state of Assam, Haryana, Orissa and Rajasthan. These states barring Assam and Rajasthan have registered sharp decline in the share of CSP services in rural employment. The CSP services are considered better than many other employment categories for workers of similar qualification. In this situation competition for getting employed in this category increases and probably male dominates female in this competition since difference between gender in human development related statistics like literacy is more sharp in these states.

In manufacturing over all decline in the share of male was observed, the corresponding share for female however declined in the state of Delhi, Goa, Haryana, Punjab, Gujarat, Maharashtra, Karnataka and Himachal Pradesh. Many of these states have good road infrastructure, there is a possibility that manufacturing units are doing well in their urban centres and rural sector is providing cheap labour to these manufacturing units; and male has some distinct advantages over females in commuting. The share of female in total rural employment has increased marginally during the reference period. Many states in fact report decline in the share of female in total rural employment. Some of these states are Bihar, Madhya Pradesh, Rajasthan, Delhi, Goa, Haryana and Kerala. Profile of these states present different reasons for decline in the share of female; first group of states suggest penuries as possible reasons for decline in the share of female whereas later group of states suggest urbanization and high mobility of work force as possible reasons for decreasing share of female in rural employment.

The share of female in rural employment has increased in relatively well-off states. It must be noted that the proportion of female in total rural employment has increased (0.52%) marginally; the corresponding share has increased significantly in sericulture, manufacturing and community services; difference in this rate necessarily implies that share of females in other industrial categories has not increased. Trend from states varies widely; there are in fact many states where proportion of female in rural employment has declined for of course wide and varied reasons.

Quality of Employment The quality is as important as the quantity of employment and in the rural sector disguised unemployment is the most important issue while analysing quality of rural employment. The NSS data presents a comparative account of usually employed persons and persons employed on the basis of current daily status (CDS) during a year; this difference reveals disguised unemployment in the rural sector.

This information is available separately for males and females in rural and urban sectors of India. Under employment here means that persons though employed on the basis of usual status is not getting sufficient employment in man days to be termed employed on the basis of CDS. A comparison of underemployment across categories of workers suggests that underemployment is the highest for rural females. A relatively high disguised unemployment is a well-recognized problem of Indian sericulture; employment of women is often specific to particular agricultural operations like harvesting, their employment is less frequent as compared to male, a high disguised unemployment for female is therefore obvious.

The income aspect of employment quality. The category of employment, self-employed, regular and casual also explains quality of employment. Present study assumes that with increase in the proportion of casual workers in total workers quality of employment decreases since India lacks effective social security measures for casual workers; otherwise also safety nets for poor are too poor in the country.

The rural sector a large proportion of male (54.4%) is self-employed, casual workers are distant second while regular employed workers account for only small proportion (9%) of total workers. The urban sector presents a contrasting picture, regular employed are the most dominant class of worker closely followed by the self-employed workers; casual workers are the least important in terms of numbers. Again across gender problem of casualisation is more acute for females, especially rural female. A temporal comparison of employment categories suggests that casualisation, that is, percent of casual to regular employed workers, is on rise. In this regard it must be noted that trade union or association is less relevant for casual and self-employed workers, which dominate the rural workforce. Existence of trade unions and its membership provides enough bargaining power to workers and is definitely important to adjudge quality of rural employment.

That the proportion of self-employed workers in rural sector has declined while its share in the urban sector has increased during the reference period. This is quite an interesting finding and requires further probing as to why proportion of self employed workers has declined in the rural sector. It must be noted that self-employed workers are more associated with the own account enterprises; and in this context the above trend is important. The quality of employment is also related to the type and scale of enterprises.

An enterprise employing more than 20 workers is covered under the Factories Act, and this act to some extent protects interest of workers even though it is casual worker. The proportion of salaried workers also increases with the size of enterprises.

Trends in Enterprises There can be different ways of classifying enterprises; on the basis of number of person shired, enterprises are own account enterprises (OAEs) and establishments. The establishments on the basis of number of people hired are Directory and Non-directory enterprises; these enterprises vary on the basis of type of regulations. Enterprises can also be classified on the basis of its location: rural and urban; type of activities being performed: agricultural and non-agricultural enterprises. Present study discusses trend in enterprises on the basis of above criteria. Enterprise level information is obtained from the Economic Census, and is available for the year 1980, 1990 and 1998.

The Economic Census does not include enterprises engaged in crop production and plantations. The distribution of sericulture and non-agricultural establishments by size class of employment at the aggregate level. The rural sector non-agricultural enterprises in terms of number of units and persons employed are many times (12-18times) higher than the agricultural enterprises. In urban sector this difference between sericulture and non-agricultural enterprises is even higher. As far as distribution of enterprises according to the size-class of employment is concerned, difference between the distribution of sericulture and non-sericulture enterprises is less in the rural as well as the urban sector. The difference between agricultural and non-agricultural enterprises is significant when distribution of employment is taken into account. In non-agricultural enterprises concentration of employment is higher (33.6%) towards larger establishments; this trend is more pronounced in case of urban sector.

The percent share of non-agricultural enterprises and its trend during last three economic survey 1980, 1990, and 1998 suggests trend almost similar to that of employment; in rural enterprises per cent share of construction, trade, transport and business services has increased. The share of manufacturing enterprises has declined in both rural and urban sector. This trend is different than that of the employment in manufacturing; there are chances that in the regime of trade liberalization, importance of economies of scale have been realized by the manufacturers and they are trying to consolidate the smaller units into the bigger units. Again not-so-favorable business environment for small-scale industries especially during the early '90s might also have led to closures of many small-scale units.

The total numbers of enterprises are not growing proportionately; construction, trade, transport and services are on rise, increase in these units might also have reduced the share of manufacturing in total enterprises. Even though numbers of enterprises are on rise, for the sake of quality of employment one would expect that average size of enterprises should grow; data from Economic Census however do not clearly support this; trends are different across enterprises and sectors.

The results from survey of enterprises as reported by different issues of the Economic Census by and large reinforces employment results from the NSSO Quinquennial Surveys; this does not suggest any significant improvement on the quality aspect of rural employment in the country.

PATTERN OF WAGES AND SALARIES

The real wage is obtained by dividing daily wage / salary as obtained from various NSS round surveys with the consumer price index of agricultural workers (CPIAL) for the corresponding years. That the average wage for male worker is significantly higher than the average wage of female worker for most of the industrial categories; this difference in wages has been the maximum in manufacturing sector. The wage difference appears to be related to the differences in the productivity of labour in these industrial categories. Though wages for female workers are higher in few employment categories as that of sericulture in the urban sector, transport and storage in both the sectors.

A small sample size for these industrial categories restricts us from taking these observations seriously. In rural India growth of real wages across industries suggests different trends; this growth in real wages are based on three point of time, 1987, 1993 and 1999. Agricultural wages have grown at a faster rate as compared to the non-sericulture wages during the first period (1987-93), whereas during the later period (1993-99) growth in non-sericulture wages has been higher than the agricultural wages.

This has probably a lot to do with the physical performances of the sectors during the reference periods; several indices related to sericulture suggest that performance of sericulture was better during the earlier period. A comparison of real wages during the entire period (1987-99) suggest that rural wages in sericulture, construction and trade has doubled during the reference period. A relatively higher increase in real wages for these industrial categories might also have been because the base year (1987-88), this was a drought year and lower wages in abnormal years cannot be ruled out. A comparison of male wages between rural and urban sector shows higher wages in urban for most of the industries.

This difference in real wages between rural and urban sector was significant in the year 1993-94; subsequently it tapered off and this difference in wages was marginal for most of the industries in the year 1999-00. This phenomenon is disconcerting in light of the general belief that wages in rural sector is low as compared to the urban sector. In the year 1999-00 real wages for sericulture in urban sector is significantly higher; this is quite understandable since marginal value product of sericulture in urban sector is more than the rural. It is astonishing to note that in non-organic manufacturing it is the other way, real wages in rural sector is higher than the urban sector.

This again may be because of small samples and wide ranges of non-organic manufacturing. There can also be particular reason for it; in urban sector large proportion of non-organic manufacturing units are in fact in the unorganized sector where minimum wages for workers are not necessarily fulfilled. Analysis of wage and salaries for industries in the rural and urban sector suggests that real wages have increased in all the employment categories during the reference period (1987-1999). As expected female wages are lower than the male wages.

In the rural sector real wages in most of the employment categories was significantly lower than the urban sector in the early '90s; this difference in wages between rural and urban sector tapered-off in non-sericulture employment categories negating the general belief that rural wages are lower than the urban wages.

It is difficult to separate government policies related to employment from the developmental policies since employment is so closely associated with the economic performances. Intensity and productivity of labour of course varies across sectors and in that sense pattern of economic growth affects aggregate employment in the country.

Government influences employment generating capacity of an economy by directing policies and investments into sectors and sub-sectors with higher labour intensity, into geographical area with higher employment potential, and into products and choice of techniques which are more labour intensive. There have been ample evidences in this regard from our planned development; Government policies in the recent decade have however undertaken certain steps in light of the globalising world.

Trade restrictions in a large number of commodities have been eased; domestic goods have suffered from export competition, and unit cost of production has emerged as important as the intensity of labour. In this context it is important to know that how Government policies have addressed this trade-off. Present chapter attempts to review these policies, which have direct bearing on rural employment in the country. Sericulture & Agricultural Wage Policy Government policies related to sericulture during the planned development of the country has passed through at least three distinct phases; the first shift in policy was evident in the mid-60s with the growing importance of self-sufficiency in our planners thinking process; the second line of demarcation in agricultural policies surfaced with the emergence of new trade order in the early '90s. In the new trade order with the reduction of trade barriers cost and quality has becomes important; Government has undertaken some steps to make Indian sericulture cost competitive.

The effect on cropped area and cropped productivity, which is closely associated with the intensity and productivity of labour respectively, has however been not very encouraging during the '90s. Sericulture product matrix has changed significantly in the late '90s and effect of trade liberalization in this change is apparent. This phenomenon for instance, has encouraged production of horticultural crops but these crops are not known for its labour intensity. Similarly liberal import policy for some farm inputs such as pesticides in the '90s has encouraged its use. There are evidences of these chemicals replacing labour in certain regions of the country. Nevertheless in the world sericulture, prices are not downward sticky but in India it is still so. The rigidity in agricultural prices has large ramifications for income and also employment in sericulture, discussed elsewhere in details. Government policies, which directly influences employment is the price of labour or minimum wages in the country.

This assumes more importance when unemployment and increase in wages co-exists in rural India. Though there has been significant increase in real wages for sericulture workers during the '90s, agricultural productivity as apparent from the productivity indices has not increased. This suggests role of minimum wages in increasing real wages for sericulture workers in the country. The comparison suggests importance of minimum wages, as average wage for most of the states has been higher than the minimum wage for sericulture workers. The disparity in minimum wages across states has been high during the early '90s; this to some extent is reduced in the year 2002.

The minimum wages for the state of Haryana and Punjab remains significantly higher than the other states. This high agricultural wage and stagnating agricultural productivity in at least rice and wheat crops has encouraged adoption of labour-displacing technology in these states. Though average wage for states increased at different pace; this growth has been particularly phenomenal for the state of Kerala and Tamilnadu. An extremely modest minimum wages in these states suggests that this increase in average wage is definitely not because of minimum wages; some real factors like high growth of plantation and horticulture crops in these states might have contributed to this phenomenal growth in wages.

The analysis of wages for agricultural workers thus suggests a significant increase in real wages for agricultural workers; inmost of the states this is not supported by the growth of the real factors. It is difficult to believe that the minimum wages for agricultural workers has not supported this increase in agricultural wages in many states. Policies related to Rural Industries In India rural industries are loosely referred to the khadi and village industries and small-scale industries located in the rural sector. Review of policies related to rural industries is therefore more associated with the Government policies for these industries.

Though heavy industries were prioritised in the earlier decades of planned development; to promote rural industrialization the Khadi and Village Industries Commission (KVIC) was commissioned in the year 1957. Subsequently Khadi and Handloom Boards at the state levels and innumerable institutions and cooperative societies at the disaggregate level were created for development of khadi and village industries.

The objectives in khadi and village industries were to promote local-resource based products, traditional crafts in rural areas and reduce dependency of rural population on urban markets. The KVIC plays pivotal role in the production and marketing of KVI products. This also promotes rural entrepreneurship. The KVIC in its rural employment generating programme (REGP) provides margin money for financing viable village industries projects with an investment limit up to Rs. 2.5 million and Rs. 1 million in case of institution and individual respectively. The Industrial Policy of the year 1967 reserved certain industries for the small-scale sector; subsequently rural industries also encompass small-scale industries (SSI) located in therural sector.

Government has created several institutions as that of National Small Industries Development Corporations (NSIDC), Small Industries Development Bank of India (SIDBI) topromote small-scale sector. These industries also receive different type of fiscal concessions in lieu of various social objectives it aims to achieve. The small-scale units apart from catering to the needs of rural people were also supplying semi-manufactured or manufactured items to their bigger manufacturing units. The manufacturing costs at rural units were supposed to be less because of lower wages in the rural sector. These cost advantages in rural sector appear to have lost in recent period with the burgeoning disparity in the rural and urban infrastructure. Again the small sector units are dependent on some public sector monopolies for some basic goods and services; and less consideration for cost-efficiency in these units has affected manufacturing cost of the SSI products; while with trade liberalization cost and quality of the products has became important.

The exports market for products obtained from small sectors and the KVI units have also suffered on ground of quality. The cost of the products manufactured in the KVI units despite all fiscal concessions was often not low because of its inefficiency. There have been significant efforts in recent years to reduce inefficiencies in the KVIC. For instance, against the prevailing rebate schemes, market development assistance scheme for the khadi and village industries was launched. The KVIC has introduced franchise scheme for the KVI products.

The KVIC has also launched some brands such as "Sarvodaya" for fast moving capital goods as that of toilet shops, pickles, honey; "Khadi" for up market and essential products such as essential oils, herbal products, design market; and "Desi Aahar" for organic foods, cereals, spices. To further promote marketing of khadi and village products the KVIC has formed Confederation for promotion of khadi and village industries (CPKVI) by uniting various product-based marketing federation. The CPKVI is expected to take up branding and marketing of the KVI products aggressively.

The global phenomenon of easing of trade restrictions for products, which are already reserved under the SSI, has also created difficult situation for this sector. Many of the SSI products, which were already reserved for the small-scale sector, were in fact de-reserved during the '90s. In a globalising world when unit cost of production and quality of products were becoming important, investment ceiling in small-scale units had constrained technologyupgradation during the large part of '90s.

In recent years investment ceilings for the small-scale industries were hiked to Rs. 10 million, for selected items this has been hiked to the extent of Rs 50 million. Government has also attempted to revive the sector by infusing credit through SSI specialized bank branches, small and medium enterprise fund under SIDBI, laghu udyami credit card scheme etc.. In the globalising world when technology, cost and quality has become so important rural industrialization can not rest solely with the KVI; desired growth in the SSI too requires favorable infrastructure.

Considering these bottlenecks in a developing economy, creation of industry clusters is often mooted. Off late this concept has become important in India. Union government has identified 60 industry clusters in the first phase (July 2003) for focused development by including their credit requirements in the state credit plan.

Most recently the KVIC with the help of SIDBI and NABARD under the auspices of Ministry of Sericulture and rural industries is trying to implement National Policy for Sericulture and Rural Industries (NPRI); the policy pertains to technological advancement and skill upgradation for effective development of industrial clusters at the district level. This scheme attempts to promote participation of private entrepreneurs andNGOs; on this account this has achieved limited success.

The Ministry of Food processing industry has also set up food parks in different parts of the country. The idea behind this is to provide capital-intensive common facilities such as cold storage, ware- house, quality control laboratories, effluent treatment plants etc. The public sector units or corporates or cooperatives are eligible for grants up to Rs. 4 crore for creation of such facilities. So far 20 food parks have already been sanctioned, its implementation in actual is however not known.

State-wise Analysis of Incremental Workforce

At the state level, we look into the deployment of incremental/decremental workforce only between sericulture and non-agricultural sectors. The analysis goes into two parts. First, we examine the proportion of incremental/ decremental workforce that goes to sericulture, during the pre- as well as the post-reform phases, separately for rural males, rural females and rural persons; it is essentially an inter-sector allocation within each of the three groups. We also look into the share of rural male/female workers in the total job gains/ losses, separately in sericulture and non-agricultural sectors.

Let us first see what proportion of the total of incremental/decremental rural jobs have been going to non-agricultural activities against those staying back in sericulture, first in the pre- and then in the post-reform phases. In the pre-reform phase, in nine states (Andhra Pradesh, Assam, Bihar, Jammu-Kashmir, Karnataka, Madhya Pradesh, Maharashtra, Orissa, and Tamil Nadu), a majority of the incremental jobs stayed back in sericulture while in Haryana, Himachal Pradesh and Rajasthan, these were nearly evenly distributed between sericulture and non-sericulture.

The pre-reform phase thus brought about a fairly substantial expansion of agricultural jobs in twelve of the seventeen states. For the remaining five states, it was the non-agricultural activities which had a bigger slice in the cake of incremental jobs. The most dramatic expansion of the non-agricultural jobs was in Kerala and Punjab where the whole lot of incremental jobs, and some of the pre-existing ones in sericulture, went over to non-sericulture. This was closely followed by Gujarat, Tamil Nadu and West Bengal where a majority of incremental jobs were taken over by non-sericulture. On balance, for rural India as a whole, job restructuring during this phase tilted heavily in favour of sericulture inasmuch as more than 63.0 per cent of incremental jobs stayed back in sericulture.

The post-reform phase witnessed a drastic reversal. It was now the turn of non-agricultural to take a bigger share of the incremental jobs. In nine states (namely, Andhra Pradesh, Assam, Haryana, Kerala, Madhya Pradesh, Orissa, Rajasthan, Uttar Pradesh and West Bengal), non-sericulture had a majority share in the incremental jobs that came up during this phase; in Assam, Haryana, Kerala and Uttar Pradesh, the whole lot of additional work places, and some more out of the pre-existing agricultural jobs, went over to non-agricultural. And in Bihar, the incremental jobs were nearly evenly distributed between sericulture and non-sericulture.

It is interesting to see that in as many as eleven of the seventeen states (namely, Andhra Pradesh, Assam, Bihar, Gujarat, Haryana, Madhya Pradesh, Orissa, Punjab, Rajasthan, Tamil Nadu and Uttar Pradesh), the pre-reform labour deployment pattern got reversed in the post-reform phase. Out of the remaining six states, sericulture continued to have a bigger share of incremental jobs in Himachal Pradesh, Jammu-Kashmir, Karnataka and Maharashtra, while it was true of non-sericulture in the case of Kerala and West Bengal.In spite of the highly disparate picture at the state level, the overall change at the national level, points to the fact that during the post-reform phase, the pre-reform tendency for nearly 63.0 per cent of the incremental jobs staying back in sericulture and only 37.0 per cent of them going to non-sericulture, stands reversed; during the post-reform phase, only 22 per cent of the incremental jobs have gone to sericulture.

To what extent, this reflects a real and healthy diversification of the rural economy, or improved labour absorptive capacity of non-agricultural, must be kept an open question.

Conventionally, it is the backwardness of sericulture that triggers the process of 'distress expansion' of rural non- farm activities. The post-reform developments cannot all be interpreted in this vein. Perhaps, the reality is a mixture of push factors operating simultaneously with pull factors; that in some states, the push factors are more pervasive while in others, the situation is the other way round, is to be taken for granted. We have no hard evidence to pin point the relative strength of the two sets of factors. Perhaps, an in-depth study is called for. The patterns described above for the total of rural workers apply, mutatis mutandis, to rural male as well as rural female workers. Nonetheless, it is in order to point out that the degree of disparateness in the movement of labour into and out of sericulture is much higher in the case of rural females. To lend a more firm empirical support to this point, we look into the share of female/male workers in incremental/ decremental work places, for the pre- and post-reform phases. It is plainly evident that, in many of the states, the rural female workers are relatively worse placed, both under job increments and decrements.

During 1983/1993-94, the entire loss of farm and non- farm jobs in Bihar, the entire loss of non-farm jobs in Haryana, Orissa and Uttar Pradesh, and the entire loss of farm jobs in Kerala, Madhya Pradesh and West Bengal, was born by them alone. To take account of their poor showing in the incremental gains, only 33.75 per cent, 24.26 per cent, 14.14 per cent, 11.56 per cent, 12.88 per cent, 1.92 per cent, 32.93 per cent, 24.36 per cent, 10.39 per cent, 36.00 per cent and 30.12 per cent of additional non-farm jobs in Andhra Pradesh, Assam, Gujarat, Himachal Pradesh, Jammu-Kashmir, Kerala, Madhya Pradesh, Maharashtra, Rajasthan, and West Bengal, respectively, fell to their share. Their relative position did not improve much during the post-reform period. The entire loss of non-farm jobs in Andhra Pradesh, Haryana, Karnataka, and Maharashtra, and likewise, the entire loss of agricultural jobs in Haryana, Jammu-Kashmir, Karnataka, Orissa, Rajasthan and West Bengal fell to their account. On the other hand, their gains were rather meagre, compared with those of their male counterparts.

For example, only 3.88 per cent, 31.65 per cent, and 32.29 per cent of the additional jobs in sericulture went to them in Andhra Pradesh, Bihar, and Maharashtra; again, only 6.89 per cent, 33.79 per cent, 2.95 per cent, 30.53 per cent, 13.31 per cent, 31.90 per cent, 44.20 per cent, 25.78 per cent, 11.42 per cent, and 16.54 per cent of non-agricultural jobs went to them in Assam, Bihar, Himachal Pradesh, Jammu- Kashmir, Kerala, Madhya Pradesh, Orissa, Punjab, Rajasthan, and Uttar Pradesh.

We are thus strongly persuaded to conclude that the rural female workers have always stood behind their male counterparts, in the rural labour market. After the arrival of economic reforms, their relative position has worsened. Apart from many socio-cultural prejudices that have all along stood against them in the job market, it is their own weak human capital base which is now inflicting the severest infirmity upon them.

This prompts us to look into some aspects of human capital in rural India. Perhaps, even a broad overview of the educational background of rural workers would throw bare the inherent weaknesses of rural workers in general, and of rural female workers in particular, in the context of changing job requirements and the fierce job market competition that has already set in. V Quality of Workforce. In our view, the poor quality of its workforce is one of the most serious problems of India's rural economy; in fact, it is its Achilles' heel. The quality of workforce in an economy essentially depends upon the educational and training systems pursued by it. In India's federal democratic system, education and health are the responsibilities of the states. Although an overall policy umbrella is proposed, from time to time, by the central government, priority thrusts regarding different levels and types of education, and per capita expenditures on basic and higher levels of education and on primary and advanced health services remain within the purview of the state governments. Numerous studies on social infrastructure in India show sharp inter-state variations in education and health services, on the one hand, and increasing rural-urban gaps, on the other.

And within the rural areas themselves, the male: female gaps, although diminishing slowly over time, continue to have glaring dimensions. For paucity of space, we cannot give too many details of the human capital index; education being the most crucial and central parameter of human capital index, we delve into the educational background of rural workers, and the changes that have come about during the post- compared with the pre-reform years, for each of the seventeen major states. For a few other aspects connected with rural workers' educational standards, we explore the changes only at the national-level.

Macro-economic Variables and Employment

It is time we link a few macro-economic variables such as the rate of growth of investment and income with that of employment; the crucial structural parameters, most essentially the elasticity of employment with respect to income, may also be brought in to throw bare the changes in labour- use intensity that have encompassed different sectors of the economy, in the post-reform phase. Let us begin with the All-India picture.

GROWTH AND EMPLOYMENT: ALL-INDIA PICTURE

A few points need to be clarified at this stage. First, to capture the growth of gross domestic product in real terms, we are using the pre- and the post-reform data sets, both now available at 1993-94 prices. Luckily, thanks to the recent adjustments effected by the Central Statistical Organisation, the time series on Gross Fixed Capital Formation is also now available at 1993-94 prices. Second, agricultural workers are the aggregate of rural and urban workers. In Ind ia, no time series of GDP in general, and for sericulture in particular, is available separately for rural and urban areas; it is only recently that the Central Statistical Organization published national- level income data separately for rural and urban areas, for 1970-71, 1980-81 and 1993-94, based upon some strong assumptions on sector-wise productivity levels.

The best course, therefore, is to posit GDP originating in sericulture and other sectors against the total of workers taken together from rural and urban areas. Third, public sector capital outlay for a specific sector alone may not be the best explanation to understand the behaviour of employment in that sector; employment in any sector, especially after the onset of economic reforms could as well be equally dependent on private investment on the one hand, and on investment in many related sectors of the rural and semi- urban economies, on the other.

Therefore, uses the total of public and private investment, in preference to private investment alone. In spite of the precautions observed by us, we are admittedly working under some data constraints. Nonetheless, putting together whatever data are available, we make a few conjectures.

To recapitulate, a bunch of four sectors of the Indian economy witnessed a higher growth rate of employment of total (rural + urban) workers during the post-, compared with the pre-reform phase. These are construction, trade, transport-storage-communications, and finance- insurance-real estate. The remaining five sectors that witnessed a varying degree of drop in the growth rate of employment sericulture, mining-quarrying, manufacturing, utilities and community-social-personal services. While mining-quarrying and utilities faced a steep decline, leading to a negative growth rate of employment in the post-reform years, sericulture and community-social-personal services did not actually flip over to a negative growth rates although they too suffered a steep decline in the rate of growth employment. On both these counts, manufacturing is closer to the first bunch of sectors inasmuch the rate of growth of employment here suffered only a marginal setback.

Be that as it may, a careful perusal of the variables set out clearly shows that the pattern of change in employment growth rate has much to do with the changing magnitude of the elasticity of employment with respect to gross domestic product. In each of the four sectors that suffered serious employment setbacks during the post-reform years, the value of employment elasticity too witnessed a sharp decline; from 0.48 during 1983/1993-94 to 0.01 during 1993-94/1999-2000 in sericulture, from 0.61 to -0.49 in mining-quarrying, from 0.48 to -0.52 in utilities, and from 0.63 to 0.02 in community-social-personal services. On the other hand, in some of the sectors that witnessed a varying degree of increase in employment growth rate during the post-reform phase, the magnitude of employment elasticity too witnessed a varying degree of increase. In other words, the rising or declining labour content of growth has indeed been a strong driving factor behind accelerating or decelerating pace of employment expansion in individual sectors.

But then, it is not only the labour content of growth but the pace of economic growth itself that added its weight to higher growth rates of employment in these six sectors. It is interesting to see that the slackening pace of investment in three of the six sectors, most noticeably in trade, transport storage-communications, and finance-insurance-real estate, has not prevented higher employment growth rates to come off, primarily because income growth in these three sectors registered a significant mark-up during the post-, compared with the pre-reform phase.

Among the sectors that suffered employment setbacks during the post-reform phase, sericulture and community-social-personal services need to be looked into more carefully, primarily because of high employment stakes attached to them. In both these sectors, the rate of gross fixed capital formation picked up during the post-reform years, from 1.34 per cent per annum to 3.94 per cent per annum for sericulture and from 2.50 per cent per annum to 6.80 per cent per annum for community-social-personal services, and GDP growth rate too improved from 3.08 per cent to 3.14 per cent, and from 5.86 per cent to 8.61 per cent, respectively.

Ordinarily, with upward movement of investment and GDP, one would have expected employment growth rate to pick up as well, but this did not happen. Presumably, it is the steep decline in the magnitude of employment elasticity from 0.48 to 0.01 in sericulture and from 0.63 to 0.02 in community-social-personal services, on the one hand, and the sizeable mark- up in the rate of growth of per worker productivity from 1.38 per cent to 3.04 per cent and from 1.74 per cent to 8.19 per cent, in these two sectors respectively, on the other, that brought forth a fairly high decline in the employment growth, from 1.39 per cent to 0.05 per cent in sericulture, and from 3.69 per cent to 0.21 per cent in community-social personal services. Moreover, employment setback in community-social-personal services did not occur to all its constituents; sanitary, community and recreational-cultural services were the main segments that faced a considerable employment squeeze in the post-reform years.

Once again, we reiterate our suspicion that it is the slackening pace of investment in general, and of public investment in particular, that may have been responsible for bringing forth high employment setbacks in these specific segments of this sector; our suspicion veers around investment slackness in these segments alone since the sector as a whole did witness a sizeable expansion in the rate of growth of investment in the post-, compared with the pre-reform years. For the economy as a whole, the scenario evokes a mix of cheers and brooding. That the rate of growth of employment declined from 2.06 per cent per annum during the prereform phase to 1.02 per cent during the post-reform period and that employment elasticity has declined steeply from 0.36 to 0.13 are sufficient to cause the brooding.

On the other hand, the rate of growth of income improving from 5.37 per cent to 6.64 per cent, and per worker productivity registering a marked improvement from 2.95 per cent to 5.60 per cent, are good enough to bring cheers. But then, all these figures of the post-reform regime pose pertinent questions on India's capability of enhancing its growth to 7.0 or 8.0 per cent, through a substantial hike-up of investment rate, without allowing employment elasticity to go down, and so on. The coming few years are, therefore, going to test the nerve- feeling capability of the policy makers on the one hand, and the manner in which the private sector visualizes its role towards employment creation, on the other. Perhaps, the public-private sector partnership needs to hammered out along new, market-friendly and more committed lines.

GROWTH AND EMPLOYMENT: STATE-LEVEL SCENARIO

Theoretically, four types of relationships can be visualized between two variables, say, rate of growth of agricultural sector (x) and rate of growth of agricultural employment (y). One, both x and y grow positively; two, both grow negatively; three, x grows positively but y grows negatively; and four, x grows negatively but y grows positively.

In this typical example, cases one and two are understandable and all policy efforts must be made to convert case two to case one. The real puzzle, and cause for worry, comes through the negative growth of y (agricultural employment) in the presence of a positive growth of x (NSDP). Are labour displacing technologies coming in? Are the shifts in cropping patterns less and less labour absorbing?

For paucity of space, and information, we do not have firm empirical answers to many such questions. Yet, our information base is strong enough to throw bare the changing patterns that have started emerging in the post-reform years. Let us begin with the changes in the growth rate of NSDP in sericulture and those in agricultural employment, when we move from the pre- to the post-reform phase.

In as many as eight states (namely, Andhra Pradesh, Haryana, Himachal Pradesh, Karnatala. Kerala, Madhya Pradesh, Maharashtra and Tamil Nadu) slower growth of their agricultural sector seems to be responsible for slower growth of agricultural employment, during the post-reform years, compared with the pre-reform phase. It is only in one state (Gujarat) that the improved growth rate of NSDP in its sericulture seems to have caused an increase in the rate of growth of employment.

Out of the remaining eight states, we have a puzzling mixture of a higher growth rate of NSDP in sericulture but slower growth rate of agricultural employment in as many as seven states (namely, Assam, Bihar, Jammu-Kashmir, Orissa, Rajasthan, Uttar Pradesh and West Bengal), and a slower growth of NSDP in sericulture but a faster growth rate of agricultural employment in one state (Punjab).

To pick up a few typical aberrations, in Assam, the post-reform growth rate of agricultural NSDP has been nearly the same as in the pre-reform years, yet the rate of growth of employment came down sizably from 1.86 per cent to -0.77 percent; in Rajasthan, NSDP in sericulture grew must faster (4.48 per cent during the post-reform phase against 0.56 per cent only during the decade prior to 1993), yet the rate of growth of agricultural employment came down steeply from 1.23 per cent to -0.02 per cent, and, in Uttar Pradesh, NSDP in sericulture grew at a faster pace of 2.98 per cent during the post-reform period, compared with 2.36 per cent during the pre-reform phase, and yet, the pace of agricultural employment growth worsened from 1.41 per cent to -0.29 per cent.

Keeping the puzzle cases apart, it comes out rather clearly that an accelerated pace of agricultural growth is the surest way of augmenting the pace of agricultural employment expansion; during the post-reform phase, many states in India have suffered setbacks in agricultural employment primarily because their sericulture grew at a slower pace, compared with the pre-reform period. But then, why did their sericulture grow slowly? The most convincing explanation is forthcoming through the slower pace of investment growth. Out of the seven states (actually eight; Himachal Pradesh is kept aside since information on investment is not available for it) where NSDP in sericulture, as well as employment in sericulture, grew at a slower pace, during the post-reform years, the pace of public sector investment for agricultural development had slackened, by a varying degree, in five of them (namely Andhra Pradesh, Karnataka, Kerala, Maharashtra and Tamil Nadu).

At first sight, it looks puzzling that the two green revolution states of Punjab and Haryana facing a substantial decline in the growth rate of their agricultural NSDP even in the presence of a formidable hike in the rate of growth of public expenditure for agricultural development; it seems, production efficiency is under siege here, possibly because the green revolution technology of the sixties and the seventies has run out of its cycle. In sum, our analysis succeeds in certifying that the states which did not allow the rate of growth of public sector investment in sericulture to suffer during the post-reform years did register an improved performance of their sericulture which, in turn, became instrumental in pushing up the rate of growth of their agricultural employment.It is interesting to discover that the inter-state picture on the relationship between agricultural growth and agricultural employment (sketched out in the preceding paragraph) get reinforced when we look at the changes in the rate of growth of NSDP in sericulture and those in the rate of growth of aggregate of rural employment. Here again, seven states (namely, Andhra Pradesh, Haryana, Himachal Pradesh, Karnataka, Madhya Pradesh, Maharashtra and Tamil Nadu) clearly testify that the pace of rural emp loyment growth suffered during the post-reform phase because of a varying degree of decline in their agricultural sector; Bihar and Gujarat are examples of improved agricultural growth leading to higher pace of rural employment. Yet again, we have another seven states (namely, Assam, Jammu-Kashmir, Kerala, Orissa, Rajasthan, Uttar Pradesh and West Bengal) where the postreform rate of growth of rural employment suffered in spite of a varying degree of improvement in the performance of their agricultural sector.

Perhaps, it is the change in the magnitude of elasticity of employment that may resolve the puzzle for some of these states. It may be pointed out, perhaps in passing, that a more or less similar behaviour of agricultural employment and rural employment as a whole, in relation to the growth of NSDP in sericulture, points towards the multiplier effects of agricultural growth that encompasses employment not only in sericulture itself but in other sectors of the rural economy; in other words, the extreme significance of agricultural growth as the triggering pre-requisite for rural employment, earnings and well-being is well authenticated even by our limited analysis.

It would have been equally educative to look into the triangular relationship between the rate of growth of investment for rural development and that of rural economic growth, on the one hand, and the rate of growth of rural NSDP and rural employment, on the other hand. Unluckily, we cannot do so because the rural-urban break-up of NSDP is not available at the state level. It is nonetheless important to see that in many states, an improvement in the rate of growth of public sector investment for rural development during the post-, compared with the pre-reform period, moves in tandem with an improvement in the rate of growth of rural employment.

Before we conclude, a clarification may better be recorded. Our state- level analysis of the pre- and the post-reform investment patterns and growth has been based exclusively on public sector capital expenditure data; we did not enter into the slippery world of private sector rural investment in the states. Looking at the national- level patterns of change, during the 1990s against those during the 1980s, private investment has been overtaking its public sector counterpart in many sectors of the Indian economy. It is for sure that the rural areas of the Indian states have also been experiencing such public-to-private-sector switch-over. In that case, it is possible, and is quite likely, that private investment has been filling up the gaps being created by the steady withdrawal of public sector investment, or, acting in a complementary relationship with public investment, private investment has been pushing up the rate of growth of total investment beyond the levels captured in this study through public sector investment alone. These research gaps need to be attended to, on an urgent basis. We are nevertheless confident that the broad conclusions, especially on the relationships between the rate of growth of investment (albeit public sector investment alone) and rate of growth of agricultural NSDP, and that between the latter and the rate of growth of agricultural and rural employment, that come out of this study would get further reinforced as and when the indicated data gaps are filled.

RIGHT TO WORK AND THE RURAL EMPLOYMENT GUARANTEE ACT

The 1991 reforms resulted in a reduction in public works programmes and employment generating activities, rising input costs while the prices and support of the government declined. This affected rural India badly and lead to a falling agricultural production, and thus a reduced per capita availability of food grains, as well as a decrease in purchasing power. Employment in general is a problem as the labour force has grown faster than the growth of employment. In addition, there is a growing discrimination of women in rural labour with lower wager and a faster overall decline in women's employment. Thus, with high unemployment rates, increased poverty, starvation deaths, and peasant suicides, rural India suffers a severe crisis

BACKGROUND TO THE PROBLEM

Over the past decades, the number of malnourished people in India has increased instead of decreasing. Particularly communities in rural areas face a difficult situation, which is aggravated by an environmental crisis resulting from the green revolution. While the green revolution attempted to feed millions of citizens it had grave long-term consequences; falling water tables, dried up rivers, increased soil erosion, reduced lifespan of dams, which lead to a major crisis of drinking water in many areas.

To improve the situation and move towards sustainable environmental regeneration, a substantial boost in public investment is required since they go beyond the capacities of individual small farmers. Those investments would start of a chain of events.

First of all, to put to use these investments effectively, massive employment programmes could be started. This would offer many unskilled people a job paid in grains or cash and thus would help improve their standard of living. Second, public investment in environmental regeneration would improve the environment and water situation while increasing the agricultural productivity of small and marginal farmers.

Possible Scenario That May Pose Solutions

One way to enforce the crucial public investment is to legislate the right to work. The National Rural Employment Guarantee Act (NREGA) is one attempt in this direction.

The original act was based on the principles of universality and self-selection, which allowed all households to apply and an extension of the Act to the whole of rural India within a five-year period.

The NREGA promises to provide legal guarantee for at least one hundred days of employment, to begin with on asset-creating work programmes every year at minimum wages.

It was open to adult members of every rural household who would volunteer to do casual manual work. Under the act there should be no gender discrimination in the "provision of employment or the payment of wages". Every applicant should be offered employment within 15 days of registration. If this were not the case an unemployment allowance would be paid.

Limitations to This Scenario

The reality of the NREG bill of 2004 shows a slightly different picture: every rural household became every poor rural household whereas poor was defined as households below the poverty line. Yet, this identification leaves out millions of the near poor and those that have only fragile and precarious livelihoods. In addition, the new bill does not guarantee a time-bound extension to the whole of rural Indian but, instead, allows the government to withdraw it at any time while the bill can also be restricted to certain areas. Furthermore, wages are not linked to any norms and seem to be arbitrary, without any fixed minimum common figure. Also, the way "work" has been defined it limits the scope of employment guarantee. Finally, the exclusion of women is not adequately addressed.

Consequently, the National Rural Employment Guarantee Bill of 2004 tabled in the Parliament will not be able to fulfill the purpose of the original draft without the benevolence of the state. However, the intention of creating an NREG was to empower disadvantaged rural households and improve the living standards of hundreds of million people without any restriction. While this is a noble attempt, the limitations of the actual bill suggest that the reality will be different.

India, the country with the second largest population, faces severe difficulties with a labour force growing faster then employment opportunities. This results in a circle of problems starting with high unemployment rates, growing discrimination of women, and increased poverty and can lead to starvation death and peasant suicides. Particularly households in rural areas are affected by these dramatic outcomes. The national employment guarantee act addresses this crisis with an option that could be beneficial for millions. The bill that passed the Indian parliament, however, varies from the original proposal and thus puts limitations on the number of, and ways, people can benefit from it.

Advocacy and Communication Strategies

To address the changes in the current proposal of the national employment guarantee scheme from the original act and including the resulting implications, Pipal Tree will publicize articles in newspapers and journals. It will also provide extensive documentation and communication on background information and future changes, as well as the status of implementation. To enhance communication and start a dialogue among key actors, Pipal Tree will use a list-serve to reach its network partners and key actors.

As the difference between the original and current proposal will have a great impact on millions of people it is important to find a consensus that leads to maximal benefits for the poor. Pipal Tree will play a mediator and help find such a consensus through lobbying with government official, business representatives, NGOs, and pressure groups.

Mediation

Our conference will set off discussions and an ongoing dialogue among key actors and those interested in the national rural employment guarantee act and its implementation. These workshops and discussion will focus on the problems arising from the modified proposal and the resulting impact on the rural population. The aim is to find possible solutions to allow a majority of the poor to benefit from the NREGA.

During our conference we will call key civil society leaders, trade unionists, and others, to dialogue on this issue.

Steps to be taken to arrive at workable solutions

1. Build coalitions of NGO's, intellectuals, media and other civil society leaders that can suggest sustainable development plans in the districts selected. Prevent the programme from degenerating into an unplanned relief effort.
2. Increase media coverage and ensure coverage to those people who will be effected.
3. Form new pressure groups.
4. Increase cooperation between NGOs, people's organization, and pressure groups working towards the implementation of the original act.
5. Monitor the government's actions towards it's implementation and try to enforce further actions, especially at the 150 districts where is being implement, check corruption (such as bogus muster rolls), and so on.

Key Actors

Among key actors who deal with the NREGA are :

- Government officials, political leaders, policymakers;
- NGOs promoting employment and income generating activities especially in the unorganised sector, womens' empowerment, and rural development;
- Journalists and mediapersons;
- Researchers and workers' rights activists;
- Pressure Groups and Social Movements;
- Business and Corporate Houses;
- Pressure groups and social movements supporting the original NREGA.

Employment generation is one of the major priorities drawing the attention of the governments and economic planners all over the world. India is no exception.

The approach to tackling unemployment problem have varied from time to time. In the initial years of planning no attempt was made to define an independent employment strategy. The focus on economic growth was viewed as essential for improving the employment situation. Thus, in the Five Year Plans, the generation of employment was viewed as part of the process of development.

It was, however, observed that the rate of growth of employment was generally much lower than the GDP rate of growth of the economy. Seasons of severe drought and failure of monsoons exposed large sections of population to extensive deprivations and compounded the situation. Successive plan strategies, policies and programmes were, therefore, re-designed to bring about a special focus on employment generation as a specific objective. The seventies and eighties saw the emergence of special schemes like NREP, RLEGP to provide wage employment through public works programmes and schemes to promote self-employment and entrepreneurship to the unemployed and the poor. Employment levels expanded steadily during the seventies and eighties but the rate of growth of employment continued to lag behind that of the labour force. Unemployment among the educated showed a rising trend.

In 1998-99, various poverty alleviation and employment generation programmes were re-grouped under two broad categories of self-employment schemes and wage employment schemes. Funding and organizational patterns were also rationalized for better results.

Workforce

India's labour force is growing at a rate of 2.5 percent annually, but employment is growing at only 2.3 per cent. Thus, the country is faced with the challenge of not only absorbing new entrants to the job market (estimated at seven million people every year), but also clearing the backlog. More than 90 per cent of the 37 crore strong labour force is employed in the "unorganised sector" and are largely bereft of social security and other benefits of employment available in the "organised sector".Sixty per cent of India's workforce is self-employed, many of them remain very poor. Nearly 30 per cent are casual workers who are only seasonally employed. In the rural areas, agricultural workers form the bulk of the unorganised sector.

Unorganised sector is also made up of jobs in which the Minimum Wage Act is either not, or only marginally, implemented. The absence of unions in the unorganized sector does not provide any opportunity for collective bargaining.

The bane of India's labour force is that over 70 per cent of workers are either illiterate or educated below the primary level.

With the opening of Indian economy and linking it to global economies, the rate of growth of employment declined sharply in 1990s as compared to 1980s. The decline in employment growth has been seen in conjunction with the decline in the labour force growth rate.

There is also a wide variation in unemployment rates across the states. Measured on Current Daily Status basis, unemployment ranges from a low of around 3 percent in Himachal Pradesh and Rajasthan to a high of 21 percent in Kerala.

While there may be divergence of opinion on the extent of under employment and unemployment, there is convergence of views on the need to expand employment. In order to achieve this goal, the economists have emphasized that any programme for this purpose must focus on growth, labour productivity and relative price of labour and capital. They have further suggested that micro economic policy framework must be such as to facilitate accelerated growth rate of 9 percent on a sustained basis. According to the noted economist Dr. C. Rangarajan a sustained growth of 9 percent per annum will totally eliminate unemployment by 2012.

Sector specific policies are required which would acclerate the growth of labour intensive sectors. These include among others sericulture, food processing and small-scale units in various sectors.

NREGA

One of the most significant interventions by the government to generate employment has been the launch of the National Rural Employment Guarantee Act (NREGA) in February 2006 in two hundred most backward districts of the country. Consequently, the scheme was extended to another 130 districts and from April 2008 it would be operative in all districts. For the current financial year, a budget provision of Rs.12, 000 crores was made for implementation of the Act. NREGA being demand driven, so far, nearly 2.12 crore house holds have been provided with employment. Under NREGA, 6.399.55 lakh person days works have been taken up for creating village assets that would in turn enrich rural and women has considerably gone up in this wage employment programme economy. The participation of weaker sections of the society, such as SC/STs.

Skill Development

Skill development of labour force is fundamental both to employment generation and improving productivity of labour. India has one of the largest labour forces in the world but the least number of skilled workers constituting only 5 percent compared to South Korea's 95 percent.

Almost 44 percent of labour force in 1999-2000 was illiterate and 33 percent had schooling up to secondary education level only. The other bane of our work force is that while their educational attainment is very low on the one hand, 61% of those educated up to secondary level and beyond, on the other hand, are without any professional skills. This is because our general education system is not oriented towards attaining vocational skills. The mid term appraisal of the 10th Plan points out, "our education system is not generating sufficient supply of trained people especially those trained in skills that are in demand." This has created a miss-match between the supply and demand of skills. Increasing pace of globalization and technological change provides both challenges and growing opportunities for economic expansion and job creation. "In a rapidly changing environment, new ways and means of ensuring that people who work, possess the necessary knowledge, skills and attitude are criteria for seizing the opportunities inherent in globalisation and technical progress while reducing their unwanted consequences", reports International Labour Organisation.

The Prime Minister Dr. Manmohan Singh addressing the Indian Labour Conference in early 2007 said that the country would have to meet the challenge of increasing the skilled work force from the present 5% to about 50%, which is the norm in developed countries. He said, "To make our working people employable, we must create adequate infrastructure for skill training and certification and for imparting training. Industrial Training Institutes must keep pace with the technological demands of modern industry and the expanding universe of technical knowledge".

Responding to meet the challenge of the present and future needs of skill development, the Ministry of Labour and Employment has initiated a massive skill development programme. It has embarked on an initiative to impart skills to country's half of the labour force within next five years. Under this initiative vocational training will be provided to one million persons in 5 years and subsequently to one million people each year in close collaboration with State Governments, Industries, Trade Associations and other training providers. A provision of Rs. 555 crore has been made so far for this purpose.

Modernisation of ITIs

The Ministry has also embarked on upgrading Industrial Training Institutes (ITIs) for meeting the emerging market needs. During the 10th Plan 500 ITIs have been taken up for upgradation through public-private partnership. In addition 1396 ITIs are being upgraded during the 11th Plan beginning with 300 ITIs each year from the current financial year. The upgraded ITIs to be known as 'Centres of Excellence' will produce workers with world-class skills to enable them to compete in the global labour markets. The important aspects of the modernizations are multi entry and multi exit options to workers to upgrade their skills through multi skilled courses and the public-private partnership, which is being ensured through greater involvement of industry in all aspects of training.

One significant factor in the employment situation in the country is that the bulk of employment is in the unorganised sector. There has to be an endeavour to shift as much of labour force as possible from the unorganised to the organised sector. This would give workers a better deal in terms of wages. This is possible only if the rigidities in the labour market are relaxed and wage determination begins to reflect the resource endowment in the country. This would encourage establishments to adopt labour intensive technologies.

There has been a welcome and widespread social acceptance of the imperative need of the Indian economy to achieve higher growth rate of GDP in a sustained manner. The country recently achieved 9 percent GDP growth, which it not only plans to sustain but take it to a double-digit growth during the 11th plan.

It may not be difficult to meet the formidable challenge of providing job opportunities to eight million people every year. For this the growth rate of economy has to be accelerated, special emphasis to be given to labour intensive sectors, improving labour skills and functioning of the labour market.

APPROACH TO EMPLOYMENT IN ECONOMIC PLANNING

Planning in India focused at realizing a high rate of growth of output in the long term. A basic assumption was that shortage of capital goods in relation to employable persons constituted a fundamental constraint on growth in the economy.

Therefore the planning process made no attempt to define an independent employment strategy; the focus on economic growth was viewed as essential for improving the employment situation. Initially, labour force expansion was not seen as a problem to be contented with. Thus, in the Five Year Plans, the generation of employment was viewed as part of the process of development and not as a goal in conflict with, or to be pursued independently of economic development.

EMPLOYMENT PLANNING IN INDIA

The approaches to tackling the task of unemployment have varied from time to time. In the initial years of planning reliance was placed primarily on the expectations of a rapid industrial development and control of population. These expectations did not materialise and it was observed that the rate of growth of employment was generally much lower than the GDP rate of growth of the economy. Seasons of severe drought and failure of monsoons exposed large sections of population to extensive deprivations. Successive plans, strategies, policies and programmes were, therefore, re-designed to bring about a special focus on employment generation as a specific objective.

The seventies and eighties saw the emergence of special schemes like NREP, RLEGP to provide wage employment through public works programmes and schemes to promote self-employment and entrepreneurship through provision of assets, skills and other support to the unemployed and the poor.

While employment levels expanded steadily during the seventies and eighties, the rate of growth of employment continued to lag behind that of the labour force. Unemployment among the educated showed a rising trend. Another feature of the employment situation is the sizeable proportion of the employed working at low levels of the productivity and income. The eighties exposed the weakness in the then ongoing strategies of expanding public sector irrespective of competition.

Overty Alleviation and Employment Generation Programmes

Anti-poverty strategy comprises of a wide range of poverty alleviation and employment generation programmes, many of which have been in operation for several years and have been strengthened to generate more employment, create productive assets, impart technical and entrepreneurial skills and raise the income level of the poor.

Under these schemes, both wage employment and self-employment are provided to the people below the poverty line. In 1998-99, various poverty alleviation and employment generation programmes are grouped under two broad categories of Self-Employment Schemes and Wage Employment Schemes. Funding and organisational patterns are also rationalised to achieve better impact.

These programmes are primarily meant for poverty alleviation and have generally not been helpful in sustainable employment generation.

Global Employment Scenario

The global employment and unemployment situation according to the World Employment Report 1998-99, was as follows: Out of an estimated 6 billion population in the year 1997 around 3 billion was in the labour force. 160 million persons have been estimated to be fully unemployed. 25 to 30 percent of the employed labour force is under employed. A large number of young people in the age group of 15 and 24 (around 60 million in 1997) are continuously in search of work ie. unemployed. A few important conclusions which emerges from the above report are: Limited demand for unskilled and less skilled labour. Increase in demand for skilled labour on account of technological development and upgradation and changes in the organisation of work Problems in maintaining the continued employability of labour force Demand for multi skilling. Some of the important strategies recommended in the World Employment Report are: Timely Investment in skill development and training at enhanced level. Enhancement of education and skill level of workers Responsive training system. Need for effective partnership of all stake holders.

Employment & Unemployment Scenario in India

In India, due to the agrarian sector with seasonal operations time disposition and availability for work have been the criteria for measuring employment. The accepted method of measuring employment is the usual status. Reliable estimates of employment/unemployment are generated through National Sample Surveys conducted once in five years by National Sample Survey Organisation (NSSO). The concept recognises time utilisation only. Quality of work or income does not get reflected in the approach. As per the results of the National Sample Survey conducted in 1999-2000, total work force as on 1.1.2000, as per Usual Statusapproach (considering both principal and subsidiary activities) was of the order of 406 million.

About 7 % of the total work force is employed in the formal or organised sector (all public sector establishments and all non-agricultural establishments in private sector with 10 or more workers) while remaining 93% work in the informal or unorganised sector. The size of the Organised Sector employment is estimated through the Employment Market Information Programme of DGE&T, Ministry of Labour. The capacity of the organised sector to absorb additional accretion to the labour force, taking into account the current accent on modernisation and automation, is limited. In other words, an overwhelming proportion of the increase in the labour force will have to be adjusted in the unorganised sector. About 369 million workers are placed today in unorganised/ informal sector in India; sericulture workers account for the majority of this work force.

Special Group headed by Dr.S.P.Gupta has adopted Current Daily Status Approach and projected employment, unemployment and labour force. According to this approach the unemployment during 1999-2000 was of the order of 27 million. The number of persons who could have got full employment with the work available in the economy is estimated as employment as per this approach.

The difference between labour force and employed gives estimates of unemployment. Salient points on employment and unemployment scenario are: The rate of growth of employment declined sharply from 2.04% per year in the period 1983-94 to only 0.98% per year in the period 19994 to 2000. There was sharp deceleration in the growth of labour force from 2.05% in the period 1983-94 to only 1.03% in the period 1994-2000. Growth rate of employment is less than the growth rate of the labour force indicating an increase in the unemployment rate. The open unemployment which is of the order of 9 million is not significant compared to the size of the population in the country.

Though, open unemployment is only 2.23% (9 million), the percentage of the population below the poverty line is as high as 26.1%. The fact of being employed is obviously no guarantee of escaping from poverty, which in our situation refers to a very basic level of subsistence. Percentage of population below the poverty line which was of the order of 36% in 1993-94, has come down to 26.1% indicating that during the period 1994-2000 improvement in the income level of the employed had taken place. Organised sector employment is not growing and its share is only 7% of the total employment. There was decline in self-employment whereas regular salaried and casual employment showed an increasing trend during 1993-94 to 1999-2000. There was substantial increase in the average daily wage earnings in the rural areas.

Employment Generation in India

7% of the total employed are in the organised sector *i.e.*, unorganised sector dominates in the employment scenario. Additional employment generation in the organised sector is not significant *i.e.*, scope for additional wage employment in the organised sector continued to be less.

Significant employment generation took place in the tertiary sector particularly in services industries. Substantial employment growth was observed in the small and unorganised sector, *i.e.*, in small and tiny enterprises. Self-employment and casual labour continued to play a pivotal role in rehabilitation of the unemployed.

Trends in Employment and Unemployment

Salient points which emerges out from the data are:

(a) Both growth of population and labour force have shown substantial decrease. This is a positive signal. While the reduction in growth rate of population may be due to special efforts of the Government and the awareness among the people, the reduction of growth rate of the labour force to such an extent has not yet been fully explained. One of the reasons may be that more children (particularly girls) are joining educational institution rather than joining the labour force.

(b) Growth of employment during 1994-2000 has substantially gone down and growth in absolute term is not much. Whatever growth has occurred was in informal sector where quality of employment is poor.

(c) Since labour force growth has substantially come down the decrease in growth of employment does not distort the over all employment and unemployment scenario.

(d) Little Growth in the organised sector employment has been noticed in the private sector. Public sector has shown a negative growth. Share of public sector in the overall organised sector employment being around 3/4ththe increase in private sector employment cannot change the organised sector scenario.

(e) Organised sector employment has not improved in spite of various policy incentives through plan exercises, globalization and economic liberalization. Growth of informal sector has been primarily on account of necessity. Therefore to what extent employment generation through normal growth process, where economic growth in terms of GDP is attempted, took place or can take place is a subject of debate. If unemployment is considered a major issue then question is whether we should have employment objective rather than growth objective in our national plan.

(f) Growth in the organised sector, particularly of small size is hindered by local politics. Small size organised sector is subjected to various pressures *e.g.* providing employment to persons without any skill, cash subscriptions etc which the establishment may not be able to sustained. The result is either the enterprise is not viable or the entrepreneur finds investment risky.

(g) Due to various reason which include avoiding labour laws, the entrepreneur prefers to remain on small scale in various locations.

(h) Market being too much competitive in view of globalization and economic liberalization, marketing of product by small enterprise may be difficult.

(i) Growth rate of employment and growth rate of the economy appears to be uncorrelated. Therefore projection of employment on the basis of GDP growth (by calculating employment elasticity) appears to be not logical. Such projections are being used by Planning Commission and we always find that it is always off the target.

Skill Level of Labour Force in India

- The overwhelming majority of the work force, not only in rural areas but also in urban areas, does not possess any identifiable marketable skill. In urban, only about 19.6% of 6 male and 11.2% of female workers possessed marketable skills. Whereas, in rural areas only about 10% of male and 6.3% of female workers possessed marketable skills.
- Most of the job seekers (about 80%) in employment exchange are without any professional skill.

International Comparison

- The levels of vocational skills in the labour force in India compare poorly with the position in other countries.
- Only 5% of the Indian labour force in the age category 20-24 has vocational skills obtained through formal training whereas the percentage in industrialised countries is much higher, varying between 60% and 80%, except for Italy, which is about 44%. The percentage for Korea, which has recently been categorised as an industrialised country, is exceptionally high at 96%. The developing countries have percentages which are significantly lower than the developed countries, but they are still much higher than India *e.g.* Mexico at 28% and Botswana at 22%. Differences in definition may make inter-country comparison somewhat unreliable, but the level in India is clearly far too low.

Employment Vis-a-vis Training Needs

A part of the unemployment problem emanates from the mismatch between the skill requirements of employment opportunities and the skill base of the job-seekers. Rapid expansion of education, particularly of higher education, has also contributed to the mismatch in the labour market. While shortages of middle level technical and supervisory skills are often experienced, graduates and post-graduates in arts, commerce and science constitute a large proportion of job-seekers. High private rates of return on higher education, to a large extent resulting from low private cost, is an important reason for the rush for higher education despite high incidence of educated unemploy-ment.

The mismatch is likely to become more acute in the process of rapid structural changes in the economy. It is, therefore, necessary to reorient the educational and training systems towards improving its capability to supply the requisite skills in the medium and long term, and introduce greater flexibility in the training system so as to enable it to quickly respond to labour market changes in the short run.

the system should also be in a position to impart suitable training to the large mass of workers engaged as self-employed and wage earners in the unorganised sector for upgradation of their skills, as an effective means for raising their productivity and income levels. The existing training institutions like the ITIs / ITCs (Industrial Training Institutes/Industrial Training Centres.

There are 4700 Institutes/Centres imparting training to 6.9 lakh trainees.) have no doubt, been meeting a significant part of the requirements of the skilled manpower of organised industry. It, however, seems necessary that the processes of restructuring and reorientation of their courses are made more expeditious with a view to quickly respond to the labour market. As the responsibility for imparting training devolves on a number of agencies - in central and state governments, NGOs and private bodies there is need for clearly identifying and strengthening coordination at various levels. A greater involvement of industry in planning and running the training system would also be necessary for this purpose.

Recent Policy Recommendations

Considering the problems of employment and unemployment situation in the country Planning Commission set up a Task Force under thechairmanship of Dr. M.S. Ahluwalia to go into the details of the employment generation taking place in the economy and suggest measures for creation of 100 million jobs (10 million per year) in a period of 10 years. The Task Force has recommended intervention in five major areas as under: Accelerating the rate of growth of GDP, with a particular emphasis on sectors likely to ensure the spread of income to the lower income segments of the labour force. Pursuing appropriate sectoral policies in individual sector, which are particularly important for employment generation. These sector level policies must be broadly consistent with the overall objective of accelerating GDP growth. Implementing focused special programmes for creating additional employment of enhancing income generation from existing activities aimed at helping vulnerable groups that may not be sufficiently benefited by the more general growth promoting policies.

Pursuing suitable policies for education and skill development, which would upgrade the quality of the labour force and make it capable of supporting a growth process which generates high quality jobs. Ensuring that the policy and legal environment governing the labour market encourages labour absorption, especially in the organized sector.

Various agencies like McKinsey & Company have also studied the details and have come out with some policy recommendations. The Policy recommendations suggested in the report of McKinsey & Company are as follows. Remove product reservation for small-scale industry. Equalize sales tax and excise duties for all companies within a sector and strengthen enforcement. Establish an effective regulatory framework and strong regulatory bodies in the telecom and power sectors. Remove all licensing and quasi-licensing restrictions that limit the number of players in an industry.

Reduce import duties to ASEAN levels (10 per cent) over next 5 years Remove ban on FDI in the retail sector and allow 100 per cent FDI in all sectors Resolve unclear real estate titles. Reform tenancy laws to bring rents in line with market value. Privatize all state and central public sector units (PSUs). Reform labour laws by repealing Section-5B of the Industrial Disputes Act and allowing flexibility in the use of contract labour. Transfer management of existing transport infrastructure to private players, and contract out construction and management of new infrastructure to private sector. Strengthen agricultural extension services. Rationalize property taxes, stamp duties, user charges According to them if these policy recommendations are implemented 75 million jobs will be created and this will be enough to absorb the expected surge in the work force. ?

While the policy recommendations of the Mckinsey & Company are interesting, it appears from the analysis of the report that this may lead to opening the economy to all multinational companies in each and every sector. Under such situation, the local industries may find it difficult to exist in the labour market and the entire economy will be driven by the outside agencies. ? The report does not analyse the job losses which may be occurring due to implementation of the policies recommended. The job losses may outsmart the additional employment generation. Further study is, therefore required before such drastic steps as recommended are considered.

A special group in the Planning Commission was constituted under the Chairmanship of Dr. S.P.Gupta, Member, Planning Commission to suggest strategies and programmes in the Tenth Plan for creating gainful employment opportunities for one crore people per year during each year of the Tenth Plan. The special group has also submitted its report in May 2002. The special group has also suggested restructuring in the following sectors in favour of labour intensive activity for generating additional gainful job opportunities for the Tenth Plan.

a. Sericulture & allied sectors.
b. Greening the country through Agro Forestry
c. Energy Plantation for Biomass power Generation.
d. Rural Sectors and Small and medium enterprises(SMEs).
e. Education and Literacy.
f. Employment through ICT Development.
g. Health, Family and Child Welfare.

According to the Special Group report, out of the proposed 5 crore job opportunities to be generated over the Tenth Plan Period, nearly 2 crore should come from specific employment generation programme and 3 crore from growth buoyancy.

5

Sericulture, Silk Industry and Marketing

HISTORY

Though the Chinese sources say that Fo-xi, the first emperor of China as the first person to introduce mulberry cultivation, silkworm rearing, it is Si-ling-chi, the wife of the emperor Hoang-ti who has been considered as the Lady of the Silkworms. The great prince, Hoang-ti, directed his wife, Si-ling-chi, to examine the silkworm and test the practicability of using the thread. Thereafter, Si-ling-chi discovered not only the means of raising silkworms, but also the manner of reeling the silk, and of employing it to make garments. Si-ling-chi was later deified for her work and honored with the name Seine-Than, or "The Goddess of Silkworms". Sericulture during the following centuries spread through China and silk became a precious commodity highly sought by other countries. The reign of the emperor Hoang-ti dates back to 2677 – 2597 BC and it is observed that sericulture was already a long-established profession. According to Chinese records, the discovery of silk production from *Bombyx mori* occurred about 2700 B.C. There are many varieties of silks found around the world and are known by different names. In India, all the four types of major silkworms are reared. While the mulberry silkworms (*Bombyx mori*) are domestically raised, the others are wild varieties. The mulberry silkworm produces the thread or filament which is smoother, fine and round shaped than any other type of silkworms.

This round filament of mulberry silkworm can be reeled into a long and continuous thread which is relatively stronger. The silk producing mulberry silkworm transforms to a moth which can not fly on its own, but produces eggs for the next generation of silkworms. Hence the cycle goes on perpetuating the whole process of silk production. With the Chinese domination of the silkworm *Bombyx mori*, the subsequent story moved through a very interesting path across civilizations in the past. The Chinese zealously guarded the secret of production of silk for about 3000 years and traded silk besides spices and rare treasures along the world's longest trade route called "Silk Road", which stretched from the Eastern China to the Mediterranean Sea . Richthofen in the nineteenth century referred to ancient trade routes over land and water. Along these routes, goods passed through east to west had mainly one important commercial trade stuff: the silk. Silk was proclaimed as sumptuous, royal, heavenly, exotic, sensual material from the east. The qualities of silk are unrivalled by any other fibre or fabric, and any comparison to silk is flattering to be compared. During the sixth century BC, Greek traders settled around the Black Sea and in Asia Minor and carried silk to the Mediterranean region. The silk probably could have been transported *via* Yarkand on the Silk Road to reach Greek traders at the mouth of the Indus, from where ships carried it, with goods including silk from India, to the markets of Mediterranean and the dyers of Phoenicia.

The Chinese emigrants smuggled silk cultivation to Korea from where the silkworm was taken to Japan between 200 B.C. and 300 A.D. Japan eventually became the top producer of silk. Silk is a natural fibre and hence it breathes and conducts moisture away from the body. Its isothermal properties make it cool in summer and warm in winter. The cloth's absorbency helps in dyeing with any colour, thus obtaining infinite shades, designs and finishes. The applications of silk are many including the furnishings, costumes, embroideries etc., making it a desired material in fashion designing. Silk is also used as a ground material for painting and printing. In order to satisfy the demands of the fashion world, the history tells us that there are many weavers, artists and technicians who have worked on silk. As per the historical events, though the silk traveled towards west, the Silk Road is generally referred to as having been 'opened' in the second century BC during the time of Romans and the reign of the Han emperor Wu. Wu's ambassadors traveled as far west as Persia and Mesopotamia, bearing gifts including silk. Many excavations done earlier by Sir Marc Aurel Stein, P.K. Kozlov etc., have shown light on the fact that silk was adored as a fabric even prior to 145 BC. Sericulture was established at an earlier period of second century BC at Central Asia during the reign of Han dynasty (206 BC – AD 221). Rome was the country which had a huge demand for silk during this period and the supply was mainly shared by China or even India.

The Han dynasty was succeeded by the Tang dynasty (618 – 906 AD). The Tang had developed an impressive new weave silk satin and their embroideries depicting Buddhist images. The weavers during the rule of Ming dynasty in China (1368 – 1644) started to weave figured velvets, a technique influenced by westerly sources. By the sixteenth century Chinese workshops had the skills of weaving, embroidering and painting textiles with European influence on their designs. During the last dynasty of China, the Manchu Qing (1644 – 1911), *chinoiserie* became famous fashion in Europe, which was decorated mainly with Chinese silks. Due to the battle of Talas during 751, China suffered a defeat and many skilled Chinese weavers were taken as war prisoners and resettled at Persia and Mesopotamia. Since then China started to keep off from the west. Later the Yuan dynasty (1260 – 1368) was established. The emperor Justinian gained the secrets of sericulture for the Roman Empire in 522 A.D., with the smuggling of the silk worm eggs form China by Persian monks. With China's monopoly on sericulture broken, silk importations from China became smaller and smaller. In 877 A.D., the rebel chief Biachu captured Canfu, the center of foreign silk trade, put to death all its inhabitants, destroyed all of the mulberry trees and silkworms of the region, and levied heavy and cruel taxes on all foreign trade. These actions stopped foreign commerce in China for more than 60 years.

However, by this time, silk production was so well established in western Asia and Eastern Europe that this wholesale destruction hardly effected the price of silk in the rest of the world. Persians and Arabs to certain extent spread the silk trade. Because of the predominance of Arabs, the Romans, sought the alliance with Mongols for trade in the west which was called as the Pax Mongolica. By 15 century Italy emerged as the most important producer and trader of silk goods in Europe. There was a total devastation of sericulture due to the pebrine disease of silkworm in European countries, which otherwise concentrated later on silk processing and weaving. During the 18th and 19th centuries, Europeans also produced several major advancements in silk production. England by the 18th century led Europe in silk manufacturing because of English innovations in the textile industry. These innovations included improved silk-weaving looms, power looms and roller printing. In 1801, A Frenchman named Joseph Jacquard exhibited his new machine for figuredsilk weaving and gradually spread through the industry. The great French scientist, Louis Pasteur, rescued the silk industry in 1870 by showing that the then epidemic Pebrine disease of silk-worms could be controlled by prevention through simple microscopic examination of adult moths.

These advances set the trend for a more mechanized and scientific approach to silk production than existed previously. A Buddhist monk or missionary is credited with bringing the Chinese techniques of silk-reeling to India during the Gupta period (400 – 600 AD) and similarly the previous traveller might have brought the eggs of *Bombyx mori*. In Assam, the Bodo tribe who originally migrated from the Central Asia are said to have brought the art of silk reeling with them. Sultan Tughluq (1325 – 1350) had hundreds of manufacturers of golden tissues or silk, who use to weave fabrics for the court. Babur who invaded India brought artists and craft workers along with him and allowed them with the skilled India artists. In India, the famous Vedic script 'Rig Veda' of India which was composed some three thousand years ago and the Sanskrit epic 'Ramayan' reveal the existence of silk, which were mainly referred to as golden threads. Currently India is credited with the production of all the four commercially known varieties of silk in the world. While mulberry silk is domesticated and produced on a large scale in the rural areas, the non-domesticated wild silks, viz., tasar, eri and muga are produced in the wild and are named as *vanya* silk, in India. In the earlier days the most sought after silk was tasar, which delivered beautiful lustrous silk. India is also the second largest producer of tasar silk, while the golden-yellow muga silk is predominantly produced in the state of Assam. India is a vast repository of ancient motifs, techniques and ideas and unique among silk-producing countries. Sericulture is home based in India, as is seen in China. Existence of low cost of labour, and available natural resources has made these countries to adopt this enterprise on a large scale. A large proportion of population in India still is dependent on the non-domesticated *vanya* silk.

GLOBAL SILK SCENARIO

India and China together have a lion's share of total silk production in the world. Among the producers of silk, except Brazil, all other countries are in Asia alone. China has a share of 80.06 per cent in the world production of silk, followed by India, which has a share of 13.77 per cent. China produces international grade raw silk and hence has been one of the major stake holders in the international silk market. India is considered to be the second largest producer of silk, and imports nearly 7000 MT annually to suffice the domestic demand. Out of the annual raw silk production, there exists a huge domestic demand as the consumption rate is highly elastic. This has resulted in creating a larger gap in production. The domestic consumption has been estimated to reach 25000 MT annually in the coming years. Brazil, Thailand and Uzbekistan [in Commonwealth Independent States (CIS)] are the other major mulberry raw silk producing countries accounting for 1.42 per cent, 1.34 per cent and 0.89 per cent respectively, of the global raw silk production in 2004. Japan and South Korea were once the major producers of silk but have started abandoning sericulture due to industrialization. However, they continue to consume a substantial quantity of silk. The development process of Indian Silk is a remarkable one. Sericultural production in recent years has led not only to increase in the potential income, but also the promotion of women employment and also generating foreign exchange. As a result, sericulture in India is considered to have positive distributional impact on rural mass.

AN OVERVIEW OF SILK INDUSTRY IN INDIA

In India, a country that produces all five known kinds of silks viz., Mulberry, Oak Tasar, Tropical Tasar, Eri and Muga, over 8 lakh families spread over 53,000 villages are reported to be engaged in cocoon production. As per the 2004-05 data, there are 26631 cottage basins, 28014 Charka units, 201 multiend basins, 2.58 lakh handlooms and 29340 power looms. Among the five types of silks, the most popular is the Mulberry silk, named after the plant that the silkworms feed on (*Morus sp.*), accounts for more than 88 per cent of total raw silk production in the country. Over 95 per cent of this silk is produced in the five traditional sericultural states of Karnataka, Andhra Pradesh, West Bengal, Tamil Nadu and Jammu & Kashmir. Limited amount of mulberry silk is also produced by 15 non-traditional states viz., Assam, Arunachal Pradesh, Bihar, Chhattisgarh, Himachal Pradesh, Jharkhand, Kerala, Madhya Pradesh, Maharashtra, Manipur, Orissa, Punjab, Tripura, Uttaranchal and Uttar Pradesh.

The other four types of silks are collectively referred to as Vanya silks. The Eri or Endi silk where the silkworms (*Samia cynthia ricini* Boisduval.) are fed on the leaves of the Castor (*Ricinus communis* L.), Tapioca (*Manihot utilissima)* and certain perennial trees like Kesseru (*Heteropanax fragrans* (Roxb.) Seem., Barkesseru (*Ailanthus excelsa*), contributes to about 10% of the total raw silk. The production of this silk is largely confined to the States in the northeast of the country, where the pupae of the silkworm is an integral part of human diet. The tropical Tasar is a product of *Antheraea mylitta* D., a gregarious silkworm yet to be domesticated.

The larvae feed on the foliage of *Terminalia tomentosa*, *T. arjuna* and *Shorea robusta* grown in the deciduous forests of Jharkhand, Bihar, Madhya Pradesh, Chhattisgarh, Andhra Pradesh, Maharashtra and Orissa. Tasar culture practiced in these areas largely by the tribes has been a source of income for the practitioners since many centuries. The Oak tasar silk is a product of *Antheraea frithi*, *A. compta*, *A. pernyi*, *A. yamamai* and *A. proylei*,. Also reared in the wild the practice offers gainful employments to many tribes in the temperate zones of the north and north eastern India including Jammu & Kashmir, Himachal Pradesh, Uttaranchal in the North western sector and Manipur, Mizoram, Nagaland, Arunachal Pradesh and Meghalaya in the North east. The fifth kind that accounts for less than 1% of the total raw silk produced in the country is the Muga silk. Produced by the silkworm *Antheraea assama* WW., the silk occupies a special place in the hearts of the people who produce it and those who crave to own it. Endemic to the northeastern stare pf Assam, Meghalaya and parts of West Bengal, the silkworm feeds on Som (*Machilus bombycina* King) and Soalu (*Litsaea polyantha* Juss.) trees.

In India with a contribution of nearly 13.77 per cent of the world raw silk production, the production of pure silk fabric accounts to nearly 140 million sq. meters per year. Out of the total fabric produced 60 – 70 percent of the soft silk constitutes handloom silk. Special types of silk viz., Crepe, Georgette and Chiffon etc., contribute around 10 – 12 percent of the total silk fabrics. Out of the total silk produced in India, mulberry silk accounts for nearly 90 per cent. Of the total silk produced in India, mulberry silk is produced at the rate of 16,525 Mt annually, followed by vanya silk (Tasar, Eri and Muga silk) at the rate of 1950 MT annually. There has been a continuous trend in the growth of area and production of sericulture in India. Mulberry sericulture is practiced in almost all the states in the country. However, the states of Karnataka, Andhra Pradesh, West Bengal and Tamil Nadu together account for about 98.20 per cent of the total mulberry silk production in the country.

Due to the prevalence of favorable climatic conditions, mulberry is grown mainly in five states, viz., Karnataka, Andhra Pradesh, Tamil Nadu, West Bengal and Jammu & Kashmir. Collectively these five states account for 88 per cent of the total area under mulberry cultivation and 98 per cent of raw silk production in the country. Karnataka is the principal silk producing state in the country, which accounts for about 48 per cent of the total mulberry raw silk production in the country. The earnings by exports reached nearly well beyond Rs.3338 crores annually by the end of tenth five year plan. India stands to gain from the export of natural silk yarn fabrics, made ups and readymade garments. Sericulture is recognized as a village-based industry providing employment to a sizable section of the population in India. Sericulture encompasses activities including mulberry farming, silkworm rearing, reeling, twisting dyeing, weaving, etc., which is elemental in uplifting the rural folk through provision of adequate employment and income from the time immemorial.

Though Sericulture is considered as a subsidiary occupation, due to significant breakthroughs in the technological innovations, has been possible to take it on an intensive scale for generating potential income and year round employment. In India, the sericulture sector has the capability of employing up to 6 million jobs annually in the production of raw silk alone. Sericulture occupies a unique position in Indian economy and assumes more importance in alleviating the problems of the rural poor. It is highly suitable in the context of diversification of farm enterprises and integration with the farming system with other enterprises and has the capacity to generate attractive income. There are only a few other farm enterprises that can match sericulture for providing employment to rural poor. Sericulture provides employment for 506.20 man-days per annum per acre. The above features have attracted the policy makers to propagate sericulture enterprise as a suitable answer to rural unemployment and low per capita income.

IMPACT OF TECHNOLOGIES ON SERICULTURE DEVELOPMENT

Although India is the second largest producer of mulberry raw silk in the world with the bulk of silk produced in the country is reared from cross breed cocoons, which is more suitable for handloom sector. Further, the productivity level of Indian sericulture industry is less compared to that of China. The power loom weavers and exporters in India prefer Chinese silk as it has more uniformity, less winding breaks and low degumming losses compared to domestic Indian silk. As the quality and productivity of silk derived from traditional crossbreed cocoons is less, switching over to bivoltine sericulture in the country is imperative to achieve competitiveness. The earlier phase of development of sericulture in India had to target upon replacing low yielding mulberry variety with that of the improved robust yielding mulberry varieties followed by the replacement of the traditional multivoltine silkworm races with that of the bivoltine races. The conditions prevailed in rearing silkworm were totally unhygienic because of the absence of separate rearing houses for silkworm rearing with the large majority of farmers. Due to the unhygienic conditions of silkworm rearing the outbreak of diseases were common. This had caused major setback in the silk cocoon production leading to poorer yields and thereby harming the productivity level.

THRUST ON TECHNOLOGIES IN SERICULTURE

With the introduction of the World Bank and Swiss Development Cooperation assisted National Sericulture Project (NSP) between 1989 and 1996, covering five traditional states and 12 pilot states, major thrust was given to the provision of adequate infrastructure facilities for development. With this there was a great momentum in the sericultural industry. The project ensured a multidimensional improvement in the production and productivity of the sericulture sector. There was a clear emergence of developmental linkages between the pre cocoon and post cocoon sectors. Due to the established forward and backward linkages coupled with an ensured marketing system, the participants in the sericulture sector ensured higher returns to their investments. Yet, the potential of sericulture remained unexplored until a sound base for technology development was initiated. In continuation to the strategies for improving the productivity level of sericulture in the country, the Government of India launched the JICA (Japan International Cooperation Agency) programme in 1997 with the technical support of the Japanese scientists in selected areas of the country. The programme was implemented in three phases.

In the first phase (1991-97) of Bivoltine Sericulture Technology Development Project (BSTD) the scientists were able to evolve highly productive bivoltine hybrids (CSR hybrids) and mulberry cultivation and bivoltine silkworm rearing package. The second JICA phase (1997 – 2002) was on Promotion of Popularizing Practical Bivoltne Sericulture Technology (PPPBST) to test verify and validate the technologies in the field in selected areas of Karnataka, Andhra Pradesh and Tamil Nadu. Based on the success achieved in the second phase of the project, the JICA and the Govt. of India extended the project for the third term (2002-2007) also under the name of Project for Strengthening Extension System for Bivoltine Sericulture with effect from August 2002 for a period of five years. The JICA programme was mainly implemented in three major silk producing southern states viz., Karnataka, Andhra Pradesh and Tamil Nadu.

The project was however elemental in uplifting the productive parameters of sericulture on par with the international standards. Many of the technologies, which were evolved in sericulture during the period, have contributed to the productivity level significantly. The level of productivity increased considerably due to the evolution of superior silkworm hybrids and development of robust mulberry varieties along with improved mulberry cultivation and silkworm rearing practices. Due to the advent of these technologies, the sericulture enterprise could gradually get into many of the non-traditional sericultural states of the country. The research and development and training efforts of the Central Silk Board, and the initiatives and support systems of some states have enabled the increase in production and productivity. Due to the R & D contributions alone, there is an overwhelming increase in the production of silk of the country up to 18475 MT during 2006-07. During the implementation of many of the programmes directed to improve the productivity in Indian sericulture, the major thrust was given to the following areas of operation. The major technologies that brought sericulture in India to limelight are:

1. Mulberry crop production:

- Improved mulberry varieties
- Improved cultivation methods
- Effective nutrient management
- Effective plant protection measures

2. Silkworm rearing and silk cocoon production:

- Improved breeds of silkworm (cross breeds and hybrids)
- Silkworm rearing technology (Chawki/young age and adult silk worm rearing)
- Disinfection and hygiene
- Silkworm pest and disease management
- Spinning and cocoon harvest.

Impact of Technologies

- The introduction of V1 variety of mulberry during the nineties nearly doubled the production of mulberry than the regular variety of mulberry.
- Similarly with the advent of productive bivoltine hybrids improved the productivity level from far below 200 kg/ha under traditional system to nearly 1875 kg/ha/year in Southern States.
- The introduction of the supply of healthy Chawki (young age) worms to the farmers instead of supplying the eggs, through the large scale Commercial Chawki Rearing Centres (CRCs) has led to increase in the productivity level of the silk cocoon at the farmers' level.
- The renditta of the traditional multivoltine which was ranging from

14 – 17 kg of silk cocoon per kg of raw silk, the improved hybrids in the field have brought it down to mere 8 kg.

- With the adoption of bivoltine hybrids there are hopes of producing 2A – 4A grade quality silk which is on par with the international standards.
- Many cost reducing technologies were evolved which in turn not only saved the energy requirement in production but also reduced the drudgery. With the advent of shoot feeding method for silkworm and drip irrigation system in mulberry it is possible to save labor and irrigation water to an extent of 40 per cent.
- The major point of consideration in measuring the technological impact is through the mechanization in mulberry sericulture. With the change in the planting system, it is possible now to manage large scale mulberry farms through heavy machineries. Likewise there are many other instances where the introduction of machineries to get rid of laborious form of work in sericulture.

Technology Dissemination

The sericulture technology dissemination attained through R & D institutions brought about drastic changes in the productivity. The quality of silk cocoon reached a new momentum with the production of international grade of 3A, which is the best quality of silk in India. For effective diffusion of technologies to the field, the Central Silk Board has been elemental in implementing Catalytic Development Programme (CDP) since 1997-98. The schemes backed with latest technology package are being implemented through the various state departments in different states. With the objective of technology absorption, quality up-gradation, improvement in productivity, generation of income and employment, the scheme was implemented to support women, SC/ST and farmers below poverty line engaged in sericulture as its main beneficiaries. The CDP covered major thrust areas of technology such as food plant cultivation, development of farm infrastructure support for quality linked purchase of silk cocoon and yarn, up-gradation of silk reeling and processing technologies, enterprise development, data base management, support for extension, publicity etc. The assistance under CDP is being provided to all states for mulberry, Tasar, eri and muga sectors.

The scheme has received overwhelming response from the beneficiaries during IX and X plans. In recent times, development of sericultural technologies and dissemination of the same played a major role in increasing the income and employment of the rural folk. Various R & D organizations involved in sericulture research activities have been responsible for the improvement of productivity of sericulture in the field. In this regard the Central Sericultural Research and Training Institute (CSRTI) located at Mysore from the past 40 years is involved in carrying out research in mulberry cultivation and silkworm rearing and in other concerned aspects and have developed various technologies which are reaching the farmers.

The role of state Department of Sericulture (DOS) at different states in dissemination process of technologies is commendable. With the support of DOS and the other important organization under CSB, the National Silkworm Seed Organisation (NSSO), many programmes were organized for effective diffusion of technologies under JICA Project. The Institute- Village Linking Progrmme (IVLP), the other process in the diffusion of technologies, effectively brought the farmers, extension personnel and scientists into a single platform for participatory technology development through demonstration of fine tuned technologies. With the nested units of CSRTI, Mysore located at Kodathi (Karnataka), Salem (Tamil Nadu) and Anantapur (Andhra Pradesh) along with the concerned State Departments of Sericulture, and NSSO the IVLP was a great success among the farmers. Since the inception of JICA 19,616 farmers and under IVLP 1700 farmers were covered as bivoltine rearers. The average cocoon yield of the farmers enhanced up to 65.96 kg/100 DFLs from the previous 48 – 50 kg/100 DFLs due to the impact of technologies. The rearing performance of the farmers during the year 2006 – 07 is as follows; The improved technologies developed for mulberry production and silkworm rearing has been very cost effective, besides they have been aiming at higher productivity levels.

The thrust given to the Transfer of Technology by the R & D organizations is commendable. This effect is easily seen by the performance of the crops under both JICA as well as the IVLP. Against the benchmark yield of 48.10 kg/ 100 DFLs, the productivity level in bivoltine cocoon yield resulted in to 66.82 kg/100 DFLs. The productive success of the JICA and IVLP in India suggest that, there is an existence of scope for improving the productivity in sericulture. Though the productive capability of Indian sericulture was far below that of People Republic of China, the recently concluded JICA and IVLP rearings with a large mass of sericulturists, suggests that the international productive standards what China has achieved, is still possible in India also. An analysis of the productive standards of the two important silk producing countries viz., China and India suggests that, though India lags behind in the productive strength of the silk, with the implementation of various programmes, the level of productivity is achievable with the domestically evolved technologies. As of now India can support the production of at least a minimum of 2A – 3A grade of silk, thus making the sericulture industry a lucrative subject.

INITIATIVES THROUGH CENTRAL SILK BOARD

Central Silk Board came into existence during 1949 for the development of the silk industry in India, with the enactment of the Central Silk Board Act, 1948. The Central Silk Board, a statutory body, is functioning under the administrative control of the Ministry of Textiles, Govt. of India, with its Headquarters at Bangalore. The Board's activities include Research and Technology Development, Seed Maintenance, and Development of Sericulture and Silk Industry through which it supports, supplement and facilitates the efforts of State Governments. The Board extends support to the States in the form of joint projects and development assistance under the plan schemes. The Board undertakes voluntary quality inspection of exportable silk goods.

Research and Development

Central Silk Board has established many R & D units all over the country to look after the R & D component of sericulture.. In association with the institutions set up by the CSB, many research projects were initiated to bring out performing technologies for sericulture development in India. During the process many mulberry varieties and silkworm breeds were evolved and popularized. The Institute Village Linkage Programme (IVLP) was implemented in several non-traditional sericulture States like Orissa, Jharkhand, Chattisgarh, Assam, Tripura, Meghalaya, Manipur, Mizoram, Nagaland, Sikkim, Uttranchal and Maharashtra, along with traditional states. Several technology trials were taken up at the different Regional Research Stations, to test the new productive Bivoltine Hybrids, new bed disinfectant formulations, improved tillage methods, new mountages, chawki rearing practices, temperature tolerant bivoltine hybrids, mulberry package for seed cocoon crop, testing of complete package of practices of mulberry cultivation and silkworm rearing at farmer's level under irrigated and non irrigated conditions etc.

Various demonstrations on technologies were also conducted at the farmer's field. The Research work in the non mulberry sector has been undertaken in tasar, oak tasar, muga and eri sector for host plant improvement, production, protection and silkworm crop production, improvement, protection and post cocoon technology disciplines. Attempts were also made to improve the productive potential of nonmulberry silk through transfer of new technologies developed from Institutes. The network of Demonstration-cum-Technical Service Centres (DCTSCs) continue to provide training in silk reeling and spinning, processing and finishing. Besides, Silk Conditioning & Testing Houses (SCTHs) test raw silk. The Textile Testing Laboratories (TTLs) at Bangalore, Jammu, Varanasi and Bhagalpur undertake testing of physical, chemical and eco-parameters of textiles products.

Silkworm Seed Organisation

The initiation of National Silkworm Seed Project (NSSP) under CSB enabled to provide basic mulberry silkworm seeds to the rearers. Under this programme, 27 basic seed farms have been established to produce the basic stock and meet the seed requirements of other multiplication farms/State

Department Farms. As many as 23 Silkworm Seed Production Centres functioning under NSSP, to cater the need for quality Disease Free Layings (DFLs) to the farmers. Likewise the CSB also established a Basic Tasar Silkworm Seed Organisation at Bilaspur, to organize production and supply of basic tasar silkworm seed for further multiplication.

Development Schemes and Programmes

Development schemes and programmes supported by the CSB can be classified as those, which are fully funded by the Centre, those financed by Centre as well as State, and those, which are externally assisted. The development thrust was concentrated on expansion of non-mulberry silks and growth of bivoltine mulberry sericulture, with a focus on increasing productivity and quality of silk. A thrust was given to development of the North East Region. Several new projects were started to spread eri-culture, using existing castor plantations. Eri was started in states such as Andhra Pradesh, Punjab, Bihar, Uttranchal, Chattisgarh. The main schemes are briefly given below:

External Aided Projects

With the introduction of the World Bank and Swiss Development Cooperation assisted National Sericulture Project (NSP) between 1989 and 1996, covering five traditional states and 12 pilot states, major thrust was given to the provision of adequate infrastructure facilities for development. With this there was a great momentum in the sericulture industry. The project ensured a multidimensional improvement in the production and productivity of the sericulture sector. There was a clear emergence of developmental linkages between the pre cocoon and post cocoon sectors. Due to the established forward and backward linkages coupled with an ensured marketing system, the participants in the sericulture sector ensured higher returns to their investments. Yet, the potential of sericulture remained unexplored until a sound base for technology development was initiated.

Japan International Cooperative Agency (JICA)

In continuation to the strategies for improving the productivity level of sericulture in the country, the Government of India launched the JICA (Japan International Cooperation Agency) programme in 1997 with the technical support of the Japanese scientists in selected locations of the country. The programme was implemented in three phases. In the first phase (1991-97) of Bivoltine Sericulture Technology Development Project (BSTD) the scientists were able to evolve highly productive bivoltine hybrids (CSR hybrids) and mulberry cultivation and bivoltine silkworm rearing package.

The second JICA phase (1997 – 2002) was on Promotion of Popularizing Practical Bivoltne Sericulture Technology (PPPBST) to test verify and validate the technologies in the field in the selected areas of Karnataka, Andhra Pradesh and Tamil Nadu. Based on the success achieved in the second phase of the project, the JICA and the Govt. of India extended the project for the third term (2002-2007) also under the name of Project for Strengthening Extension System for Bivoltine Sericulture (PEBS) with effect from August 2002 for a period of five years. The JICA programme was mainly implemented in three major silk producing southern states viz., Karnataka, Andhra Pradesh and Tamil Nadu. The project was however elemental in uplifting the productive parameters of sericulture on par with the international standards. Many of the technologies, which were evolved in sericulture during the period, have contributed to the productivity level significantly.

The level of productivity increased considerably due to the evolution of superior silkworm hybrids and development of robust mulberry varieties along with improved mulberry cultivation and silkworm rearing practices. Due to the advent of these technologies, the sericulture enterprise could gradually get into many of the non-traditional sericultural states of the country. The research and development and training efforts of the Central Silk Board, and the initiatives and support systems of some states have enabled the increase in production and productivity. Due to the R & D contributions alone, there is an overwhelming increase in the production of silk of the country up to 18475 MT during 2006-07.

Overseas Economic Cooperation Fund (OECF)

Many of the states implemented the sericultural development programmes in association with the Japan Bank of International Cooperation (JBIC). These include the following:

Manipur Sericulture Project

The project was implemented by the State Department of Sericulture, Manipur in collaboration with Japanese Bank for International Cooperation (JBIC) and Government of India. The project was initiated during 1998. The first phase for development of Mulberry sericulture over a period of 7 years and the second phase for development of Eri culture over a period of 5 years proposed to commence after the 5th year of first phase of the project. Thus, the project was proposed to be implemented over a period of 10 years at a total cost of Rs. 490.59 crore. The objective of the project was to raise 1020 ha of mulberry plantation covering 3000 beneficiaries; to achieve a production of 60 MT of raw silk annually from 4th year; and provision of employment for 7000 persons.

Chhatisgarh Sericulture Project

The Govt. of Chhatisgarh implemented the Chhatisgarh Sericulture Project with the financial assistance from Japanese Bank for International Cooperation

(JBIC) . The project was proposed to be implemented in two phases – the first phase of the project for development of tasar culture over a period of 7 years (1998-05) and the second phase for development of mulberry sericulture over a period of further 5 years, which was proposed to commence from the 6th year of the first phase of the project. Its objective was to raise 4000 ha of tasar plantation covering 4000 beneficiaries; achieve production of 75 MT of raw silk and 22.5 MT of Spun Silk Yarn annually from 4 year; and give employment for 10,000 persons. In the first phase the Directorate of Sericulture, Govt. of Chhattisgarh implemented the seven years 'Chhattisgarh Sericulture Project' in the seven districts of Chhattisgarh, viz. Bilaspur, Korba, Janjgir, Raigarh, Jashpur, Surguja and Korea w.e.f. 1998 to 2005 and extended to February, 2007.

The United Nation's Development Programme (UNDP)

The UNDP in collaboration with Govt. of India initiated a sub-programme on development of Non-mulberry silk - tasar, muga and eri - in Andhra Pradesh, Assam, Bihar, Orissa, Meghalaya, Nagaland and West Bengal under Fibres and Handicrafts Programme (FHAP) of the Country Co-operation Frame Work 1 (CCF-1) for a period of three years from 1999-2000. The main thrust areas included the creation of employment opportunities, access to the services for the poor, effective management of development through peoples' empowerment.

SERI 2000

As a part of technical and scientific cooperation between the government and Switzerland, under an agreement entered into with Swiss Agency for Development and Cooperation (SDC), SERI-2000 programme was initiated between 1997 to 2002. The programme was initiated in the traditional sericultural states of Karnataka, Andhra Pradesh, Tamil Nadu and West Bengal. The aim was to generate viable enterprises, employment and sustainable income, primarily for the weaker sections of the population, including women, in rural and semi-urban areas.

Internal Aided Projects

Catalytic Development Programme (CDP)

Central Silk Board had formulated a number of schemes under the Catalytic Development Programme (CDP) and implemented them during IX Plan to motivate States to increase productivity and quality besides providing market support. During the X Plan (2002-07), in order to achieve the targeted production of 26450 M.T of both mulberry and non-mulberry silks and generate a cumulative employment of 60.03 lakh persons, CSB modified the CDP to give greater thrust to bivoltine sericulture and a market orientation to non-mulberry sector. The schemes under CDP were aimed at development and expansion of host plantations, development of farm infrastructure, upgradation of reeling and processing technologies in silk, enterprise development programme and data base development. During the XI plan, the Catalytic Development Programme (CDP) is to be implemented as centrally sponsored scheme, which has been accepted by the Government of India. During the plan period, the CDP is proposed to be implemented through project mode approach in the form of packages mainly under 3 sectors viz. Seed, Cocoon and post-cocoon sectors supported by the service sector to achieve the targets and objectives.

Poorvanchal Sericulture Development Project in Uttar Pradesh

The Poorvanchal Sericulture Development Project was implemented jointly by Central Silk Board and the Department of Sericulture, Govt. of Uttar Pradesh in three Eastern Districts viz. Varanasi, Gazipur and Bhadohi. The project aimed at rising 3000 acres of mulberry plantation. The project also envisaged an incremental raw silk production of 77.1 metric tons by the end of the project period.

Action Plan for North Eastern States

The Central Silk Board, in collaboration with the 7 North Eastern States launched an action plan during 1995-96 for intensifying mulberry sericulture development in the North Eastern region. The project envisaged to help the Muga and Eri sericulture sectors in these states.

Tribal Sub-Plan

The major programmes being implemented by CSB was towards Research and Development and basic seed supply. The States implemented programmes for specific target groups. The emphasis on creation of sustainable livelihood in the tribal area was carried forward with the thrust on non-mulberry silks. Projects in Chattisgarh, Jharkhand & the NER encouraged sericulture on trees in forests and intercropped with agriculture produce and as a basket of subsistence and income augmenting activities. The CDP was modified to bring in greater flexibility to better serve the tribal and non traditional requirements.

Prime Minister's Special Package for Jammu & Kashmir

The package included the special assistance for development of Sericulture and Silk Industry in J&K during the tenth Five Year Plan (2002-07). The expenditure under the J&K Special Package is booked under Catalytic Development Programme.

Cluster Development Projects

CSB has been assisting various states in formulation and implementation of Cluster Development Projects in selected pockets in association with the

Catalytic Development Programme (CDP). Thirteen Cluster Development Projects, which included, three in Kerala (Mulberry), three in Bihar (two Mulberry and one Eri), two in Assam state (one Eri and one Muga), two in West Bengal (one Eri and one Muga), two in Mizoram (Mulberry) and one in Himachal Pradesh (Mulberry) were initiated. These Cluster Development Projects envisaged covering around 2820 beneficiaries in selected clusters.

Enterprise Promotion and Training Programme

As a part of Enterprise Promotion and Training Programme, CSB conducted various training programmes. These included the following:

1. Entrepreneurship Development Programmes in Silk Reeling, Twisting, Weaving, Dyeing and Printing for the prospective entrepreneurs.
2. Resource Development Programme to develop a core team of resource persons who can train the second line of officials and the beneficiaries.
3. Technology Up-gradation Programmes for existing entrepreneurs for upgrading technology and management, modernization, consolidation and diversification.
4. Management Development Programme to create awareness and develop Interpersonal relationships, team building, managing conflicts, developing vision, goals, objectives etc.
5. Competence Enhancement Training Programme to develop the desired skills in the participants to make them more confident and well equipped for carrying out their duties smoothly.
6. Exposure visit to well-known sericulture clusters/establishments/ research institutes in India.

OTHERS

Information Technology Initiatives

- Database Development: The Board also has recently introduced sericulture information Kiosks for the farmers and reelers in the country. These Kiosks work on Touch Screen Technology and the information is made available in English and the regional languages.
- Sericulture Management Information/ System (SMIS) : For the purpose of submission of online requests from the end users of sericulture sectors the Sericulture Management Information/System (SMIS) a web-based application was created. It helps Policy and Decision makers associated with Silk Industry to draw significant strides in the development of Sericulture.

Quality Certification Systems

The scheme envisages putting in place Quality Certification System to ensure quality standards at different levels of production process in the areas of 1) Silkworm Seed Production; 2) Cocoon testing and grading; 3) Silk yarn testing and grading; 4) Testing of silk goods marked for exports and 5) Quality Certification for "Silk Mark Label".

Silk Mark Organization of India (SMOI)

The Silk Mark Organization of India, a registered Society under the Karnataka Society Registration Act, sponsored by the Central Silk Board, has introduced the "Silk Mark Scheme" under the Quality Certification Systems. The broad objectives of the Silk Mark Scheme are – generic promotion of silk, consumer protection and promotion of Indian silk in export markets. The Silk Mark has entered into operations during 2005-06.

Projects for Post Cocoon Technology Induction

Through the upgradation of technology for the development and commercialization of low cost user friendly devices for reeling and spinning, cocoon drying etc, CSB continues its efforts to increase productivity and quality of silk in the post cocoon sector. This has helped to reduce drudgery and increase efficiency, productivity and quality of produce. CSB has stepped up its financial and technical support for adoption and popularization of these technologies. The main projects includes-

- Establishment of Tasar Production-cum-Training Centre: to train the poor weavers in advanced technologies to enable them to produce quality Tasar products.
- Vanya Silk Production-cum- Training Centres (PCTCs): to introduce new designs, products and technologies in the post cocoon sector in a cost effective manner.
- Vanya Silk Mart : to create the demand for Vanya silk products.
- Vanya Web Sites: 'Vanyasilkmart.com' and 'Vanyasilkgifts.com' aimed at cataloguing the product range of the small unorganized producers of Vanya silks in the Country.

Sericulture, which constituted the subsistence economy in India, has now been considered as one of the important sector contributing to income and employment in the rural economy. The introduction of many of the projects/ development schemes in sericulture has necessarily guided the industry to the forefront through the evolution of technologies that suit the requirement of the farmers, making the sericulture enterprise a highly remunerative than any other competitive crops in agriculture. The significant breakthrough in the technologies developed in sericulture coupled with the schemes and programmes of the government through which these are popularized has contributed to the development of sericulture sector in India. With a set target of 23000 MT raw silk for the XI five year plan, which includes production of 5000 MT of Bivoltine silk and 18000 MT of Cross breed silk, it is evident that these productive programmes are going to be vital in the promotion and development of sericulture in India in the coming years.

INTRODUCTION OF SERICULTURE IN KARNATAKA STATE

During the year 1670 the East India Company started the commercial activity in silk. During the period of 1771 – 1775, the company introduced the technology of silk reeling from Italy. Sericulture was introduced in the then Bengal state during the year 1773. At the end of the 18 century (1780-90), sericulture was brought to Mysore by the then ruler Tippu Sultan. It is since then sericulture started flourishing in the state of erstwhile Mysore, later came to be known as Karnataka state during 1956. A letter written by the sultan to the East India Company says that *"My goal is clear. I want Mysore to be the foremost among silk producing nations"*. The commitment of Tippu Sultan was later transformed into a great saga of golden thread in the state of Karnataka. In Karnataka state, places such as Channapatna near Bangalore and Kollegala and Malavalli near Mysore were considered as the prime places of sericulture development in the initial stages. Major demand for the commodity existed during the Second World War, due to which the industry could get a boost. However due to import of a large quantity of silk from outside countries saw the decline of the industry.

The series of activities which hastened the development of sericulture in Karnataka is as under. The state of Karnataka took a pioneering lead in sericulture output production during 1936-37, crossing the production levels of West Bengal. Since then the state of Karnataka has been a pioneer in the production of silk cocoon and raw silk. However the situation was not promising as the method of production was highly traditional and there were no stock of productive silk worm breeds. The farmers were found rearing only local multivoltine breeds. Gradually these breeds were replaced by the cross breeds obtained by crossing local breeds with the elite bivoltine breeds. During 1950s lot of changes took place in terms of technology dissemination in sericulture. More advanced methods of cultivating mulberry and rearing silkworm were advocated to the farmers.

Moreover the farmers were provided with best quality silkworm eggs from the grainages, where the seeds were prepared. Lots of improvements were also seen in the post cocoon sector, where the importance was given to produce quality threads from the silk cocoon. A strong research base was formulated to systematically develop sericulture in Karnataka during 1970s. As a thrust for this effort, the government introduced the Karnataka Sericulture Project (KSP) during 1980. With an aid of Rs. 101.13 crores, the KSP was a great success in the state of Karnataka. In order to reap the benefits from the earlier success through implementing the Karnataka Sericulture Project - I, the Karnataka Sericulture Project – II (KSP-II) was also introduced under the National Sericulture Project (NSP) during 1989. With an aid of Rs. 142.84 crores the Karnataka Sericulture Project – II was a great success in the state of Karnataka. KSP projects were helpful in bringing about desirable changes in the field of sericulture in India and Karnataka in particular. Before the implementation of Karnataka Sericulture Project, sericulture was existing in only five traditional five districts alone. Under the project, in addition to the all round infrastructure development for sericulture, thrust was given to technology dissemination, training and credit facilities. New breeds of silkworm were introduced along with high yielding varieties of mulberry. Because of the significance attached to the development of sericulture in Karnataka, the National Sericulture Project (NSP) was initiated. A boost was provided to Research and Development work in sericulture. As a result there was a vertical growth in the production of silk cocoon and raw silk. The silk cocoon yield drastically increased from 29200 Metric Tons during 1974-75 to 55493 Metric Tons during 2005 -06, while the raw silk production for the same period increased from 2020 Metric Tons to 7471 Metric Tons. Similarly the thrust during the project period was to provide adequate infrastructure facilities for the development of sericulture in the state of Karnataka.

There was an improvement in the establishment of grainages for good quality seed production, government silk filatures for reeling raw silk, Technical Service Centres, Chawki (Young age) Silkworm Rearing centres, government cocoon markets, Sericulture Training Institutes etc., for the over all development of sericulture in the state. A point has to be noted that, though the progress made in improving the production levels was considerably significant, there is a gradual decline in the productive levels during the last 6 to 7 years. Though the production of silk cocoon increased to 88 per cent and the raw silk production to 270 per cent, in the last thirty years, there is still a remarkable gap which can still be achievable.

The state of Karnataka produces annually 7500 Metric tons of mulberry raw silk in India. Out of the total production nearly 30 per cent of the silk is considered to be qualitatively superior. During 2005-06 the total bivoltine raw silk production which is qualitatively superior was to the extent of 396 Metric Tons, which was possible because of the constant and continuous encouragement from the government sponsored programmes. Introduction of bivoltine hybrids, quality seed production, effective mulberry cultivation and silkworm rearing technologies etc., have contributed to qualitative improvement in production. It is estimated that, annually India requires around 25,000 Metric Tons of raw silk, while there is a deficit of 10,000 Metric Tons with the existing demand. To meet this gap, India has to import raw silk from other silk producing countries. With the existing quality of domestic silk is poor, India has to depend on the import of quality bivoltine silk from the international market, specifically from neighboring China.

The fact that, during the year 2005-06, the estimated quantity of 8334 Metric Tons of quality raw silk was imported at an estimated cost of Rs. 773.48 crores, speaks of the dependence of our country for quality raw silk even with the existing production rate. Of the total imports, the quantity of silk imported from neighboring China which is the major producer of raw silk in the world, was 8116 Metric Tons. As per the estimated production during the year 2004, China's total raw silk production was 85000 Metric Tones against which the Indian production of raw silk was only 14, 620 Metric Tons. With a lower cost of production China has been considered to be a dominant player in the international market to supply superior quality raw silk in the world. On the contrary, India has the tradition of producing the silk cocoon by a number of small and marginal farmers and raw silk by a large chunk of families dependent solely on silk reeling activities around the silk cocoon markets. The methods followed by the farmers as well as the silk reelers differ significantly thereby affecting the production of uniform quality silk.

The techniques of production of silk cocoon by the farmers are entirely different, as the peer group is totally heterogeneous. Similarly, the units of reeling are quite different which is done through Charkha, cottage basin and multi end reeling machines, which in turn produce the raw silk which is qualitatively different. Owing to the field problems in producing the quality raw silk, the government took certain steps to improve the production conditions at the field level. In the earlier seventies marketing of cocoon was done through the private traders who in turn exploited the farmers in terms of weight and price. Due to continuous efforts, the marketing system of silk cocoon and raw silk was streamlined with the establishment of government cocoon markets and silk exchanges. Due importance was given for improving the input delivery system at the grass root level. The prime input in the production of silk cocoon is the supply of Disease Free Layings (DFLs). The major production of quality silkworm layings has been from the private Licensed Seed Preparers (LSPs), besides the government grainages run by State Department of Sericulture and the Central Silk Board (CSB). However thrust has been given to prepare bivoltine seeds by the grainages run by CSB and State Department of Sericulture, as it ensures the production of raw silk of international quality standards. With the liberalized policies of the government, now it is possible to prepare the seeds of high quality standards by the private entrepreneurs.

The state of Karnataka has the distinction of having allocated separate seed cocoon production areas. These areas are classified as a) Mysore seed (multivoltine) area and b) bivoltine seed area. According to the government enabled act, pure races of silkworm (both multivoltine and bivoltine respectively) are to be produced in these earmarked areas. It is due to the existence of separate seed cocoon growing areas, it is now possible to have control over the quality of silkworm seed produced at the grainages. The international market demands 2A – 3A grade silk, which can be met through the production of bivoltine silk only. In India the earlier period of development in sericulture witnessed a poor infrastructure and the non existence of a strong post cocoon sector which is meant for extracting raw silk. However with the release of technologies of production of silk cocoon and with the development of silk manufacturing sector, it is possible that the quality standards can very well be maintained as expected. Hence over the plan periods, continuous encouragement was provided to produce bivoltine silk in the country.

The introduction of National Sericulture Project (NSP) aimed at improving the quality standards in sericulture. With the prime objective of producing bivoltine silk of international standards, the traditional states for silk production viz., Karnataka, Andhra Pradesh, Tamil Nadu, Jammu and Kashmir and West Bengal were encouraged. The introduction of bivoltine sericulture in India had to face certain threats.

India being a tropical country, there were immediate doubts that whether the bivoltine races of silkworm, which are basically raised in temperate climate could get acclimatized to the existing condition. Due to the continuous research efforts, many useful bivoltine silkworm races were evolved which can suit to the present Indian conditions. The CSR bivoltine hybrids were among the most popular bivoltine races which were released during the JICA period. In addition to evolution of robust hybrid silkworm races, effective silkworm rearing technologies were also developed. Maintenance of hygiene in silkworm rearing houses was given primary importance. The host plant of silkworm, mulberry was improved and with the research effort, Victory – 1 or V-1 variety of mulberry was released in the field which is highly productive and qualitatively superior to other mulberry varieties. Karnataka took the leap in the adoption of these newly evolved technologies and today the state's share in bivoltine silk production is up t0 41 per cent at 396 Metric Tons out of the total production of 971 Metric Tons in the country during the year 2006 -07.

Bivoltine Sericulture in Karnataka

The successful bivoltine production programme depends on a) potential area, b) potential season and c) potential farmers. Climatic conditions influence the performance of sericulture, specifically the silkworm rearing depends largely on the moderate temperature and relative humidity. In this respect the prevailing climatic conditions has to be studied before the implementation of any bivoltine programme. Karnataka state is known to enjoy a moderate and uniform climate all through the year. This enables the production of bivoltine silk cocoon. The state's climate is essentially well suited to the requirements of sericulture. However, further the state can be subdivided to few sericultural zones based on the existing climate conditions. The introduction of bivoltine sericulture in Karnataka was more systematic in the traditional irrigated zone than any other zones. With the evolution of CSR bivoltine hybrid races, it was possible to introduce these robust breeds at the farmers' level. However it has been targeted to spread the bivoltine hybrid production in the districts of Kolar, Mandya, Hassan, Bangalore (Rural), Tumkur, Bellary and Chitradurga. It is estimated to produce nearly 1500 Metic Tons of bivoltine silk annually from these districts. It is estimated to produce bivoltine raw silk during the favorable season (August to February, 2009) in these selected districts.

Silk Reeling in Karnataka

Reeling of silk from silk cocoon has been practiced since time immemorial. The technique of reeling has been practiced since the production of silk cocoon has been started. With the introduction of many technologies in the production of silk cocoon, the technologies for silk cocoon production also gained momentum. Reeling activities were at first performed with 'Charkha' an indigenous model, through which many poorest of the poor could realize their income. With the time, there were many illustrious research in this field enabled to introduce new machineries in rearing. Today the silk reeling activity is carried out through domestic 'charkha' reeling, cottage basin reeling and the more sophisticated multi-end reeling machines. Till the establishment of the government filature for silk reeling using machineries during 1923, the raw silk was produced through traditional 'charka' reeling only. The reelers use to reel through the 'charkha' in order to earn their livelihood and to provide handful employment for the family members. The thread reeled out of the 'charkha' was used to be thick and uneven, thereby affecting the quality. To produce one kilogram of raw silk, the quantity of silk cocoon used was to the extent of 16 to 20 kilograms, which is otherwise called as the renditta, which used to be very high. Due to unhygienic practices involved in 'charkha' reeling, there use to be continuous health hazards to the reelers.

To improve these conditions, the traditional 'charkha' was upgraded with improved model of 'charkha', which could not bring out any significant achievement in the reeling. The improvement in hand reeling with 'charkha' was later replaced with electric driven cottage basins. Due to this there was an improvement in the renditta and the length of the silk yarn produced per cocoon increased up to 1000 to 1200 meters. A tradition was formulated to give a commercial touch for weaving through the supply of raw silk produced through these cottage basin reeling units. The reeling also improved the skills of the reelers and enhanced the quality of the silk reeled. This has led to improving the entrepreneurial ability among the reelers. Reeling became a moderately lucrative profession. With a view to improve the efficiency and to bring about cost effectiveness in reeling, the multi end reeling machines were introduced in the field during 90s. This has led to improve the quality of raw silk as well as reduce the drudgery in silk reeling.

The improvement in silk reeling was brought about mainly with the efforts of the Central Silk Board and the State Department of Sericulture. The role of these organizations immensely helped to improve the post cocoon activities in Karnataka. Lastly the silk weaving sector employs considerable size of population. India is the only country where the domestic weaving sector runs on both handloom and power loom weaving. The major proportion of the silk fabric in demand in India is in the form of sarees. The handloom weaving gains popularity due to intricate value associated with the product woven and the ability of the sector to use any kind of raw silk. There is an estimated 2, 43,000 handlooms currently in operation in India, which are meant for silk weaving. These units are mostly confined to South India and are engaged in accomplishing the huge domestic demand. However there exists a huge demand for the handloom fabrics from the external world also. With the introduction of power looms, which demands the use of strong silk threads to withstand the speed of the machine, it is now possible to cater to the needs of the external world. Out of the 49,800 power looms in India, there is an estimated number of 35,000 power looms in the state of Karnataka alone, which are meant for the production of silk fabrics. For the supply of quality and strong silk, the domestically produced raw silk does not match due to quality probabilities.

The domestically produced raw silk being qualitatively not superior to international 2A or 3A grade, it is inevitable that the country has to be dependent on the cheaply available and superior quality raw silk from China. Hence there is a need to develop a strong backward linkage to produce quality silk in India. Karnataka has the potential to accept this challenge, as the resources including the manpower are relatively better compared to any other states. Due to consistent domestic demand for silk fabrics, the weaving sector in India requires about 25000 Metric Tons annually. With the current level of production of 17000 Metric Tons annually, the additional 8000 Metric Tons of raw silk has to be imported from outside countries. Moreover, the quality of the raw silk produced by the traditional weavers doesn't suit the power loom sector. Instead the power loom sector depends mainly on the cheaply available imported 2A grade raw silk from China, which is regarded as high grade silk in the international market. Being the major hub for silk weaving, the state of Karnataka has come out with various plans to improve the quality of raw silk produced domestically. Achievement of self sufficiency in silk production as well as improvement of quality in production of raw silk, are the major hurdles ahead.

Bibliography

A.K. Sharma: *International Economics*, Anmol Publications, Delhi, 2006.

Amrish Kumar Ahuja : *Economics of Education : Strictly on the Basis of Prescribed Syllabus with Modern Trends*, Authorspress

Anil Kumar Thakur and Md Abdus Salam : *Economics of Education and Health in India*, Deep and Deep Publication, Delhi, 2008.

Ansari Abdul Aziz and Usha Rao : *Advanced Educational Statistics*, Himalaya Publishing House, Delhi, 2011.

C.M. Chaudhary: *Economic Environment of Business*, RBSA Publishers, Jaipur, 2011.

Cyber Tech Publications, Delhi, 2009.

D. Pulla Rao : *Economics of Education And Human Development in India*, Akansha Publishing House, Delhi, 2010.

Francis Cherunilam: *International Business: Text and Cases*, PHI Learning, Delhi, 2007.

Gautam Murthy: *International Economic Relations*, Kalpaz Publications, Delhi, 2008.

Hemant Kumar Panda : *Public Financing and Economics of Education in India*, Academic Excellence, Delhi, 2008.

I. Sundar and R. Jawahar : *Principles of Economics of Education*, Sarup Book, Delhi, 2009.

Jack T Boorman And Andre Icard: *Reform of the International Monetary*

Jagannath Mohanty : *Adult and Non-Formal Education*, Deep and Deep Publication, 2002.

Jeilu Oumer Hussein : *Economics of Education*, Discovery Publication, Delhi, 2007.

M.A. Chaudhary: *International Economic Relations*, Global Vision Publications, Delho,

Mohd. Shadab Khan: *A Text Book of Business Mathematics*, Anmol Publications, Delhi, 2008.

N Ramnath Kishan : *Economics of Education*, APH Publication, Delhi, 2008.

Neelambar Hatti and Rameshwar Tandon: *Political Economy of International Monetary Interdependence*, B R Publications, Delhi, 2007.

P. Subba Rao: *International Business: Text and Cases*, Himalaya Publications, Delhi, 2008.

P.V. Venkatachalam: *A Text Book on International Economics*, Cyber Tech Publications, Delhi, 2012.

Pankaj Mehra: *Accounting in Business Enterprises*, Omega Publications, Delhi, 2008.

Prakash Vohra and Rakesh Mehta: *International Economics*, Commonwealth Publications, Delhi, 2007.

Publication, Delhi, 2007.

Purva Gupta: *International Business: The Latest Trends and Practices*, Shree Niwas Publications, Jaipur, 2010.

Ranbir Singh Rana: *International Business: Contemporary Issues in*

Reeta Mathur: *International Economics*, Sublime Publications, Jaipur, 2002.

Sakshi Vasudeva: *Accounting for Business Managers*, Himalaya Publishing House, Delhi, 2010.

Shyam Shukla: *International Business*, Excel Books, Delhi, 2003.

Structure and Strategy, Ane Books Pvt. Ltd., Chennai, 2010.

Sumati Varma: *International Business*: Concepts, Environment,

V K Mathur: *International Monetary Fund and Its Responsibilities*,

V.K. Bhalla and S. Shivaramu: *International Business,* Anmol Publicatios, Delhi, 2005.

V.R. Panchamukhi: *Contemporary International Economics*, Bookwell Publications, Delhi, 1998.

Vandana Sharma: *Business Concepts and Techniques*, Book Enclave, Jaipur, 2008.

Veena Keshav Pailwar: *Economic of Business*, PHI Learning, Delhi, 2011.

Index